THE POLITICS
OF TAXING
AND SPENDING

THE POLITICS
OF TAXING
AND SPENDING

PATRICK FISHER

LYNNE
RIENNER
PUBLISHERS

BOULDER
LONDON

Published in the United States of America in 2009 by
Lynne Rienner Publishers, Inc.
1800 30th Street, Boulder, Colorado 80301
www.rienner.com

and in the United Kingdom by
Lynne Rienner Publishers, Inc.
3 Henrietta Street, Covent Garden, London WC2E 8LU

Library of Congress Cataloging-in-Publication Data
Fisher, Patrick (Patrick Ivan)
  The politics of taxing and spending / by Patrick Fisher.
    p.   cm.
  Includes bibliographical references and index.
  ISBN 978-1-58826-644-6 (hardcover : alk. paper)
  ISBN 978-1-58826-619-4 (pbk. : alk. paper)
  1. Taxation—United States. 2. Government spending policy—United States.
3. Budget deficits—United States. I. Title.
  HJ2381.F57   2009
  336.73—dc22

                                                2008040203

British Cataloguing in Publication Data
A Cataloguing in Publication record for this book
is available from the British Library.

Printed and bound in the United States of America

 ∞ The paper used in this publication meets the requirements
     of the American National Standard for Permanence of
     Paper for Printed Library Materials Z39.48-1992.

   5 4 3 2 1

CONTENTS

TABLES AND FIGURES

Tables

Figures

THE POLITICS
OF TAXING
AND SPENDING

1

THE DISCREPANCY BETWEEN TAXING AND SPENDING

THE SUBSTANTIAL BUDGET DEFICITS THAT THE US GOVERNMENT produces are in large part due to the disconnection between taxing and spending decisions. While people often think of fiscal policy along the lines of traditional budgetary balance or deficits, budgeting is better recognized as consisting of two distinct and separate issues: government expenditures and revenue policy.[1] The relationship between taxing and spending varies considerably across functions. Indeed, whether one focuses on expenditures or revenues can lead one to completely different interpretations about the politics of public budgeting.[2]

Yet even though taxing and spending decisions are largely made separately, they inevitably affect each other. For example, if taxes are cut but spending is not, the result is a generational tax shift. Large deficits will lead to larger future payments on interest to the national debt. Thus, by definition, tax cuts that produce large deficits will lead to an increase of future government spending.

The tax side of the budget therefore needs to be considered equal to the spending side of the budget in its political and economic importance. Most critics of the federal budget process place the blame for skyrocketing deficits on the inability of policymakers to curtail spending.[3] One can just as easily argue, however, that it is the inability of policymakers to tax enough that makes it so difficult for the government to balance the budget.

Despite ups and downs, overall federal revenues and outlays as a percentage of gross domestic product (GDP) have been relatively stable since the 1960s (see Figure 1.1). Revenues in particular have been re-markably steady. From 1965 to 2005, federal tax collections aver-aged 18.2 percent of GDP, with a high of 20.9 percent in 2000 and a low of 16.3 percent in 2004.[4] Outlays were a bit more volatile. As a share of national income, expenditures averaged 20.1 percent, reach-ing a high of 23.5 percent in 1983 and a low of 17.2 percent in 1965. This level of expenditures is projected to remain roughly the same over the next decade; for 2007 to 2016, outlays are projected to be between 19 and 20 percent of GDP.[5]

This book examines taxing and spending like policymakers largely do: by treating them separately. By examining taxing and spending in-dependently, the goal is to establish that the decisionmaking process for each side of the budget is distinctive. The politics of taxing, simply put, is considerably different from the politics of spending.

The Political Context of Taxing and Spending

It is critical to study policymakers' taxing and spending decisions for reasons of democratic accountability.[6] Government budgets reflect

Figure 1.1 Total Revenues and Outlays as a Percentage of GDP, 1965–2007

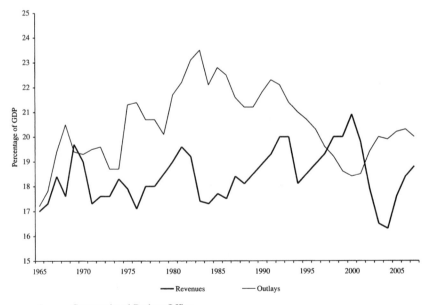

Source: Congressional Budget Office.

values and influence the environment in which we work just as household budgets reflect our values and shape our personal lives. By debating how to tax and spend scarce resources, policymakers must define what they stand for and what they stand against.[7] Certainly, taxing and spending decisions are as significant as ever. The degree by which the budget now dominates the federal policy process can be seen in an analysis of news coverage of Congress and the budget. A recent study found that the number of *New York Times* stories on Congress and the budget has increased dramatically since the 1970s, from about 5 percent in the early years of that decade to about 20 percent today.[8]

The federal budget process does not make balancing revenues with expenditures easy. As dictated by the Budget and Accounting Act of 1921, the president initiates the process by submitting a budget to Congress within fifteen days of the start of the legislative session. Congress then follows the procedures set forth by the Congressional Budget Act of 1974. After the president submits the budget to Congress, congressional committees hear testimony from the various executive departments. After the hearings, Congress passes a budget resolution that lays out its taxing and spending priorities for the next fiscal year. The targets of the budget resolution become guidelines for the various authorizing and appropriating committees that write specific taxing and spending bills. The congressional budget resolution, however, has only limited utility as a mechanism for balancing the budget. The resolution is only a congressional declaration of budgetary goals, not a statute. As a result, it cannot make or change laws. The resolution sets forth spending totals and broad priorities, but does not identify specific programs.[9] Thus it can reduce overall spending levels, but cannot actually cut programs from the budget.

The budget reconciliation process, on the other hand, is designed for Congress to make specific program cuts. Reconciliation is the process by which Congress tries to bring revenue and spending, under existing laws, into conformity with levels set in the budget resolution. Enactment of a reconciliation bill changes revenues or spending laws. Reconciliation is an optional process that is not activated every year. It is most likely to be used if the president's budget recommends spending cutbacks and if Congress wants to take active steps to reduce spending.[10] Major budget shifts today tend to take place through the reconciliation process, which has evolved into the principal means for Congress to enact deficit reduction legislation. The major budget shifts of 1981, 1990, 1993, and 2001 were all enacted through the reconciliation process.

The reconciliation process has generally made the budget process much more complicated. In one area, however, the reconciliation process has brought about a significant change that has made budgetary politics easier: a reconciliation bill cannot be filibustered in the Senate.[11] However, since the president still has veto power over the budget, this rule has worked to enhance his budgetary powers. While the president only needs to muster a majority of Congress to support his budget proposals, Congress would have to muster a two-thirds majority in both houses to pass the budget without presidential approval.

Traditionally the budget process was seen as being a rather sedate process of incremental bargaining among political actors, and attracted little political attention. The rise of large budget deficits, the increase in ideological distance between Democrats and Republicans in Congress, and budget reforms enacted by the Congressional Budget Act of 1974 have created an entirely different process. Today the budget is at the heart of the political process; it is the means by which policymakers attempt to implement most of their agenda.[12] For example, after the Republicans won control of Congress in 1994, they relied heavily on the budget process in attempting to implement their agenda of cutting taxes, balancing the budget, reforming welfare, cutting Medicare and Medicaid, terminating programs, and sending power back to the states.[13] For the Democrats, after winning back control of Congress in 2006, it was through the congressional power of the purse that they tried to establish a timetable for withdrawing troops from Iraq, by threatening to cut off funding for the war unless US involvement ended by a certain date.

From the end of World War II until the early 1970s, congressional tax committees were able to keep revenues roughly equal to expenditures by virtue of the strong growth of the US economy. This system of spending and taxing worked well as long as revenues were increasing due to economic expansion. The arrival of large deficits in the 1970s, however, significantly impacted Congress's ability to enact major legislation. Without the ability to offer targeted tax cuts and district spending benefits, it has become more difficult for Congress to secure the votes necessary for passage of budgetary as well as nonbudgetary issues.[14]

Public accountability requires that public money be spent as agreed, and that the government report accurately to the public on how money is spent. Public acceptability, on the other hand, means that policymakers who make budget decisions are constrained by what the public wants.[15] Raw, policy-specific facts, such as the size of the federal budget deficit, have a significant influence on the public's political judgments. Rather than diluting the influence of new information, general knowledge appears to facilitate the incorporation of new policy-specific information into political judgments.[16]

Yet the inconsistencies of taxing and spending policies are clearly related to public opinion. Counterintuitively, people who want the government to spend more money on specific programs are more likely to support tax cuts than those who do not. At the same time, those who feel that the government is wasteful in spending taxpayer money are markedly less supportive of tax cuts than those who hold more optimistic views of government efficiency.[17]

Ironically, taxing and spending lends itself to compromise much more than other areas of public policy. For example, if one faction suggests an income tax rate of 30 percent and another of 40 percent, a rate of 35 percent is a logical and relatively easy-to-achieve compromise. Other issues do not readily lend themselves to such compromise. With the war in Iraq, for example, one could legitimately argue that a compromise position was the worst possible, because it achieved no one's goals yet put American lives at risk. The problem from a balanced budget perspective is that taxing and spending compromises are largely made separate from one another.

The Partisanship of Taxing and Spending

Since the Great Depression, Democrats and Republicans have generally favored different fiscal, monetary, regulatory, and macroeconomic policies.[18] This polarization has accentuated since the 1960s, and the parties are now ideologically further apart on economic issues than they have been at any time since World War I.[19] The intensifying nature of budgetary partisanship is in part due to institutional factors, such as the evolution of macrobudgeting.[20] More important, however, are the growing partisan differences on economic issues.[21] The changes in congressional voting patterns over the past century can be traced to corresponding changes in the economic interests of their constituents.[22] From a budgetary perspective, this is potentially problematic because countries with higher levels of party polarization have higher deficits in election years, while the opposite is true for low-polarization countries; as a result, more polarized countries experience larger electoral cycles in fiscal policy.[23] Partisanship, however, is not an infallible predictor for budgetary decisions. Congressional budget votes, for example, often split one or both of the parties, in part because legislators have to defend parochial interests.[24] Government taxing and spending decisions, therefore, are never wholly ideologically consistent on all points.[25]

High-income voters have consistently been more prone to identify with and vote with the Republican Party than have low-income Americans, who disproportionately support the Democrats. Though this has been the case since the Great Depression, as the parties have become more differentiated in fiscal and economic policies, they have cued the voters to vote more on the basis of income. Economic issues such as measures to balance the budget, therefore, may now be viewed as a defining ideological difference between the parties. But just because partisan elites have become more polarized does not mean that mass partisans have necessarily followed suit.[26]

As the parties have moved apart ideologically, they have also become more homogeneous internally.[27] Democrats, in particular, are much more unified on economic issues today than they were in the 1960s and 1970s, when the party was split among northern liberal and southern conservative camps.[28] This is in large part due to a switch of partisan allegiances in the southern United States. As the region has moved from a one-party system dominated by the Democrats to a two-party system, it has seen a dramatic increase in the income effect on vote choice. Outside the South, however, the income effect has leveled off since the 1990s.[29]

The modern conventional justification for public debt emerged with John Maynard Keynes. Government, he believed, must take an active role in promoting full employment through both fiscal and monetary policy. To Keynes, classical economics failed to recognize that the market cannot by itself adequately maintain consumption demands and coordinate investment decisions.[30] Thus, Keynesian economics justified deficit spending in the short term. In fact, many leading economists saw the balanced budget norm as the main obstacle of rational economic policy making.[31] Over the long term, however, Keynesian economics held that government should reduce the public debt in times of economic prosperity by increasing taxes, cutting government spending, or both.

Keynesianism was embraced by New Dealers during the Great Depression as a means of stimulating an economy in dire straits. Once Franklin Roosevelt endorsed the concept of short-term deficit spending in order to stimulate the economy after he was elected president in 1932, the Democrats became the party associated with Keynesian economic principles and the Republicans largely remained unfettered from their historical belief in balanced budgets. By criticizing the large deficits of New Deal policies, the Republican Party began to be seen as the party that put a higher emphasis on balanced budgets, and this belief was reinforced by the election of Dwight Eisenhower as president in 1952 on a platform stressing the importance of balancing the budget. After World War II, however, federal budget deficits were relatively small under both Republican and Democratic presidents. Democrats may have embraced Keynesian economic principles, but they still tended to support the balanced budget norm, which was overwhelmingly supported by the American public. Between 1950 and 1965, for example, the US government produced surpluses only four times—in 1951, 1956, 1957, and 1960—but deficits during this period tended to be small, only exceeding $7 billion (1.7 percent of GDP) once, in the recession year of 1959. From 1965 to 2005, however, the federal government produced surpluses only five times: 1969, 1998, 1999, 2000 (when the surplus reached a record $236 billion, or 2.4 percent of GDP), and 2001 (see Figure 1.2). In every other year during that period, the federal government produced deficits. Though the deficit levels of the 1960s and 1970s were relatively small by today's standards, many of the annual deficits since the 1980s have been staggeringly large. In 2004, for example, federal

Figure 1.2 Federal Deficit, 1965–2007

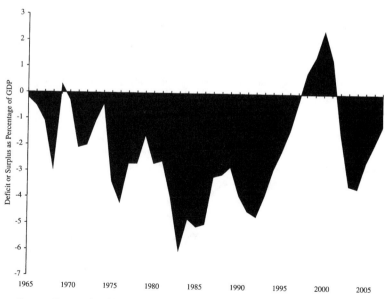

Source: Congressional Budget Office.

outlays were $2.29 trillion and revenues were $1.88 trillion, producing a deficit of 3.6 percent of GDP ($413 billion). As a percentage of GDP, the largest deficit of the past half century came in President Ronald Reagan's second budget year, 1983, when the deficit reached 6 percent of GDP ($208 billion).

From the New Deal era to the election of Reagan as president, it was widely held that Republicans put a higher premium on balancing the budget than Democrats. Republicans traditionally saw reducing the national debt as a means to reduce taxes in the long term. To be "conservative" on fiscal policy meant being averse to deficits. The large deficits of the 1980s, however, recast American politics, and the Republican Party's historical image as the antideficit party changed with the election of Reagan as president. Though conservatives and Republicans still tend to support budgetary balance in the abstract, they are less willing than previously to support the concept when presented with the specifics. Since Reagan's election, the emphasis for many in the party has moved toward cutting taxes rather than reducing the deficit. For numerous Republicans, supply-side economics promises short-term stabilization effects by promoting economic growth as well as the long-held goal of smaller government. In this way, Republicans can avoid the problem of limiting government and also supporting countercyclical spending.[32]

The Republicans' embracing of tax cuts as the foremost economic priority has changed the way that Democrats view deficits. Democrats increasingly support deficit reduction as an important means in itself—at least when it is defined in their terms.[33] Republican attempts to cut taxes and move toward budget deficit are seen by many Democrats as long-term means to reduce the spending that benefits Democratic constituencies. For many Democrats today, therefore, eliminating the deficit is simply a means to an end: protecting entitlement programs and restoring the government's credibility.

Balancing the budget has come to be seen as a means by which Democrats can maintain spending levels, while Republicans increasingly believe that large deficits will force spending cuts in the future. The Democrats first began trying to make large deficits an issue during the Reagan administration. Beginning with Walter Mondale's run for the presidency in 1984, the Democrats came to be more widely seen as the antideficit party, moving away from the Keynesian position that dominated the economic beliefs of the party in the postwar era. Since 1984, every major Democratic presidential candidate has condemned deficit spending.[34] Democrats' historical support for a countercyclical budget policy that makes redistribution an ongoing achievement of stabilization gave way to the perception that budget deficits were becoming unmanageable and needed to be curtailed. It is also possible that Republicans began to see budget deficits as less negative, because deficits tended to favor creditors, mainly Republicans, over debtors, mainly Democrats. Thus, by the 1980s, Democratic concern about deficits could have been a reflection of the belief that Democratic constituencies wre losers in deficit spending.[35]

This trend can be seen worldwide. Prior to the 1970s, parties of the political left were more likely to produce larger deficits than parties of the right. Since the 1970s, however, many parties on the right have pursued policies that have led to large deficits.[36] The supply-side economic policies of some governments on the right have produced very large deficits, while socialist and social democratic governments increasingly have adopted rather conservative fiscal policies. Overall, the political persuasion of a government appears to have little relationship to deficits, with several conservative governments producing large deficits and several social democratic governments producing relatively small deficits.[37]

In the United States, constituent Republicans and Democrats react differently to societal and individual economic concerns. Republicans tend to be more supportive of budgetary balance than Democrats, and this belief intensifies as perceptions of the national economy worsen. Democrats, on the other hand, support budgetary restraint when they believe the economy is strong, but tolerate deficits during periods of perceived economic recession—the classic Keynesian approach. Republicans, however, are more driven by personal pocketbook concerns than Democrats: when times get tough economically at the individual level, Republicans become much less committed to government frugality.[38]

The fact that congressional Republicans are relatively supportive of deficit reduction suggests that many might prioritize deficit reduction if the White House were to support balanced budget legislation. On the other side of the aisle, congressional Democrats might be less likely to support deficit reduction if not prodded to do so by the White House, as during the Bill Clinton administration. Thus, partisans in Congress appear to be following the lead of the executive branch in determining the priority of deficit reduction. As a result, the White House leadership appears to be more important than ever in regard to balancing the budget.

This can be seen in the considerable partisan relationship in the different taxing and spending priorities of presidents—and the deficits that resulted from these priorities. Since the Lyndon Johnson

administration, there has been a discernible pattern of revenue and
expenditure changes by presidential party (see Figure 1.3). For all
Democratic presidents since Johnson (Johnson, Carter, and Clinton),
the growth in revenue was greater than the growth in spending compared to the previous administration. On the other hand, for every
Republican administration (Nixon, Ford, Reagan, and the two Bush
presidents), the growth in spending was greater than the growth in
revenue. The relationship between Bill Clinton and George W. Bush
is especially noteworthy: while revenue increased 26 percent more
than did spending during the Clinton administration, spending increased 23 percent more than did revenue during the Bush administration (through 2007).

The different budgetary approaches of Democratic and Republican presidents in recent years may be a result of the fact that Democrats and Republicans tend to follow the wishes of those partisans
who elected them to office. Policymakers may simply be responding
to different portions of their constituencies.[39] This can be seen in the
partisan budgetary preferences of voters in the 2000 presidential

Figure 1.3 Change in Average Revenue and Spending
                by Presidential Administration

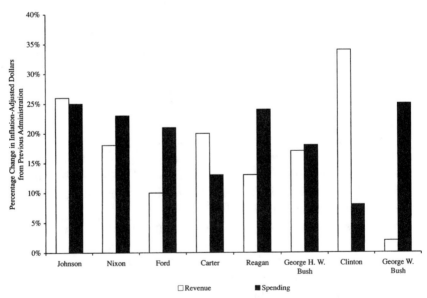

Sources: Heritage Foundation, Budget of the United States Government, Fiscal Year 2005,
tabs. 2.1 and 7.1.
Note: Data for G. W. Bush administration through fiscal year 2007.

election, during which significant partisan differences regarding tax-ing and spending proposals played a major role. An exit poll found noticeably different priorities between those who voted for Al Gore and those who voted for George W. Bush. Gore supporters argued that tax cuts should be a low priority for the next president, while Bush supporters strongly supported tax cuts.

Of those who claimed that tax cuts should be the top priority for the next president, 70 percent voted for Bush. Of those who claimed that prescription drugs, education, and Social Security should be the top priority, most cast their votes for Gore.[40] This may explain why Bush made tax cuts the major focus of his new administration despite opinion polls showing that the American public overall tended to be ambivalent toward the necessity of reducing taxes. Bush may have simply been responding to his political base, who strongly supported tax cuts.

The evidence indicates that Democratic presidents have been more successful at balancing the budget than Republican presidents, but does this partisan relationship also exist within Congress? The evidence is mixed, depending on the measures analyzed.

Congressional Support for Deficit Reduction

There is no consensus regarding how to measure congressional sup-port for deficit reduction. Looking at Congress as an institution, it is easy to critique the US legislature as doing an exceedingly poor job of balancing the budget. At the same time, however, the vast major-ity of those in Congress claim to support balanced budget principles. Almost all members of Congress claim to be against budget deficits and in favor of balancing the federal budget, at least in the abstract. When it comes to supporting the actual policies that would lead to expenditures and revenues being in balance, however, federal legis-lators often abandon balanced budget principles. The explanation of policy position variation across members does not explain aggregate budget decisions by Congress. Yet, looking at individual members of Congress, it is clear that not all are equally responsible for large deficits. The problem then becomes how to measure individual sup-port for deficit reduction.

A popular explanation for the inability of Congress to consistently produce balanced budgets is that its members are unwilling to make tough choices, thus undermining the budget process. If Congress were willing to cut spending or raise taxes, the deficit problem would abate and the process would stabilize.[41] Legislators, however, are expected to carry out those acts that gain the most votes and lose the fewest votes.[42] The problem is that American voters tend to favor lower taxes, greater government spending, and also a balanced budget.[43] That the American public tends to have contradictory opinions on the necessity of a balanced budget therefore complicates life for representatives. The difficulties that members of Congress face in budgeting are a direct result of the nature of a representative democracy; deficits may to a large degree simply be the result of the nation's representatives following the dictates of their constituencies.[44]

Members of Congress can avoid making politically difficult decisions by blaming the president, the bureaucracy, and interest groups as the real culprits for unbalanced federal budgets. For citizens, it is difficult to assess whom to blame for deficit spending. Accountability becomes a problem. One way to determine the degree to which members of Congress support balanced budget principles is to discriminate between legislative votes on taxing and spending. The analysis in this book utilizes congressional vote scores as provided by the Concord Coalition, an interest group that promotes deficit reduction.

The Concord Coalition is an antideficit group whose official mission is "to challenge national office holders to make the tough political choices required to balance the federal budget and keep it in balance."[45] It was founded in 1992—during which the deficit reached a record high (at the time) of $290 billion—by the late senator Paul Tsongas (D-MA), former senator Warren Rudman (R-NH), and former secretary of commerce Pete Peterson. Former senator Sam Nunn (D-GA) joined Rudman as a cochair of the coalition in 1997, and was replaced by former senator Robert Kerrey (D-NB) in 2001.

The Concord Coalition purports to champion the general interest by advocating fiscal responsibility and reform of entitlement programs, in order to ensure their viability and fairness for future generations. It was founded on the premise that when faced with the dilemma of balancing the budget, too few legislators summon the courage to make the necessary difficult decisions. As a result, the coalition's goal is to encourage politicians to change course through lobbying legislators and educating constituents.

In order to influence the political process, interest groups such as the Concord Coalition publish ratings of members of Congress. The Concord Coalition began publishing deficit reduction scores during the 104th Congress (1995–1996) and continued to do so through the

107th Congress (2001–2002). The coalition's "fiscal responsibility scorecard" rated each legislator on a scale of 0 to 100. Votes deemed to have significantly impacted deficit reduction were assigned various weights according to their relative importance. The Concord Coalition calculated the raw score by adding the weighted values of a legislator's "fiscally responsible" votes and dividing that number by the total weighted value of all votes cast by that legislator. Votes in which the legislator did not participate were excluded. "Fiscally responsible" votes were those that (1) reduced the deficit and protected the surplus, (2) supported actions that addressed long-term generational pressures on the federal budget, (3) kept budget enforcement procedures strong, (4) opposed enactment of new permanent claims on the federal budget that would be difficult to finance in the future, or (5) reduced or eliminated unnecessary or wasteful programs.

The fact that the Concord Coalition considers the tax side of the budget to be equal to the spending side of the budget in political and economic importance is a beneficial attribute of its scores—the coalition measures legislators' tendency to support deficit reduction in terms of both taxing and spending. To the Concord Coalition, "fiscal responsibility" is voting in favor of reduced spending or increased taxes, and voting against increased spending or reduced taxes. Thus the coalition's congressional vote scores can be seen as a means of measuring legislators' willingness to support the principles of balancing the budget from both the revenue side of the budget and the expenditure side of the budget.

Though the Concord Coalition's ratings will be utilized throughout this book, by no means should these ratings be viewed as irreproachable indicators of legislators' intentions. The imperfection of interest group ratings is partly due to the fact that they are based on a relatively small number of roll calls. Votes made on the floor of Congress may hide many important decisions made earlier in the legislative process, such as those made in committee. Many proposals do not make it out of committee, and of those that reach the floor, less than half are voted on in both the House and the Senate. Thus the estimates of influences on decisions generated from roll-call data will be much too large, because they do not account for the probability that a proposal receives committee approval and is subject to a roll call.[46] Interest group ratings are thus influenced by the distribution of the roll calls selected, which makes legislators appear to be more extreme than they actually are.[47] Furthermore, votes may be the result of pressures of party leadership and zealous constituents rather than the true positions of legislators.[48] Yet, though imperfect, interest group vote scores can provide a good indication of legislators' behavior in office over the long run.

In recent years, a number of constitutional amendments have been proposed to force the federal government to balance the budget. Since 1982, there have been five votes on balanced budget amendments in the House and seven in the Senate. Though the details of the amendments sometimes varied (usually with exceptions for time of war or a change in economic conditions), the overall goal of supporters of such amendments was to constitutionally require the federal government to produce a balanced budget. While four out of the five votes in the House (the exception being in 1982) achieved the required two-thirds majority to send the amendment to the states for ratification, only in 1982 did the Senate pass the amendment with a two-thirds majority.

In regard to the partisan divide on amendment votes, Republicans tended to overwhelmingly favor balanced budgets while Democrats generally opposed them. The amendment votes therefore tend to lend support to the argument that congressional Republicans are more supportive of balancing the budget than congressional Democrats. Thus the votes tend to reinforce the traditional stereotype of the Republican Party being the balanced budget party, and congressional Republicans have in the past used their voting record on balanced budget amendments as a wedge issue to differentiate themselves from Democrats.

The actual merits of a balanced budget amendment, however, are hotly contested. For one, it is unclear what the practical effects of such an amendment would be. Balanced budget amendment votes have been criticized by many as being purely symbolic, since they deal with the process, not tangible outcomes. Many Democrats have argued that these are phony proposals that are simply used to win political points. It is certainly plausible for someone to support the concept of balancing the budget while opposing a change to the Constitution. Many supporters of deficit reduction through means other than amending the Constitution, for example, often argue that such an amendment would give the judiciary too much power over fiscal policy, weakening the ability of the legislative and executive branches to implement the type of deficit spending necessary to extricate a potential budgeting crisis.[49]

Furthermore, even if a balanced budget amendment were enacted, it would remain unlikely that the federal government could balance the budget every year, even if it wanted to. Producing a balanced budget requires accurate forecasting of revenues and expenditures. These forecasts depend upon accurate forecasting of economic conditions, which is an inexact science. Inaccurate forecasts can play an important role in increasing the deficit. Deficit estimates are almost inevitably subject to seemingly large swings, even when they are made only a month before the end of the fiscal year. The projections for the fiscal 1993 deficit, for example, ranged from $352 billion in January 1992, to $327 billion in January 1993, to $285 billion in September 1993; the actual deficit was $255 billion.[50] Deficit projections for 1993 decreased as the economy proved to be healthier than expected, and interest rates dropped to record lows. Conversely, the economy wreaked havoc with 1990 deficit figures; even though the 1990 budget summit produced a deal that generated huge budget savings, higher deficits resulted as the savings were overwhelmed by the recession.[51]

A better way to measure the parties' support for balanced budget legislation in Congress is to compare the partisan dynamics of the Concord Coalition's vote scores. Comparing the mean vote scores of the parties during the 104th to 107th Congresses (1995–2002), we find that Democrats and Republicans do indeed have noticeably different voting records on deficit reduction measures, in both houses of Congress (see Figure 1.4). An interesting characteristic of the effect of partisanship on the vote scores, however, is that the direction of partisan influence is not consistent. That is, in some years, Republican have higher deficit reduction scores; in other years, Democrats have higher deficit reduction scores. During the 104th Congress, for example, House and Senate Republicans scored about 60 in terms of "fiscal responsibility," while congressional Democrats scored close to 40. For the 106th Congress, however, the ratings were reversed, with congressional Democrats scoring close to 60 and congressional Republicans near 40. This suggests that both the Democrats and the Republicans can legitimately claim—at least—to be the party more likely to support balancing the budget.

The fact that the Concord Coalition's congressional roll-call vote ratings do not fit nicely on the standard left-right political spectrum is atypical of interest group ratings.[52] This suggests that the political dynamics of deficit reduction are different from those of other issues. Most interest groups that issue ratings tend toward the exterior—or the extreme—of legislators. This means that interest group ratings tend to polarize legislators, moving them away from moderate positions.[53] The Concord Coalition's scores, on the other hand, appear to

Figure 1.4 Congressional Support for Deficit Reduction by Party

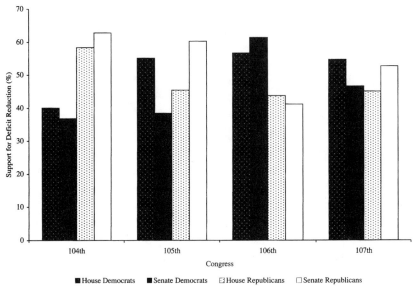

Source: Compiled by author.
Notes: Figures represent the mean Concord Coalition vote score (%) for each Congress. Data for the 104th, 105th, and 106th Congresses are composites of individual-year vote scores.

work against more ideologically extreme legislators. This is consistent with another study that found that it was indeed the more moderate legislators who were more supportive of deficit reduction, suggesting a polarization of fiscal policy as it relates to ideology.[54] The highest scores given by the Concord Coalition, for example, included legislators from across the political spectrum, both Republicans and Democrats.[55] In the 107th Congress (2001–2002), for example, the senators who received the highest scores were Lincoln Chafee (R-RI), Russell Feingold (D-WI), Thomas Carper (D-DE), Judd Gregg (R-NH), Bob Graham (D-FL), and John McCain (R-AZ); the representatives who received the highest scores were Gene Taylor (D-MS), Jeff Flake (R-AZ), Charles Stenholm (D-TX), Ed Royce (R-CA), and John Shadegg (R-AZ).

The Disconnection Between Taxing and Spending

Why does partisan support for deficit reduction vary so greatly from Congress to Congress according to the Concord Coalition's ratings?

The variance in partisan ratings may simply be a result of the number of votes on tax policy relative to the number of votes on spending policy in a particular Congress. Which party is seen by the Concord Coalition to be a better advocate of balanced budget policies may thus simply be a product of whether a spending or taxing issue is being debated.

As demonstrated in Figure 1.5, there is a clearly partisan pattern to taxing and spending votes. While House Democrats supported deficit reduction (as defined by votes on which the Concord Coalition took a position) on 72 percent of tax legislation votes during the 104th to 107th Congresses, House Republicans supported deficit reduction on only 9 percent of tax legislation votes. On legislation concerned with expenditures, however, House Republicans voted to support deficit reduction on 45 percent of votes, compared to 30 percent for House Democrats. In the Senate, the figures were similar: Democrats supported deficit reduction on 63 percent of tax votes but on only 33 percent of spending votes, while Republicans supported deficit reduction on only 21 percent of tax votes but on 48 percent of spending votes.

Figure 1.5 Partisan Support for Deficit Reduction: Taxing Versus Spending Votes

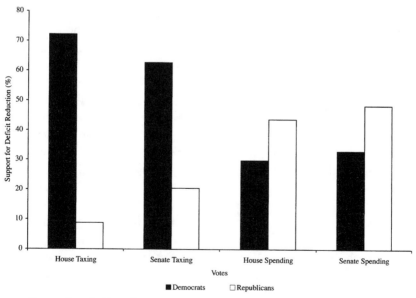

Source: Compiled by author.

Note: Data represent the average percentages supporting the Concord Coalition's positions on taxing and spending votes for the 104th–107th Congresses (1995–2002).

Thus, while the Concord Coalition's vote scores suggest that Democratic and Republican support for deficit reduction tends to vary from Congress to Congress, there is a consistently significant difference between the two parties in regard to taxing and spending votes that would reduce the deficit. Democrats are more supportive of reducing the budget deficit on taxing and spending votes. Overall, more than 70 percent of the votes the Concord Coalition chose for its rankings were for bills that dealt solely with spending. There was notable variation from Congress to Congress in the proportion of tax votes versus spending votes, with the proportion of spending votes ranging from 64 to 80 percent.

It may be that these changes in taxing and spending ratios from Congress to Congress represent a reaction of the Republican-controlled Congress to the surpluses from 1998 to 2000, and a reaction to changes in the White House's budget priorities. After the 1994 elections, in which the Republicans took control of Congress, annual deficits were still relatively high. Thus the Republicans, even though they publicly supported significant tax cuts, accorded higher legislative priority to cutting domestic spending. With a Democrat in the White House, congressional Republicans may have decided they would be more successful passing legislation that reduced spending than enacting tax cuts. Immediately after the Republicans took control of Congress, therefore, they received higher Concord Coalition vote scores, because they controlled the legislative agenda and supported a number of measures to reduce federal spending that Democrats opposed. The budget agenda changed, however, with the arrival of surpluses beginning in 1998. With the advent of federal budget surpluses, the Republicans made a more concentrated effort to reduce taxes, and the Democrats, playing defensively, voted against the tax cuts, arguing that the surplus would be better used for domestic programs and reducing the national debt. George W. Bush's election as president in 2000 may have reinforced this pattern. With a Republican in the White House, congressional Republicans saw an opportunity to accord tax cuts a greater priority, which lowered their vote scores, while Democrats' opposition to tax cuts garnered them higher scores.

To a significant degree, therefore, which party is the better advocate of balanced budget policies is determined by whether a spending or a taxing issue is being debated. While Republicans are consistently better supporters of balancing the budget on spending votes, Democrats are better on tax votes. An important difference in the levels of support on taxing and spending legislation between the parties in both the House and the Senate, however, is the degree by which they support the Concord Coalition's position. While the Democrats are overwhelmingly more likely to support the coalition's position on tax legislation, the Republicans are only somewhat more supportive on spending legislation. The data presented in Figure 1.5 emphasize the degree by which the Republicans have become an antitax party in Congress.

Consequently, the Republicans will generally be seen as the better advocates of a balanced budget when it comes to attempts to keep spending down, but the Democrats will be seen as the better defenders of a balanced budget when it comes to tax legislation. The Republicans' emphasis on tax cuts during the George W. Bush administration, for example, suggests that Democrats, perhaps by default, can be regarded as the stronger supporters of balancing the budget. Though the Democrats by no means dominate the Concord Coalition's ratings, the coalition's vote scores do lend some support to the Democrats' claims to be the party of fiscal responsibility. To a considerable degree, congressional Republicans now seem to have placed tax reduction ahead of balancing the budget.

For the population as a whole, as mentioned previously, constituent Republicans tend to put a higher priority on maintaining a balanced budget than do constituent Democrats.[56] Among federal policymakers, however, evidence lends credence to the Democrats' arguments that they are the better balanced budget party. The fact that spending votes outnumber tax votes by a good margin in the Concord Coalition's vote scores tends to work in favor of Republicans, but the Democrats more than hold their own in the rankings due to the Republicans' overwhelming lack of support for deficit reduction through increased taxes. Overall, however, the Concord Coalition's scores tend to be low for both parties; most of the votes on which the coalition advocates a position are defeated, sometimes by overwhelming margins.

The extremely partisan nature of taxing and spending votes has significant public policy implications. An advantage of a partisan budget process is that the parties can potentially produce comprehensive budgets. It might be that Democratic and Republican policymakers negotiate for what they hold most dear—for Republicans that would mean reduced taxes and for Democrats that would mean increased spending (especially on entitlements). But since balancing the budget is not a foremost priority for either party, it is abandoned.

To a surprising degree, taxing and spending decisions in the United States are disconnected from one another. Discussions of the federal budgeting process usually consider taxing and spending decisions in tandem. A problem with this approach is that it underestimates the degree to which the political dynamics of taxing are different from the political dynamics of spending. This book will therefore treat taxing and spending as separate entities. The decisionmaking process for taxes, simply put, is considerably different than that for spending. This analysis can further separate budget decisions by looking at how decisionmaking is different for increasing revenue and spending levels than it is for cutting revenue and spending totals. From a budgetary perspective, the political dynamics of adding are much different from those of subtracting. There is no consistent coalition of support for balancing the budget in terms of both taxing and spending.

The budget process in the United States is problematic and subject to many conflicting pressures. Budgeting, by its very nature, requires policymakers to think of the well-being of society as a whole in order to make macro-level decisions for a nation of more than 300 million people. The large budget deficits that currently plague the federal government suggest that there are overwhelming barriers to cutting spending and increasing taxes—and correspondingly balancing the budget. The disconnection between taxing and spending demonstrates that the budget is not as comprehensive as it should be.

Notes

1. Andrew Taylor, "The Ideological Roots of Deficit Reduction Policy," *Review of Policy Research* 19 (2002): 11–29.

2. Christopher Wlezien and Stuart N. Soroka, "Measures and Models of Budgetary Policy," *Policy Studies Journal* 31 (2003): 273–286.

3. Allen Schick, *The Capacity to Budget* (Washington, DC: Urban Institute, 1990); Dennis S. Ippolito, *Why Budgets Matter: Budget Policy and American Politics* (University Park: Pennsylvania State University Press, 2003); Aaron Wildavsky and Namoi Caiden, *The New Politics of the Budgetary Process,* 5th ed. (New York: Longman, 2004).

4. Congressional Budget Office, *The Fiscal and Economic Outlook: Fiscal Years 2007 to 2016* (Washington, DC, 2006), p. 4.

5. Ibid., p. 8.

6. John W. Burns and Andrew J. Taylor, "A New Democrat? The Economic Performance of the Clinton Presidency," *Independent Review* 5 (2001): 387–408.

7. David G. Levasseur, "The Role of Public Opinion in Policy Argument: An Examination of Public Opinion Rhetoric in the Federal Budget Process," *Argumentation and Advocacy* 41 (2005): 152–167.

8. David W. Brady and Craig Volden, *Revolving Deadlock,* 2nd ed. (Boulder: Westview, 2006), pp. 64–65.

9. Schick, *The Capacity to Budget,* pp. 88–89.

10. Allen Schick, *The Federal Budget Process: Politics, Policy, Process* (Washington, DC: Brookings Institution, 1995), pp. 82–83.

11. Brady and Volden, *Revolving Deadlock.*

12. Eric Patashnik, "Budgeting More, Deciding Less," *Public Interest* 138 (2000): 65–79.

13. Ibid.

14. Brady and Volden, *Revolving Deadlock.*

15. Irene S. Rubin, *The Politics of Public Budgeting,* 5th ed. (Washington, DC: Congressional Quarterly, 2006), pp. 18–19.

16. Martin Gilens, "Political Ignorance and Collective Policy Preferences," *American Political Science Review* 95 (2001): 379–396.

17. Larry Bartels, "Homer Gets a Tax Cut: Inequality and Public Policy in the American Mind," *Perspectives on Politics* 3 (2005): 15–31.

18. Burns and Taylor, "A New Democrat?"

19. Keith T. Poole and Howard Rosenthal, *Congress: A Political-Economic History of Roll Call Voting* (New York: Oxford University Press, 1997).

20. Lance LeLoup, *Parties, Rules, and the Evolution of Congressional Budgeting* (Columbus: Ohio State University Press, 2005).

21. Mark D. Brewer and Jeffrey M. Stonecash, *Split: Class and Cultural Divides in American Politics* (Washington, DC: Congressional Quarterly, 2007), pp. 42–43.

22. Sam Peltzman, "An Economic Interpretation of the History of Congressional Voting in the Twentieth Century," *American Economic Review* 75 (1985): 656–675.

23. James E. Alt and David Dreyer Lassen, "Transparency, Political Polarization, and Political Budget Cycles in OECD Countries," *American Journal of Political Science* 50 (2006): 530–550.

24. Poole and Rosenthal, *Congress.*

25. Andrew T. Cowart, "The Economic Policies of European Governments, Part I: Monetary Policy," *British Journal of Political Science* 8 (1978): 285–311.

26. Kara Lindaman and Donald P. Haider-Markel, "Issue Evolution, Political Parties, and the Culture Wars," *Political Research Quarterly* 55 (2002): 91–110.

27. Gary C. Jacobson, *A Divider, Not a Uniter: George Bush and the American People* (New York: Longman, 2007), p. 24.

28. John Coleman, *Party Decline in America: Policy, Politics, and the Fiscal State* (Princeton: Princeton University Press, 1996).

29. Nolan McCarty, Keith T. Poole, and Howard Rosenthal, *Polarized America: The Dance of Ideology and Unequal Riches* (Cambridge: Massachusetts Institute of Technology Press, 2006), chap. 3.

30. John Maynard Keynes, *The General Theory of Employment, Interest, and Money* (New York: Harcourt Brace Jovanovich, 1937), pp. 372–374.

31. Patashnik, "Budgeting More, Deciding Less."

32. Steven Schier, *A Decade of Deficits* (Albany: State University of New York Press, 1992), p. 26.

33. Taylor, "The Ideological Roots of Deficit Reduction Policy."

34. Patashnik, "Budgeting More, Deciding Less."

35. Joseph White and Aaron Wildavsky, *The Deficit and the Public Interest* (Berkeley: University of California Press, 1989), p. 412.

36. Cowart, "The Economic Policies of European Governments."

37. B. Guy Peters, *The Politics of Taxation* (Cambridge: Blackwell, 1991), pp. 118–123.

38. David C. Barker and Stephanie T. Muraca, "'We're All Keynesians Now'? Understanding Public Attitudes Toward the Federal Budget," *American Politics Research* 31 (2003): 485–519.

39. Morris Fiorina, *Representatives, Roll Calls, and Constituents* (Lexington, MA: Lexington, 1974).

40. Gallup Exit Poll of 2000 Elections (November 7, 2000), national survey of 13,130 adults.

41. Schick, *The Capacity to Budget.*

42. Anthony Downs, *An Economic Theory of Democracy* (New York: Harper and Row, 1957).

43. Patrick Fisher, *Congressional Budgeting: A Representational Perspective* (Lanham: University Press of America, 2005), chap. 6.

44. Ibid., chap. 7.

45. Concord Coalition, "About Us," September 2, 2005, http://www.concordcoalition.org/about.html.

46. Peter M. Vandoren, "Can We Learn the Causes of Congressional Decisions from Roll-Call Data?" *Legislative Studies Quarterly* 15 (1990): 311–340.

47. James M. Synder, "Artificial Extremism in Interest Group Ratings," *Legislative Studies Quarterly* 17 (1992): 319–345.

48. John W. Kingdon, *Congressmen's Voting Decisions,* 3rd ed. (Ann Arbor: University of Michigan Press, 1989).

49. Taylor, "The Ideological Roots of Deficit Reduction Policy."

50. George Hager, "Plummeting Interest Rates Help Trim Deficit," *Congressional Quarterly,* October 30, 1993, p. 2955.

51. George Hager, "Latest CBO Figures Support Clinton Deficit Projection," *Congressional Quarterly,* September 11, 1993, p. 2376.

52. Poole and Rosenthal, *Congress.*

53. Ibid.

54. Taylor, "The Ideological Roots of Deficit Reduction Policy."

55. Patrick Fisher, "Who Are the 'Deficit Hawks'? An Analysis of the Concord Coalition Congressional Vote Scores," *American Review of Politics* 24 (2003): 343–360.

56. Barker and Muraca, "'We're All Keynesians Now'?"

2

THE POLITICS OF TAXING

TOTAL TAX REVENUE FOR THE US GOVERNMENT IS NOW MORE than $2 trillion annually. With so much money at stake, it is important to scrutinize the manner in which this revenue is being raised. The need for tax revenue has always been a source of tension between governments and their citizens. Many important changes in governing structures throughout history have been a direct result of the need for greater tax revenue. In early modern Europe, for example, taxation led to representation when monarchs were compelled to relinquish some of their authority to parliamentary institutions in exchange for the ability to raise new taxes. Similarly, the American Revolution began as a rebellion against British taxes.[1] Determining the level of taxation is a crucial link between citizens and their governments.[2] The relationship between taxes and democracy may go so far as to explain the one-person, one-vote standard of most democracies. A democracy in which each person has one vote restricts the ability of majorities to excessively tax minorities.[3]

Taxes have been a subject of political controversy since the United States was founded. The Constitution provides in Article I, Section 8, that "the Congress shall have power to lay and collect taxes, duties, imports and excises, to pay the debts and provide for the common defense and general welfare of the United States." This provision represents an extensive grant of fiscal authority to Congress, because it covers almost any common form of taxation imaginable. The constitutional framers, fearing potential abuses by the executive branch to control the power of the purse, ensured that any tax proposals had to be passed by the people's branch of government, the legislative branch, and originate in the House, the only branch originally elected by the public. Over time, however, Congress has delegated much of its taxing power to the presidency, because it serves individual members' interests.[4]

Research has found that the American public is largely unaware of the particulars of tax policy.[5] Nonetheless, public opinion plays an important role in determining tax priorities. It has been found, for example, that presidential tax initiatives are related to public opinion over time.[6] Correspondingly, policy-specific facts, such as federal income tax rates, have a significant influence on the public's political judgments, and general knowledge appears to facilitate the incorporation of new policy-specific information into political judgments.[7] Following public opinion, however, is not always clear because Americans tend to have contradictory opinions concerning taxes. Voters want more benefits for the same or lower taxes.[8] Evidence also suggests that Americans do not always hold opinions consistent with their own self-interest in regard to tax policy.[9] Knowledge about the tax code, furthermore, is sharply skewed by income.[10]

Tax Rates

Individuals are responsive to the level of taxation. Dissatisfaction with particular taxes rises and falls with the toll they exert over time.[11] Citizens do not like taxes, but on the whole they like the benefits they receive from government and tend to be much more willing to pay taxes when reminded of the benefits they receive. The majority tend to favor the same or greater expenditures for programs even after the "tax price" is introduced.[12] Yet many Americans are hostile to the level of taxes that they pay, because they believe that this money is being spent wastefully or even fraudulently, or that a substantial part of it goes for services of which they disapprove.[13] Since the payment of most taxes is for services or goods that are not directly received, there remains the impression that taxes are a net loss rather than a payment.[14] The hostility toward taxes, however, does not mean that Americans are unwilling to pay them. Studies have found that, comparatively speaking, Americans are relatively obedient when it comes to paying taxes. The tax evasion rate in the United States is relatively low, though it is higher in the United States than in Scandinavian countries.[15]

Are Americans overtaxed? Certainly many Americans believe that they pay too much in taxes. The political rhetoric concerning social programs usually centers on the cost to the taxpayer, accompanied by assertions that Americans are already overtaxed. Compared to other developed countries, however, the United States collects among the lowest proportion of taxes (see Figure 2.1). As a percentage of GDP, taxes in Denmark are nearly twice what they are in the United States. The United States has by far the lowest tax rate for high-income individuals, its corporate taxes are below the mean, and its levies on goods and services are even further below the mean.

Denmark's willingness to tax considerably more than the United States is clearly a product of the country's different political culture. A society's tax regime is clearly predicted by its predominant political orientation.[16] In political as well as economic terms, taxes are the cost of providing the benefits of government. Comparatively speaking, the United States appears to be less willing to pay the costs of these benefits than other countries.

For the most part, growth in federal revenues in the United States has historically been closely tied to annual increases in GDP. Before the George W. Bush presidency, the major exceptions occurred when

Figure 2.1 Comparative Tax Rates, 2007

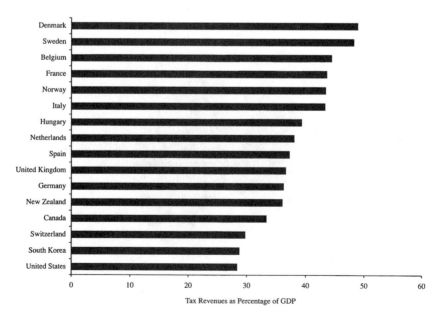

Source: Organization for Economic Cooperation and Development.

revenues dropped dramatically from the previous year following major tax cuts, as enacted under the presidencies of Richard Nixon and Ronald Reagan. During the George W. Bush presidency, however, tax revenues became much more volatile than they had been over the previous three decades, and more susceptible to swings in the stock market. Tax revenues are increasingly dependent on the fortunes of the very wealthy, who are different from other taxpayers in that much more of their income is tied not to wages but to the stock market and executive bonuses, which can vary widely from year to year.[17]

Political debates on tax policy tend to revolve around the question of how much to tax. An equally important question is what to tax. Federal revenues are derived from various sources, the most important of which are individual income taxes, corporate income taxes, and payroll taxes. In 2007, individual income taxes constituted 45 percent of federal revenues, social insurance taxes constituted 34 percent, and corporate income taxes constituted 14 percent (see Figure 2.2).

The Income Tax

From the founding of the United States until World War I, tariffs and excise taxes were the primary sources of revenue for the tiny national

Figure 2.2 Sources of Federal Revenue, Fiscal Year 2007

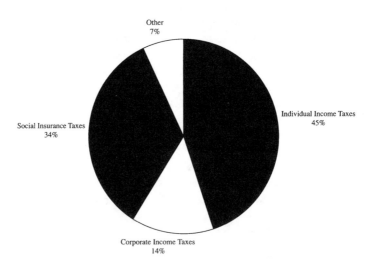

Source: Congressional Budget Office.

government. The income tax was unknown until its brief use during the Civil War. It then remained unused until 1894, when President Grover Cleveland convinced Congress to lower tariffs and substitute a modest tax on incomes to recoup revenues. The Supreme Court, however, ruled the income tax unconstitutional in the case *Pollock v. Farmers' Loan and Trust Co.* (1895). As a result of the *Pollock* ruling, the federal government ran deficits in eleven of the twenty-one years from 1894 to 1914. In reaction to the federal government's inability to balance the budget, the Sixteenth Amendment, which allowed the income tax, was ratified in 1913. Although the modern federal income tax was enabled by the Sixteenth Amendment, it was not until World War II that anyone other than the very wealthy paid it. In 1939, fewer than 4 million individuals paid the federal income tax; by 1945, that figure was greater than 42 million.[18]

Income tax rates have fluctuated considerably since the Sixteenth Amendment was ratified. In 1913, the top marginal rate was only 7 percent. This figure increased dramatically during World War I, to 77 percent, before decreasing to 25 percent in the 1920s. In order to pay for New Deal programs and later to help finance World War II, however, Franklin Roosevelt raised the individual and corporate income taxes to unprecedented levels, with the top marginal rate remaining over 70 percent until 1982.

Figure 2.3 shows the top marginal individual income rate since the Sixteenth Amendment was ratified. It contains a number of simplifications and ignores some factors—the definition of taxable income, for example, has varied substantially through the years, and taxable income can be considerably lower than actual income. Also, the income level at which the top rate takes effect has varied considerably, from $2 million in 1916–1917 and 1936–1941 to $84,300 in 1991–1992. It is clear, however, that the rate of taxation for the top income tax bracket has decreased dramatically during the past half century, falling from 91 percent in 1963 to 35 percent in 2003.

Other than actual income tax rates, other factors that influence the amount of revenue that the federal government receives through the income tax are exemptions and deductions. Tax exemptions allow individuals and organizations to forgo taxes that they would normally be required to pay. Usually, the government allows tax exemptions in order to economically promote certain activities, such as charity. Tax deductions are expenses incurred by a taxpayer that are subtracted from his or her gross income. As a result, tax deductions lower the amount of tax paid. Each taxpayer is allowed a standard deduction

Figure 2.3 Historical Highest Marginal Income Tax Rates, 1910–2007

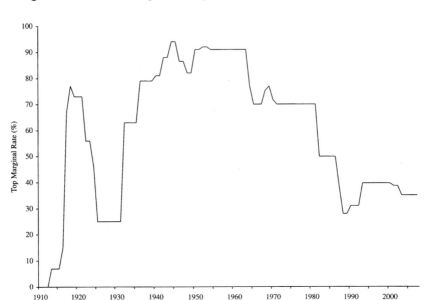

Sources: Joseph A. Pechman, *Federal Tax Policy* (Washington, DC: Brookings Institution, 1987); Joint Committee on Taxation, "Summary of Conference Agreement on the Jobs and Growth Tax Relief Reconciliation Act of 2003," JCX-54-03, May 22, 2003; Internal Revenue Service.

that increases with the number of his or her dependents. One of the furthest-reaching (and most expensive) deductions is for interest on home mortgages, which cost the Treasury an estimated $76 billion in 2006.[19]

The level of individual income tax revenue fluctuates significantly even when the marginal tax rates do not change. Historically, individual income tax revenue has been the key determinant of total federal revenues. Between 1965 and the late 1990s, individual income taxes produced nearly half of all federal revenues. Between 1992 and 2000, individual income tax revenue more than doubled, averaging an annual growth rate of nearly 10 percent and reaching a historic peak of 10.3 percent of GDP. After 2000, individual income taxes fell as a share of GDP for four consecutive years, down to 7.0 percent in 2004, the lowest level since 1951. The drop in income tax revenue began as a result of the stock market decline and the 2001 recession and was reinforced by income tax cuts after George W. Bush was elected president. With the growth in income beginning in 2004, tax revenues began rising again, a trend that is projected to continue past the Bush presidency.[20] Another factor that affects income tax revenue is inflation. When inflation pushes incomes into higher tax brackets, the result is the so-called bracket creep—an increase in taxes but not an increase in real purchasing power. Bracket creep has been problematic during periods of high inflation, such as the late 1970s.

There are many potential variations in implementation of the income tax. One of the more politically controversial features of the federal income tax today is the alternative minimum tax (AMT). The AMT was originally designed to limit the use of tax preferences (exclusions or deductions from a comprehensive measure of income) by high-income taxpayers to ensure that they paid at least some income tax. Under the AMT, a parallel tax system with its own set of exemptions and its own rate schedule was created with a limited set of tax preferences compared to those that apply under the regular income tax. Taxpayers are required to pay whichever is greater—the tax they owe under the AMT or the tax they owe under the regular income tax.[21] The AMT allows a single large exemption, which was originally designed to make sure that low- and middle-income taxpayers would not be forced to pay the AMT.

The number of taxpayers who are affected by the AMT has been growing. Historically, the share of tax filers who are subject to the AMT has been small; in 2000, only 1 percent of filers, 1 million taxpayers, qualified for the AMT. Unless the law is changed, however, the number of AMT qualifiers is expected to rise to 33 million by 2016, and revenues from the AMT over this time period are projected to increase almost sixfold, to about $81 billion.[22] The growth of the AMT is the result of two factors. First, unlike the parameters of the regular income tax, the parameters of the AMT are not indexed for inflation. Thus, over time, taxpayers face higher tax rates under the AMT even if their incomes grow only at the rate of overall increases in the cost of living. The last permanent increase in the AMT took effect in 1993, at which point the exemption for married couples was increased to $45,000. Inflation sharply reduced the real value of the 1993 exemption; if the married AMT exemption had kept up with inflation after 1993, it would have increased to almost $63,000 in 2006.[23] Second, the tax cuts enacted in 2001 and 2003 resulted in additional taxpayers becoming subject to the alternative tax, though this effect was mitigated somewhat by a temporary increase in the AMT exemption that expired in 2005.[24]

The broad reach of the tax suggests that taxpayers in larger families (who have a greater number of personal exemptions) and taxpayers with larger deductions for state and local taxes tend to be more affected by the AMT than other taxpayers. The impact of the AMT also varies among different income groups. The share of taxpayers affected by the alternative tax is projected to grow for all income groups, although the share is expected to expand the most for taxpayers with incomes between $50,000 and $500,000.[25] As a result, some tax experts believe that the problems with the AMT could force Congress to significantly revise the tax code.[26]

Along with personal incomes, the federal government taxes corporate incomes. The current corporate income tax rate ranges from 15 to 35 percent, depending upon a corporation's profits, and the effective corporate income tax rate is close to 26 percent. Most businesses are classified by the Internal Revenue Service as "S" corporations, which are not required to pay the corporate income tax. Fewer than 10 percent of all businesses, including farm businesses, are classified as "C" corporations, which are subject to the corporate income tax.[27] The profits of businesses other than "C" corporations are subject to the individual rather than the corporate income tax.

Since World War II, the corporate income tax has been an important source of federal revenue; today it is the third largest source. The relative share of corporate income taxes, however, has declined significantly since the 1950s, from 28 percent of federal revenues in the 1950s, to 21 percent in the 1960s, to 13 percent in the 2000s. This decline in corporate income tax revenue is in part due to the decline in corporate tax rates, which exceeded 50 percent for most of the 1950s and 1960s. Another reason for the decline in corporate income tax revenue is the increasingly aggressive use of tax shelters by businesses to avoid paying taxes. As a result, corporate income tax revenue as a share of the economy in the United States is lower than that in most other developed countries.[28]

Corporate income tax revenue has tended to be extremely volatile over the past couple of decades. Corporate income taxes, like those from individual income taxes, rose dramatically in the 1990s but fell sharply after the recession of 2001 reduced corporate profits. After 2003, corporate income taxes rebounded; in 2005, the $278 billion collected in such taxes was more than twice the amount collected two years earlier. As a share of GDP, however, the 2005 figure, 2.3 percent, was similar to levels of the late 1990s.[29] Projections of corporate tax revenue depend critically on projections of corporate profits, which are heavily influenced by assumptions about depreciation deductions and contributions to underfunded pension plans.[30]

The Payroll Tax

Social Security is financed by a flat-rate payroll tax. The effective payroll tax rate drops as income rises. This is due to the fact that only the first $94,200 in earned income is taxed. Since 1990, employers and employees have each paid 6.2 percent of the employees' earned income to finance Social Security and 1.45 percent to finance Medicare. Self-employed individuals pay both shares (15.3 percent). Workers do not pay the Social Security tax on wages over $94,200, but they do continue to pay the Medicare tax.

The payroll tax rate for Social Security has increased dramatically since Social Security's founding (see Figure 2.4). The original Social Security payroll tax, in 1937, was only 1 percent. This rate tripled by 1961, increased to 4.2 percent in 1970, and rose gradually in the 1970s and 1980s before leveling off at 6.2 percent in 1990. The payroll tax thus now accounts for a greater proportion of federal revenues than has historically been the case, and now represents the second largest source of revenue for the federal government. Since 1990, this tax has generated about one-third of federal revenues, or

Figure 2.4 Payroll Tax Rate for Social Security, 1935–2007

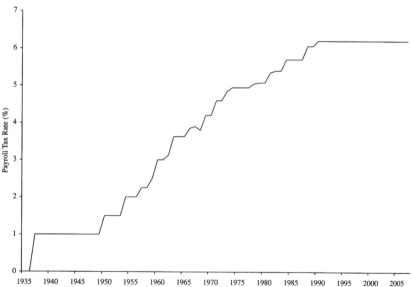

Source: Social Security Administration.
Note: The payroll tax rate is that paid separately by employees and employers.

about 6 to 7 percent of GDP.[31] Revenue from the payroll tax is projected to claim a roughly constant share of GDP—between 6.3 and 6.4 percent—through 2016. As a share of wages and salaries, which constitute the approximate base for the payroll tax, revenue is also projected to remain relatively stable, at about 14 percent.[32]

Social Security is a pay-as-you-go system, with current workers paying for existing retirees. Despite the rhetoric of politicians, Social Security taxes are used for the same purposes as income taxes—the government uses the money to meet whatever expenses are pending. It is therefore incorrect to look at the payroll tax separately from the rest of the budget.

Other Federal Taxes

Before the twentieth century, the major source of revenue for the United States was the tariff, the taxing of goods upon importation. The precedence for the federal government's reliance on the tariff goes back to the first days of the nation, when the 1st Congress passed the Tariff Act of 1789. Though high tariffs, considered economically counterproductive by free trade advocates, were often politically contentious, they provided a relatively stable revenue base for the small federal government throughout the nineteenth century. It was not until it became clear that tariffs alone would no longer provide enough revenue for the federal government to sustain itself that Congress reluctantly sought to ratify the Sixteenth Amendment in order to allow for the income tax.

Today, federal revenues from tariffs and taxes other than the income and payroll taxes amount to only about 1.5 percent of GDP.[33] Excise taxes, which are paid when purchasing particular goods or when engaging in particular activities, constitute about 3.4 percent of all federal revenues. Excise taxes generally fall into five major categories: highway, airport, telephone, alcohol, and tobacco.

The contribution of excise taxes has declined substantially, from 12.5 percent of federal revenues in 1960 to 3 percent in 2008. Revenues from excise taxes are expected to continue their long-term decline. Most excise taxes are levied per unit of good or per transaction, rather than as a percentage of value. Thus, excise revenues do not grow as fast as the nominal GDP.[34]

By far the most important excise tax in the United States today is the gasoline tax, which accounts for about half of all excise revenues.

In 2008, the federal gas tax was 18.4 cents per gallon. At the state level, gas tax rates varied considerably, with Wisconsin having the highest, at 31.0 cents per gallon, and Georgia having the lowest, at 14.5 cents per gallon.

All federal excise taxes are deposited into the Highway Trust Fund. With the passage of the Transportation Equity Act for the 21st Century in 1998, Congress established a direct link between the Highway Trust Fund and the funding transferred to states and cities for highway and transit programs. As a result, spending on all highway and transit programs decreases proportionately if tax revenue in the trust fund falls short.[35]

A more politically controversial tax, despite the fact it brings in relatively little federal revenue, is the estate tax, also known as the inheritance tax. Only a little more than 1 percent of all federal revenues are derived from the estate tax. A justification for this tax is that an inheritance constitutes an income for the recipient that is not earned in the same sense that money is earned, through work or even through returns on investment decisions. Those who oppose the inheritance tax, on the other hand, argue that taxes were presumably paid by the estate's owner while he or she was earning a living.

The federal estate tax is scheduled to be phased out by 2010 but reinstated in 2011. Before the temporary reduction currently under way, revenue from the estate tax tended to grow more rapidly than revenue from the income tax, because the credit for the estate tax, which effectively exempted some assets from taxation, was not indexed for inflation.[36] Since estate tax liabilities are paid after a lag caused by the implementation of the tax after a death, and because the gift tax remains in the tax code, revenue from the estate tax will not disappear completely, but will reach a trough in 2010 and 2011. The projected revenue in 2011 will largely result from taxable gifts that people will bestow in 2010 due to the relatively low rate of the estate tax and its planned reinstatement in 2011. These gifts would otherwise be given in earlier or later years and would therefore affect the pattern of revenue. The Congressional Budget Office (CBO) estimates that after 2011, estate tax revenue under current law will return roughly to its 2002 share of GDP.[37]

Significantly, the revenue base of the federal government does not rely on a sales tax or property tax. These taxes are utilized by state and local governments. Forty-four states levy a tax on the sale of goods and services, and this tax is their largest source of revenue. The United States is the only industrialized nation without a federal sales or value-added tax, so named because it is imposed on the "value added" at every stage of production or service. This is the single most important difference between the US tax system and the tax systems of other industrialized nations. In most European nations, for example, revenues from consumption taxes amount to about 38 percent of GDP.[38] For the United States, creation of a value-added tax would significantly increase federal revenue.

Along with the lack of a value-added tax, the United States collects less revenue than most developed countries in environmental taxes. In 2003, while Organization for Economic Cooperation and Development countries averaged 5.7 percent environmental tax revenues as a share of total tax revenues, the United States managed only 3.5 percent; by comparison, Germany's environmental tax share was 7.4 percent and the United Kingdom's was 7.6 percent.[39] Advocates of higher environmental taxes argue that a better approach would be to shift more of the tax burden into activities that are economically unproductive and reduce quality of life, such as pollution and waste disposal. Environmental charges—taxes or fees levied on firms based on the amount of pollution they release into the air, water, or soil, for example—could provide revenue and at the same time increase the efficiency of the economy.[40] Although the average level of taxation of gasoline in the United States is roughly 40 cents per gallon, for example, current research by economists suggests that the optimal gasoline tax rate—taking into account factors such as pollution and congestion effects—exceeds $1 per gallon.[41]

The Progressivity of Federal Taxes

All taxes discriminate. The public policy question is how to properly target that discrimination to raise the needed revenue. Taxes can be progressive, regressive, or proportional. In a progressive tax structure, the rate of taxation increases as income and wealth increase. For example, in a progressive tax system, a person who earns $200,000 might pay 40 percent of his or her income in taxes, while a person who earns $50,000 might pay 20 percent. The US federal income tax is currently progressive in its implementation. A regressive tax system is the opposite of its progressive counterpart, with the rate of taxation decreasing as income and wealth increase. The federal payroll tax is currently construed as a regressive tax. A proportional tax maintains an equal tax rate, regardless of income level, and does not shift the rate disproportionately to those with higher or lower incomes. A sales tax under which all goods are taxed at one fixed rate is a common example of a proportional tax (though some argue that proportional taxes on consumption are regressive, because lower-income individuals spend a greater percentage of their incomes on taxable goods).

The most important choice the federal government ever made about taxation was the decision to raise revenue by taxing personal and corporate incomes. The second most important choice was that the federal income tax be progressive, with the heaviest burden carried by those most able to pay. Advocates of the income tax as a major source of revenue tend to stress the tax's progressivity as a primary advantage.

Whether or not federal taxes are progressive depends upon the tax. The federal income tax is progressive. Payroll taxes and excise taxes, however, tend to be regressive. Figure 2.5 displays the markedly different impacts of personal income taxes and payroll taxes depending upon income. For the lowest quintile (the poorest 20 percent), the effective income tax rate is actually negative (meaning that they receive money from the federal government), because of the Earned Income

Figure 2.5 Effective Federal Tax Rates by Income Level, Fiscal Year 2007

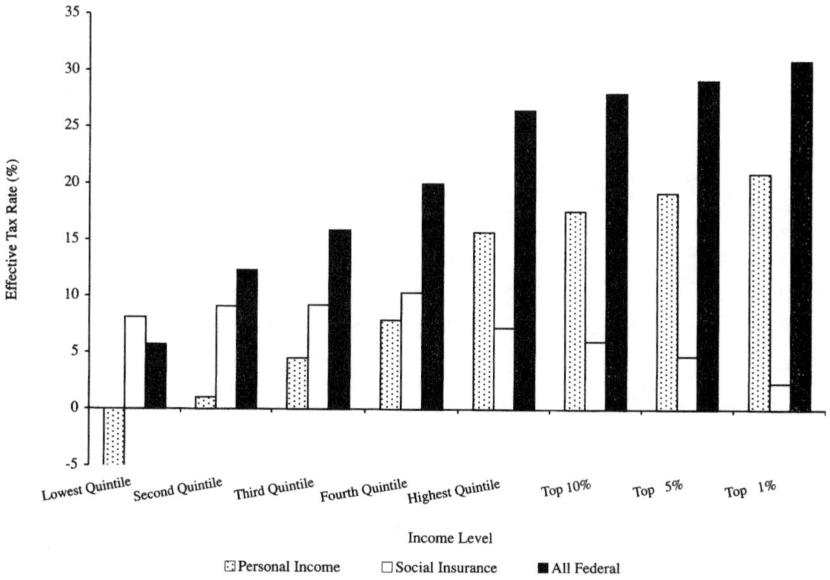

Source: Congressional Budget Office.

Tax Credit (EITC) program. For the highest quintile (the wealthiest 20 percent), the effective income tax rate is about 16 percent. With payroll taxes, on the other hand, the effective tax rate decreases as income increases, because the payroll tax is paid only on incomes up to $94,200. While the effective payroll tax rate for the lowest quintile is 8.1 percent, it is only 2.3 percent for the wealthiest 1 percent. To critics, the magnitude of the Social Security–Medicare payroll tax makes the US tax system less progressive than it should be. Due to its regressive nature, the payroll tax is arguably unfavorable to lower-middle-class Americans.[42] The total amount one contributes in all federal taxes, however, is progressive; the effective tax rate for all federal taxes is 5.7 percent for the lowest quintile and 26.5 percent for the highest quintile.

An advantage of progressive taxes from a revenue perspective is that it is easier to raise money by taxing the wealthy in this manner. It is easier for the very wealthy to enhance their income levels than other segments of the population. There is also evidence that wealth is more concentrated than it used to be, suggesting that progressive taxes can be justified on "fairness" grounds. The fairness of progressive taxes is of course debatable, but progressive tax rates have clearly impacted the concentration of wealth in the United States. Of the forty richest men in US history, for example, not one made his fortune during eras when the tax code was at its most progressive.[43]

Though surveys have revealed that substantial income redistribution has never been popular in the United States, the income tax has always been progressive in its implementation. Since an increase in the progressivity of the income tax can result in significantly higher tax revenues, increasing tax rates for the wealthy may be a relatively acceptable means of raising more revenue. But individuals do not always hold opinions consistent with their own self-interest, suggesting that taxing the rich progressively may not be the most politically feasible way to increase government revenues.[44]

Americans possess only a limited understanding of the concept of progressive taxation, complicating matters for policymakers. One study, for example, found that most Americans preferred progressive taxes when using the format of standard survey questions; but when similar questions were framed in concrete terms, a majority rejected progressive taxes.[45] In comparison, Swedes tend to have a much greater understanding of progressive taxation than Americans. This may be due to the Swedish welfare state system and the political environment exercising a substantially stronger educational influence on the meaning of redistribution. Importantly, greater understanding leads to greater support for progressive taxes—Swedes strongly support progressive taxes while Americans offer only tepid support.[46] Interestingly, however, the larger welfare states (including the Scandinavian nations) are disproportionately financed by flat-rate consumption and payroll taxes, despite the stereotype that such countries rely on highly progressive income taxes.[47]

Ideologically, the tax debate in the United States revolves around the question of equity versus efficiency. Advocates of progressive taxation measures tend to focus on the growing inequality in the distribution of income and conclude that the more affluent should pay at higher rates. Conservatives, on the other hand, argue that high marginal rates on upper tax brackets stifle innovation and initiative. They see the potential for considerable upward mobility and believe that growing income inequality is reflective of differential rewards for entrepreneurs, who should not be taxed disproportionately. Conservatives also argue that the wealthy are carrying an ever larger portion of the tax burden and that redistribution in the tax system is growing.[48]

The EITC, for example, gives partially refundable tax credits to individuals who earn wages below an established maximum, as well as to qualifying families with dependent children. If the credits exceed a taxpayer's liability, the excess may be refunded to the taxpayer, depending on the filer's earnings. The refundable portions of these credits, which are categorized as outlays, are approximately $50 billion and are projected to remain at that level until 2012.[49] As a result, there is a redistributive effect at the bottom of the income spectrum, because the poor receive more money back than they pay in income taxes. In 2005, this program distributed $39 billion to families. Since the EITC program is redistributive, it contributes to a growing percentage of filers who have no tax obligation.

Over the past half century, conservatives have been winning (incrementally at least) the battle on tax progressivity. Since the end of World War II the federal tax system has clearly moved in a less redistributive direction.[50] As Figure 2.6 demonstrates, payroll or social insurance taxes have increased substantially as a percentage of GDP, while corporate income taxes have declined in revenue importance. Since the payroll tax is a flat tax and is paid only on income up to a certain ceiling each year, it is a far greater burden on low-income households. On the other hand, corporate income taxes—much more progressive than payroll taxes—were roughly 3.8 percent of GDP in the 1960s, but fell to 1.2 percent by 2003.[51]

It can be argued that the tax shift in recent years has worked against the middle class from both ends of the income spectrum. Not only are the wealthy being taxed less, but so are the poor, meaning

Figure 2.6 Revenues, by Source, as Share of GDP, 1965–2007

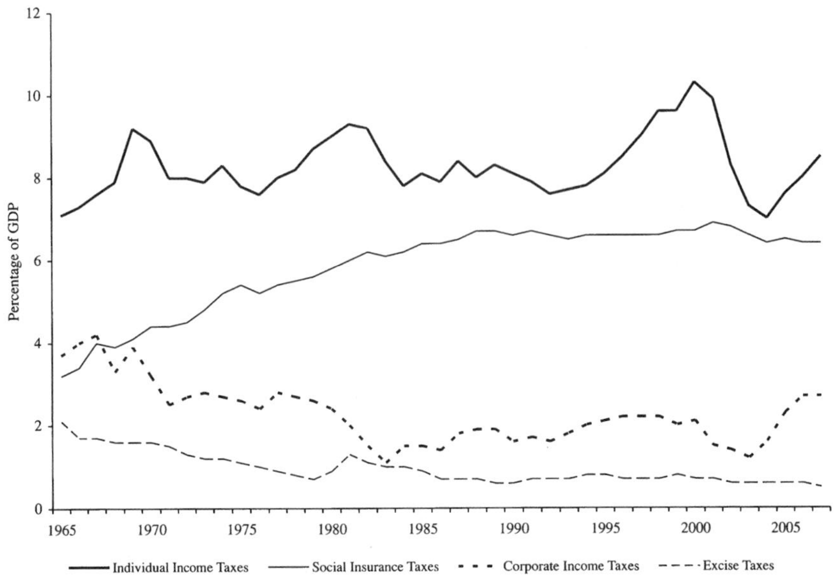

Legend: Individual Income Taxes   Social Insurance Taxes   ▪ ▪ ▪ Corporate Income Taxes   – – – Excise Taxes

Source: Congressional Budget Office.

that the middle class is now paying a larger amount of the tax burden than previously. The middle 20 percent of Americans are paying more taxes today than in 1977, while the top 1 percent are paying much less and the poorest Americans are receiving extended income tax benefits through the EITC.

The Partisanship of Taxation

Since the election of Franklin Roosevelt as president in 1932, Democrats and Republicans have generally favored different tax policies.[52] The polarization between the parties on taxes, however, is greater today than it has ever been.[53] Figure 2.7 displays the average percentage of Democratic and Republican legislators who supported the Concord Coalition's positions on tax legislation from the 104th to 107th Congresses. Examples of the Concord Coalition's stance on tax legislation included advocating against the Tax Cut Reconciliation Bill of 2001 (George W. Bush's tax cut package), against alleviation of the "marriage penalty," and against repeal of the Social Security earnings

Figure 2.7 The Partisanship of Congressional Tax Votes

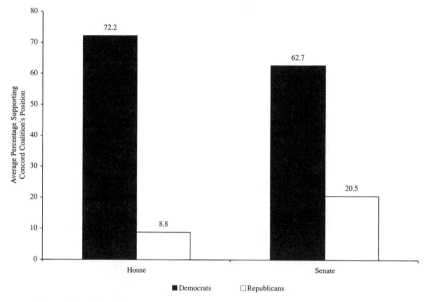

Source: Compiled by author.
Note: Data are for the 104th–107th Congresses (1995–2002).

test. There was clearly a strong correlation between a legislator's party affiliation and a legislator's votes on tax legislation. In the House, Democrats supported the Concord Coalition's positions on 72.2 percent of tax legislation, while Republicans supported the Concord Coalition's positions on only 8.8 percent of tax legislation. In the Senate, the differences were similar but not quite as dramatic: Democrats supported the Concord Coalition's positions on 62.7 percent tax legislation, while Republicans supported the Concord Coalition's positions on only 20.5 percent of tax legislation. Partisanship is thus an overwhelmingly dominant factor in congressional tax votes. Democrats in both the House and the Senate are much more likely to vote against tax cuts and much more likely to vote for tax increases.

The parties' different stances regarding taxing legislation have been historically regarded as class-based, with Democrats favoring more progressive taxes and Republicans tending to support tax cuts that give a greater share of benefits to the wealthy. Whether to reduce the budget deficit by altering tax policy can therefore be seen as a defining ideological difference between the parties. As a result of the polarization of the parties on tax policy, partisan control of Congress can potentially have significant public policy implications.[54] If changes in the tax code are largely the result of partisanship and not constituency preferences, this suggests that tax policy has become more top-down and potentially elitist, with more power concentrated in the hands of relatively few policymakers who have attained party leadership positions in Congress. Rather than basing tax decisions on the relative number of winners or losers in their constituencies, legislators may be basing their decisions on party loyalty and the partisan leanings of their constituents. For example, it has been found that the probability of congressional incumbents winning reelection decreases as they offer increased support for their party.[55] In relation to tax legislation, partisanship may be bad politics.

Notes

1. Michael Ross, "Does Taxation Lead to Representation?" *British Journal of Political Science* 34 (2004): 229–249.

2. Michael Herb, "No Representation Without Taxation?" *Comparative Politics* 37 (2005): 297–316.

3. Hans Gersbach, "Why One Person One Vote?" *Social Choice and Welfare* 23 (2004): 449–464.

4. Jasmine Farrier, *Passing the Buck: Congress, the Budget, and Deficits* (Lexington: University Press of Kentucky, 2004).

5. Sven Steinmo, *Tax Policy* (Cheltenham: Edward Elgar, 1998).

6. Christopher Wlezien, "Patterns of Representation: Dynamics of Public Preferences and Policy," *Journal of Politics* 66 (2004): 1–24.

7. Martin Gilens, "Political Ignorance and Collective Policy Preferences," *American Political Science Review* 95 (2001): 379–396.

8. Sven Steinmo, *Taxation and Democracy* (New Haven: Yale University Press, 1993).

9. Larry Bartels, "Homer Gets a Tax Cut: Inequality and Public Policy in the American Mind," *Perspectives on Politics* 3 (2005): 15–31.

10. Jacob S. Hacker and Paul Pierson, "Abandoning the Middle: The Bush Tax Cuts and the Limits of Democratic Control," *Perspectives on Politics* 3 (2005): 33–53.

11. Andrea Louise Campbell, "American Public Opinion Toward Taxes, 1939–2006," paper presented at the annual meeting of the American Political Science Association, Philadelphia, September 1, 2006.

12. B. Guy Peters, *The Politics of Taxation* (Cambridge: Blackwell, 1991).

13. Alice Rivlin, "The Continuing Search for a Popular Tax," *AEA Papers and Proceedings* 79 (1989): 113–117.

14. Steinmo, *Taxation and Democracy.*

15. Peters, *The Politics of Taxation,* pp. 210–224.

16. Charles Lockhart, "American and Swedish Tax Regimes," *Comparative Politics* 35 (2003): 379–397.

17. Edmund L. Andrews, "Those Wild Budget Swings," *New York Times,* July 16, 2006, p. WK4.

18. W. Elliot Brownlee, *Federal Taxation in America: A Short History,* 2nd ed. (New York: Cambridge University Press, 2004), p. 115.

19. Roger Lowenstein, "Who Needs the Mortgage-Interest Deduction?" *New York Times,* March 5, 2006.

20. Congressional Budget Office, *The Fiscal and Economic Outlook: Fiscal Years 2007 to 2016* (Washington, DC, 2006), pp. 80–85.

21. Congressional Budget Office, "The Individual Alternative Minimum Tax," Statement of Douglas Holtz-Eakin Before the Subcommittee on Taxation and IRS Oversight, Committee on Finance, US Senate, May 23, 2005.

22. Congressional Budget Office, *The Fiscal and Economic Outlook,* p. 90.

23. Citizens for Tax Justice, "Who Pays the Individual AMT: State-by-State Estimates for 2006," March 22, 2006.

24. Ibid.

25. Congressional Budget Office, "The Individual Alternative Minimum Tax."

26. Jeffrey H. Birnbaum, "Oregon Senator Wants to Take on the Burden of Fixing the Tax Code," *Washington Post,* July 24, 2006, p. D1.

27. Joel Friedman, "The Decline of Corporate Income Tax Revenues," Center on Budget and Policy Priorities, October 23, 2003, http://www.cbpp.org/10-16-03tax.htm.

28. Ibid.

29. Congressional Budget Office, *The Fiscal and Economic Outlook,* p. 94.

30. Ibid., p. 95.

31. Ibid., p. 80.

32. Ibid., p. 93.

33. Ibid., p. 80.

34. Ibid., p. 97.

35. Patrick Fisher and David Nice, "Variations in the Use of Grant Discretion: The Case of ISTEA," *Publius* 32 (2002): 131–142.

36. Congressional Budget Office, *The Fiscal and Economic Outlook,* p. 98.

37. Ibid.

38. Steinmo, *Taxation and Democracy,* p. 196.

39. Gilbert E. Metcalf and Ian Parry, "Tax Solutions," *Issues in Science and Technology* 22 (2006): 20–22.

40. Craig Hanson, "A Green Approach to Tax Reform," *Issues in Science and Technology* 22 (2006): 25–27.

41. Metcalf and Parry, "Tax Solutions."

42. William Quirk, "Social Security Tax and Social Security," *Society* 40 (2003): 49–56.

43. Sam Pizzigati, "Must Wealth Always Concentrate?" *Good Society* 14 (2005): 63–67.

44. Campbell, "American Public Opinion Toward Taxes, 1939–2006."

45. Jonas Edlund, "Attitudes Toward Taxation: Ignorant and Incoherent?" *Scandinavian Political Studies* 26 (2003): 145–167.

46. Ibid.

47. Junk Kato, *Regressive Taxation and the Welfare State* (New York: Cambridge University Press, 2003).

48. Jeffrey Stonecash, "The Disputed Evolution of Tax Burden," paper presented at the annual meeting of the American Political Science Association, Philadelphia, September 1, 2006.

49. Congressional Budget Office, *The Fiscal and Economic Outlook,* p. 62.

50. Nolan McCarty, Keith T. Poole, and Howard Rosenthal, *Polarized America: The Dance of Ideology and Unequal Riches* (Cambridge: Massachusetts Institute of Technology Press, 2006), chap. 6.

51. Office for Social Justice, Archdiocese of St. Paul and Minneapolis, May 24, 2006, http://www.osjspm.org/101_taxes.htm.

52. John W. Burns and Andrew J. Taylor, "A New Democrat? The Economic Performance of the Clinton Presidency," *Independent Review* 5 (2001): 387–408.

53. Patrick Fisher, "The Prominence of Partisanship in the Congressional Budget Process," *Party Politics* 5 (1999): 225–236.

54. Alberto Alesina and Howard Rosenthal, *Partisan Politics, Divided Government, and the Economy* (New York: Cambridge University Press, 1995).

55. Brandice Canes-Wrone, David W. Brady, and John F. Cogan, "Out of Step, Out of Office: Electoral Accountability and House Members' Voting," *American Political Science Review* 96 (2002): 127–140.

3

RAISING TAXES

THERE ARE TWO WAYS FOR A GOVERNMENT TO BALANCE A budget in which spending exceeds revenues: by increasing taxes or cutting spending. There are, however, considerable structural obstacles to both tax increases and spending cuts. Since cutting spending will not always be politically feasible or desirable, taxes will occasionally need to be increased to keep government expenditures in line with the desires of taxpayers. In order to produce balanced budgets, however, policymakers must overcome the obstacle of garnering support for tax increases, which is different from gaining support for spending. To gain support for spending, one can build a coalition either by spreading the money around to different groups or by promising program increases. Since policymakers hope that by endorsing spending proposals they might obtain the support they need in the future, there should be little active opposition to spending. For taxation, however, there is an inherent active opposition and no natural support. Increasing taxes is a major undertaking and requires significant efforts to create support and defuse opposition.[1] In order for legislators to support raising taxes, they must convince the public that there is a need for a tax increase and they must prove to citizens that taxpayer money will not be wasted. Increasing taxes is a hard sell politically, even if the goal of the increased taxes is to reduce the deficit.[2] Deficit reduction requires one to think in terms of the long run, which is difficult for voters as well as policymakers to do. The effects of tax increases, however, become evident immediately, and therefore are much more of a factor at the ballot box.

Policymakers are faced with the task of how to minimize political costs while maximizing tax revenue. There is a strongly perceived link between taxes and electoral success. A study of the relationship between level of the income tax and electoral outcomes in Britain, for example, lends credence to this notion: an increase in the average tax rate was found to be associated with electoral defeat.[3] Policymakers clearly fear the potential electoral consequences of raising taxes.

This aversion to risk in tax policy extends to the types of tax that policymakers are willing to raise when revenue must be increased. The repeal of established taxes is problematic because of the fear of losing revenue, while at the same time there is a reluctance to introduce new taxes due to the fear that they might have an unfavorable impact upon the electorate. By making few changes, policymakers keep past laws in effect as the best means of minimizing the political costs of taxation while maximizing tax revenue.[4] This inertia of established tax laws makes it difficult to change tax policy.

The great majority of revenue laws are thus old laws. By sustaining familiar taxes, inertia tends to make taxation politically acceptable, while new tax proposals can induce anxiety due to their unfamiliarity. When the taxation status quo fails to generate a sufficient amount of revenue to meet expected expenditure, policymakers can then resort to borrowing to fund the deficit—what has been called the "nondecisionmaking model."[5] This sidesteps the need to decide on matters that are both visible and likely to be politically unpopular. Informal rules and behavioral patterns ensure that a policy already in place will remain in effect without new decisions being made. This is not just inertia, but also a systematic bias against consideration of raising taxes.[6] The fact that the United States relies disproportionately on the income tax may also make it more difficult to introduce new taxes. The larger welfare states in the world today are disproportionately financed by flat-rate consumption and payroll taxes, complementing income taxes with significant regressive taxes, particularly sales taxes that allow these welfare states to survive budget deficits with less political backlash.[7]

Despite the best efforts of politicians, taxes are of course occasionally raised. Because anticipated political costs influence the likelihood and scale of tax changes, a reduction of political costs therefore increases the likelihood of taxes being raised.[8] Policymakers plan carefully for tax increases. Members of Congress tend to be extremely sensitive to public opinion in their districts, which has been found to have a major impact on voting in congressional elections even when congressional actions seem to contradict public opinion. Constituency pressures against tax increases constrain congressional voting behavior, as members of Congress must consider the electoral ramifications of their roll-call decisions if they desire to win reelection.[9]

Electoral risk has therefore traditionally been the best predictor of whether or not legislators will vote against controversial tax legislation, as was certainly the case with the tax increases that were adopted in 1990 during the George H. W. Bush administration. Partisanship, however, dominated the vote to increase taxes in the first year of the Bill Clinton administration, in 1993. Partisanship dominates the politics of taxation more than ever before in the United States, adding a new calculus to the process.

The 1990 Tax Increases

The experiences of the early 1980s taught the Republicans that opposing taxes was good politics, but that assailing popular domestic programs was not. Deficit levels, however, increased dramatically during the Ronald Reagan administration, eventually becoming too large for federal policymakers to tolerate. As a result, George H. W. Bush, Reagan's Republican successor, was finally forced to confront the record deficits. In the end, the tax debate in 1990 shifted to the Democrats' position. Despite having campaigned in 1988 on a pledge of "read my lips, no new taxes," Bush reluctantly agreed during a budget summit to a deficit reduction package in the Budget Enforcement Act of 1990 that would raise taxes and impose new user fees in return for cuts in entitlement programs and future limits on discretionary spending.

A number of factors accounted for the Republicans losing control of the tax issues as the parties maneuvered through 1990. Bush, concerned that a soaring deficit could severely damage the economy and hurt his reelection chances, sought Democrats' help in designing a bipartisan deficit reduction deal and, in June 1990, issued a statement that "tax revenue increases" would have to be part of any package. With Republicans deeply split over Bush's tax shift, and with polls indicating a growing public perception that Republican tax policies had favored the wealthy, Democrats seized the issue of tax equity and made it the focus of the tax debate. Democrats argued that tax changes made during the 1980s had largely benefited the wealthy and that this direction needed to be reversed.

When Republican and Democratic leaders unveiled a final budget package in September 1990, strong opposition from both the House and the Senate prevented the package from advancing. Congressional Democrats criticized the package as imposing too much of the burden on low- and middle-income taxpayers and not enough on the wealthy. Congressional Republicans complained that the package would impede economic growth by generating too many new taxes and too few breaks for investors. Congress's rejection of the package forced the Bush administration to negotiate on the Democrats' terms. The result was a set of tax provisions, under a reconciliation bill, that not only raised the top income tax rate from 28 to 31 percent, but also imposed other changes designed to shift the tax burden to the wealthy. The proposed tax distribution would be significantly different than that suggested during the budget summit, which would have resulted in relatively smaller tax increases for those with higher incomes. As Congress and the Bush administration negotiated for a compromise that would make the tax system more progressive without imposing a visible surcharge on the wealthy, they further complicated a tax system that was supposed to have been simplified by the 1986 tax reforms (a topic we will return to in Chapter 4).[10]

The deficit reduction package on which Congress and President Bush finally agreed raised taxes, imposed new user fees, and cut entitlements. Despite the unpopularity of both the bill and Congress itself at the time, few legislators paid a price for their support of the bill during the 1990 congressional elections.[11] Budget politics, however, had a significant impact on voting during those elections. Members of Congress were acutely sensitive to the electoral implications of their actions, which explains why only a handful of legislators lost their seats. The bill passed only because so few members faced opponents who posed a serious electoral threat—most were in an electoral position that afforded them the opportunity to absorb the anticipated political damage without risking their careers. While 94 percent of retiring House representatives—those who faced no electoral consequences at all—voted for the bill, only 14 percent of those representatives from competitive seats voted for the legislation. No consideration other than electoral risk—not even partisanship—appears to have affected legislators' decisions to support the bill or not.[12]

The final outcome on the 1990 deficit reduction package was far more congenial to Democrats than to the Bush administration, and it represented a clear political defeat for President Bush. The public was evenly divided when asked if "the President showed real courage by changing his mind on his 'read my lips' pledge not to raise taxes."[13] When asked whether they approved or disapproved of the measure, however, 58 percent of respondents claimed that they disapproved.[14] Furthermore, in terms of the partisan winners and losers in the process, while 49 percent of Americans claimed that the Democrats were "more right" in the debate over how to cut the federal budget deficit, only 30 percent supported the Republicans (see Figure 3.1).

Overall, the Omnibus Budget Reconciliation Act of 1990 was projected to increases revenues by $165 billion over five years, while providing new tax breaks of $27 billion.[15] These projections were soon deemed irrelevant with the election of Bill Clinton as president in 1992; Clinton was poised to raise taxes considerably more than had Bush. By raising taxes in the name of deficit reduction, Bush set a precedent that made it easier for his successor to do the same. Despite the measure's unpopularity, the 1990 tax increases arguably laid the groundwork for the significant deficit reduction that occurred after Bush left office. By helping to reduce the deficit over the long term, the 1990 budget succeeded in fulfilling its goal. From President Bush's perspective, however, the political consequences were severe. Bush compromised on policy and improved the process, but paid a price in public opinion and eventually at the polls.[16]

Figure 3.1 Who Won the 1990 Budget Battle?

"As far as you are concerned, in the debate over how to cut the federal deficit, who do you think was more right—the Democrats or the Republicans?"

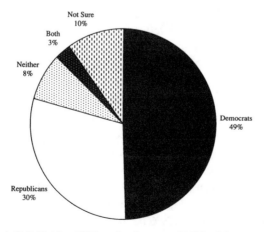

Source: Harris Poll (October 1990), national survey of 1,253 adults.

By reneging on Bush's "no new taxes" pledge, the 1990 budget contributed to his defeat when he sought a second term. The budgetary lesson of 1990, therefore, was that increasing taxes—even at a time of record deficit levels—was a hard sell politically. It was in this political environment that Bill Clinton was elected and soon set out on the same path of deficit reduction that George H. W. Bush had followed.

The 1993 Tax Increases

Despite the fact that Bill Clinton did not emphasize deficit reduction while running for the presidency in 1992, he demonstrated his intent early in office. The strong showing of Ross Perot, who won 19 percent of the vote in the 1992 presidential election while running on a strong antideficit platform, contributed to the Clinton administration's decision to focus on deficit reduction. Clinton, surprising many, showed a willingness to risk his own popularity by proposing a budgetary blueprint that relied heavily on increased taxes.

One month after his inauguration in 1993, President Clinton unveiled a proposed budget that included both significant spending reductions and significant tax increases in order to reduce the deficit. Clinton's deficit-cutting plan was the largest in history, proposing a savings of $493 billion over four years, $247 of that to come from spending cuts and $246 billion from tax increases, almost exactly a one-to-one ratio. The ratio of tax increases to spending cuts quickly emerged as the major point of conflict in Congress. Though the deficit reduction plan proposed notable spending cuts, its heavy reliance on tax increases reflected the difficulties the Clinton economic team faced in designing acceptable spending cuts.

Clinton's call for tax increases was a direct repudiation of the economic philosophies of his two Republican predecessors, and implied that the tax policies of Ronald Reagan and George H. W. Bush came at the price of high deficits. Clinton hoped that he could convince the American public that the economic expansion of the 1980s held negative consequences in the long run. The fact that the 1993 budget's tax increases disproportionately targeted upper-income taxpayers marked a return to the traditional Democratic-style budgets of the post–New Deal era. Though the two new tax brackets that were created—36.0 percent and 39.6 percent—were much smaller than the highest tax brackets under previous Democratic presidencies since the New Deal, the return to a more progressive income tax was a significant shift from the tax policies of Reagan and Bush. Overall, more than half of the new taxes were projected to apply to families making more than $200,000 a year.

With the Republicans unwilling to compromise and unable to drive the process themselves, the struggle to push the antideficit package through Congress relied on obtaining sufficient support from the Democrats. This was the case even though the proposal contained something to offend almost every Democrat; conservatives were uncomfortable with the entire range of tax increases, and liberals were uncomfortable with the $87 billion in cuts over five years in entitlement programs (mainly Medicare and Medicaid) as well as the $102 billion in cuts over five years in appropriated discretionary spending. The plan marked a major step not only away from the low-tax and high-deficit policies of Clinton's Republican predecessors, but also away from the spending-oriented policies of prior Democratic Congresses. As Clinton later articulated, "It seemed to me that, in 1992, we needed to be more conservative in things like erasing the deficit, and paying down the debt."[17] Liberals and the Congressional Black Caucus, however, endorsed the bill early on, making moderates and conservatives the critical swing voters.

The 1993 budget is among the best exhibits for the idea that drama and contingency are fundamental aspects of politics.[18] In the end, Clinton's economic plan emerged victorious, though just barely. The Omnibus Budget Reconciliation Act was approved in August 1993 without a single vote to spare in either chamber: it passed 218 to 217 in the House and 51 to 50 in the Senate (with Vice President Al Gore making the tie-breaking vote), without any Republican support in either chamber.

Democrats were buoyed by polls suggesting at least some public support for deficit reduction, even at the cost of higher taxes. In one poll taken in January 1993, for example, as many people claimed to favor tax increases to cut the deficit as were opposed.[19] Democrats hoped that citizens would realize that real deficit reduction would necessitate more taxes. After the Clinton budget was passed by Congress in August 1993, Americans were surprisingly willing to pay for the new levies called for in the budget plan. According to a poll taken after the budget plan was implemented, 52 percent of respondents said that they did not object to the new taxes, compared to 47 percent who did. There was a significant partisan effect, however: 66 percent of Republicans said they opposed the new taxes, compared to only 49 percent of Independents and 26 percent of Democrats (see Table 3.1). Interestingly, even though the new taxes disproportionately targeted the wealthy, those with the lowest incomes were actually the least willing to support the new taxes. In regard to education level, college graduates overwhelmingly supported the tax increases, while the greatest hostility toward the taxes (by a large margin) came from those who had attained some college education but had not graduated. In general, higher levels of education tend to increase appreciation for the benefits that taxes provide. Thus, despite the progressive nature of the new taxes, those at the top end of the income spectrum were actually relatively more likely to support the tax increases. The fact that those with some college education were so overwhelmingly against the new taxes was a prelude to the problems the Democrats would face in the 1994 congressional elections. This demographic group, who had disproportionately supported Ross Perot's bid for the presidency in 1992, turned strongly against Clinton after the 1993 budget.

The fact that not a single Republican in either the House or the Senate supported the 1993 budget indicates the degree to which partisanship and ideology dominated the vote on the bill.[20] Republicans saw the Clinton budget as a means of raising taxes and undoing the Reagan legacy. Democrats, though they were not enamored with the tax increases, felt that it was important to support the first Democratic

Table 3.1 Willingness to Pay New Taxes, 1993 (percentage)

"Do you object to paying the new taxes, or not?"

	Yes	No
Total	47	52
Partisanship		
Republicans	66	33
Democrats	26	74
Independents	49	50
Education		
College postgraduate	33	67
College graduate	41	59
Some college	77	20
No college	46	53
Income		
$50,000+	46	54
$30,000–49,999	47	52
$20,000–29,999	41	59
Under $20,000	49	50

Source: Gallup Poll (August 8–10, 1993), national survey of 799 adults.

president in twelve years. By embracing the plan, if only barely, congressional Democrats gambled on their political futures, betting that deficit reduction would improve the economy in the long run and improve their reelection prospects. Because they passed the budget package without a single Republican vote, Democrats hoped that they would be given sole credit for future success of the bill.

Democratic optimism that the 1993 budget would not be a political hindrance, however, evaporated as the 1994 congressional elections approached. As those elections proved, the Democrats' support for tax increases was a political albatross. Though other issues such as health care and gun control also played important roles in the 1994 elections, Democrats who supported the Clinton economic plan fared poorly in those elections despite a relatively healthy economy. Of the 228 House Democrats who sought reelection, 34 lost, including 28 who voted for the 1993 Budget Reconciliation Bill. More tellingly, not a single Republican incumbent lost a reelection bid for Congress in 1994. Even in an environment where voters were calling for deficit reduction, voting to raise taxes or cut programs proved to be a politically hazardous move for members of Congress. The passage of the reconciliation bill therefore left a mixed message. The bill was remarkably successful in accomplishing its goal of reducing the deficit, but many of those who supported it paid a heavy political price.

The Advent of Budget Surpluses

Overall, the Clinton budget was expected to reduce but not eliminate the deficit. Annual deficits under the law were expected to be about $200 billion, and since nearly $500 billion in deficits was to be eliminated over five years, the national debt was expected to rise by "only" $1.1 trillion.[21] Annual deficits, however, shrank much more dramatically after the measure was enacted than anyone predicted. The plan produced long-term deficit reduction for the first time since the 1970s. The deficit declined (or surplus increased) for a remarkable eight consecutive years, a postwar record. And in a development that would have been thought impossible in the early 1990s, there were budget surpluses from 1998 to 2001, the first time since 1969 that the federal government did not produce deficits.

The budgetary situation changed with staggering speed. To illustrate, in 1993 the Congressional Budget Office projected a fiscal 1998 deficit of $357 billion; the actual 1998 fiscal budget had a surplus of

$69 billion. By 2000, the surplus reached a record $236 billion. Surpluses emerged and continued to increase even with the tax cuts of the 1997 Balanced Budget/Taxpayer Relief Act, which reduced revenues by $81 billion over five years.[22] The elimination of nearly thirty years of federal budget deficits was a remarkable achievement and dramatically changed the dynamics of political debate over budget priorities. By the end of the Clinton presidency, surpluses had become an accepted part of the vocabulary and arithmetic of federal budgeting.[23]

The elimination of the deficit was made possible by a considerable increase in revenues after the 1993 budget was passed. The significant increase in revenues resulted from the progressive nature of the tax increases of the 1993 budget coupled with a strong economy. People with relatively high incomes did particularly well in the economic environment of the late 1990s, and as a result paid more federal taxes at a higher tax rate. After 1992, the last year the highest income tax rate was 31 percent, the federal government gained substantially more revenue from those with higher incomes. Because of the widened gap between low- and high-income earners, the federal government took in much more revenue than it would have without the 1993 tax increases.

Table 3.2 shows how federal coffers were enhanced disproportionately from taxes on those with high incomes. The individual income taxes received by the federal government from those making over $100,000 increased over 231 percent in the seven years after the tax provisions of the 1993 budget became law. Millionaires contributed more than four times as much to the US Treasury in 2000 than in 1992. In part this was due to the progressive nature of the tax increases. But deficit reduction was also aided by a healthy economy

Table 3.2 Aggregate Individual Income Tax Revenue by Income Group, 1992–2001 (in $ billions)

	$0–50,000	$50,000–100,000	$100,000–1,000,000	$1,000,000+
1992	145	140	144	47
1993	143	145	162	53
1994	141	158	179	57
1995	141	168	208	72
1996	142	178	241	97
1997	142	190	277	122
1998	133	194	314	147
1999	131	205	359	182
2000	132	216	407	226
2001	123	213	388	164

Source: Compiled by author from Internal Revenue Service returns.

that pushed up many people's incomes. The number of people making between $100,000 and $1,000,000 increased from 3,698,000 in 1992 to 10,614,000 in 2000, and the number of millionaires rose from 67,000 to 240,000 during that same period. The government taxed the economic winners of the 1990s, redistributing income while boosting its revenues.[24] Yet tax rates after the 1993 budget were by no means unprecedented; the effective income tax rate, for example, was about 24 percent, approximately the same rate as in 1980, Jimmy Carter's last year in office.[25]

Deficit reduction in the 1990s was clearly aided by a healthy economy. The fact that the economy performed so well after the 1993 Budget Reconciliation Bill was enacted is a strong defense of the success of the bill. Congressional Republicans were adamant that the 1993 budget's tax increases would result in an economic downturn. As Representative Dick Armey (R-TX) stated, the 1993 budget was "a recipe for disaster. . . . Taxes will go up. The economy will sputter along. Dreams will be put off, and all this for the hollow promise of deficit reduction and magical theories of lower interest rates." Newt Gingrich, who was House Minority Whip at the time, predicted that the bill would lead to "a job-killing recession."[26] The health of the economy after 1993 indicates that tax increases on upper incomes are not necessarily a hindrance to economic growth, and are a legitimate mechanism—if not a politically popular one—by which to potentially balance the nation's budget.

The Politics of Surpluses

For much of his presidency, Bill Clinton did not necessarily pursue a budgetary strategy consistent with producing budget surpluses. He did not commit to the concept of a balanced budget until 1995, and that was for future budgets when he would no longer be occupying the White House. Surpluses, however, arrived earlier than expected because the strong economy produced an unexpected surge in revenues. Once the first surplus did arrive, in 1998, it dramatically changed the nature of the debate over the budget.

Once the reality of long-term surplus projections set in, the White House and congressional Republicans quickly laid claim to the revenues to finance their competing agendas. For Clinton, that included new spending on domestic programs and a new Medicare prescription drug benefit. Republicans, on the other hand, rallied behind tax cuts.

Legislators were nowhere near a consensus on how the extra revenues should be distributed.

The Clinton administration and many congressional Democrats argued that Social Security and Medicare should be addressed before any tax cut. Republicans, on the other hand, continued to argue that the surplus should be used for tax cuts. In August 1999, Congress approved a budget that would reduce income tax rates by 1 percent, lower the capital gains tax, give more favorable tax treatment to retirement savings, gradually abolish the inheritance tax, eventually end the so-called marriage penalty and the alternative minimum tax, and give significant tax breaks to commercial enterprises. The Republican Congress approved the so-called Taxpayer Refund and Relief Act of 1999, but Clinton strongly opposed the tax cuts and vetoed the bill.

Even though Clinton was certain to veto any tax cut bill of the size desired by Congress, Republicans hoped the effort would increase public interest in their tax-cutting agenda and help them regain the offensive on budget and tax matters from the president. When Clinton vetoed the tax cut bill, he argued that he did so "because it ignores the principles that have led us to the sound economy we enjoy today and emphasized tax reduction for those who need it the least." Clinton attacked his opponents for taking the easy, popular way even though it was bad public policy. He stressed that he might not be taking the most popular approach by advocating the maintenance of large budget surpluses, but argued that maintaining surpluses was the best long-term economic approach.[27] In the end, Clinton appeared to win the public opinion battle, since Republicans were portrayed as supporting a tax reduction bill that mainly benefited the wealthy.

Instead of using the surplus for the broad-based tax cuts that Republicans suggested, Clinton tried to rally support for his plan to save future surpluses for Social Security and Medicare. In February 1999, Clinton suggested that 75 percent of the projected surpluses for the next fifteen years should be used to stabilize those entitlement programs. At the same time, he suggested that the surpluses, if not used for substantial new spending or tax cut proposals, could substantially trim the accumulated $5.6 trillion national debt, a policy that he argued would create financial security for future generations.

The surpluses allowed Clinton, at the end of his administration, to begin pursuing the same goals he had sought at the beginning of his presidency in 1993, though usually by different means. For example, in 1993 Clinton had proposed an expansion of the food stamp program and a Democratic Congress had approved much of his proposal. The 1996 welfare law passed by a Republican-controlled Congress cut food stamp spending, but Clinton later won restoration of some of the cuts. Essentially, the surpluses allowed Clinton to successfully adopt a more incremental approach in support of his policy goals at the end of his presidency.

The surplus deepened the rift with the Republican Party, separating the deficit hawks, who were devoted to staying within spending limits, from the supply-side tax-cutters, who argued that lower taxes would spur growth. Importantly, even with the large projected surpluses, congressional Republicans were also continuing to press for spending cuts. In October 1999, the House passed an $85 billion measure for labor, health, and education programs containing a nearly 1 percent across-the-board cut in federal spending.

A lesson of the conversion of deficits into surpluses is that fiscal prudence can reign when neither party can achieve its budgetary vision.[28] Although there were trillions of dollars in projected surpluses, a Republican Congress and a Democratic White House were not able agree on what to do with the windfall of new revenues. Republicans in Congress called for tax cuts while the Clinton White House argued in favor of using the surpluses for debt reduction and spending proposals. Due to the different priorities of the executive and legislative branches, there was no large tax cut or an expansion in spending programs. Gridlock, however, had important policy consequences. It meant that the surpluses were left intact, enabling the nation to pay down the debt that had skyrocketed over the previous three decades. Divided government thus made it easier to keep a surplus, because the opposing parties could not agree. While this approach was never put to a vote or fully debated in Congress, it resulted in an outcome that most economists considered positive for the economy over the long run. As one economist argued in 2000, the nation was "at one of those times when doing nothing—or, at any rate, doing very little— is preferable to doing something."[29] Though it would have been politically unrealistic, if the federal government had continued on this course, it could potentially have eliminated the national debt in ten to fifteen years.

The end of divided government after the 2000 elections did in fact have negative consequences for the surplus. Divided government from 1995 to 2000 blocked Republican attempts for large tax cuts and deterred Democrats from significant increases in social spending.

By winning control of both the White House and Congress in the 2000 elections, Republicans were able to pursue their desired budgetary agenda of emphasizing tax reductions. Divided government had protected the surpluses because it had produced a default fiscal policy of funding debt reduction.

The ability of the federal government to produce surpluses may have also been related to changes in public opinion. To some degree, the contradictions of citizen demands were mitigated. The public's perception of taxing and spending priorities became more supportive of deficit and debt reduction. Congress was able to produce budgetary surpluses mainly because of an unexpected windfall of revenues. But a changed climate in public opinion also aided Congress in this endeavor. This was especially true when it came to public opinion on taxation.

The fact that most Americans do not believe that upper-income earners are paying their "fair share" in taxes has important consequences for the federal government's ability to balance the budget. Though surveys have revealed that substantial income redistribution has never been popular in the United States, Americans have always strongly supported a progressive income tax.[30] And since an increase in the progressiveness of the income tax can result in significantly higher tax revenues, increasing tax rates on the wealthy is potentially a politically acceptable means of raising more revenue. The success of the progressive tax increases under the 1993 Budget Reconciliation Bill at reducing the federal deficit indicates that a more progressive income tax may be a solution to the deficit woes that have plagued the United States since the 1970s.

Since the increases in federal revenues came disproportionately from the wealthy after the top income tax rates were raised in 1993, the fact that the public did not tend to support reducing taxes for those with upper incomes increased the likelihood of surpluses. Thus, public opinion in regard to taxing the wealthy during the later stages of the Clinton administration facilitated the ability of the federal government to produce balanced budgets. When asked what should be the priorities of the federal government after budget surpluses arrived on the scene, Americans gave remarkably little support to cutting taxes, relative to other priorities. In one poll in 1999, for example, strengthening Social Security, reducing the national debt, strengthening Medicare, and increasing education funding were all deemed as higher surplus priorities than cutting income taxes (see Figure 3.2).

Even though the public was against cutting spending on entitlements, policymakers were aided in their attempts to reduce the deficit

Figure 3.2 Surplus Priorities, 1999

"Given the budget surplus, what priority should these proposals be given?"

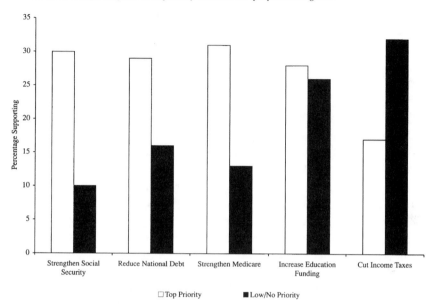

Source: Gallup Poll (August 17–18, 1999), national survey of 1,013 adults.

because the public deemed deficit reduction a higher priority than tax cuts. The increase of revenues due to the 1993 budget may have been a fluke—the revenues generated were much greater than anyone expected—but public opinion produced a hospitable environment for deficit reduction. Congressional inaction on the budget was therefore a good reflection of public opinion as the federal government produced surpluses.

It can be argued that the 1993 budget was successful—remarkably so—at reducing the deficit. After the reconciliation bill was enacted, the deficit decreased every year until 1998, at which point the federal government produced a surplus for the first time in nearly thirty years, and by 2000 the federal government was producing a record surplus of $236 billion. The elimination of a federal budget deficit may have been Clinton's greatest accomplishment as president.[31] Every year that he was in office, the economy flourished and the outlook for the federal budget improved. Despite the unprecedented reduction of the federal budget deficit throughout his presidency, however, Clinton garnered few political rewards for this achievement. According to one poll conducted in January 1998, 32 percent said that Clinton deserved no credit at all for balancing the budget. When respondents were asked who deserved more credit for reducing the deficit, the result was a virtual tie between Clinton and Republicans in Congress.[32] As had been the case in 1990, raising taxes proved to be politically problematic for the president. This was the case even though the taxes went a long way toward helping to reducing the deficit.

George W. Bush clearly inherited a much rosier budget picture than had Clinton. While Clinton was elected president in a year that produced the largest deficit of all time, Bush was elected in a year that was generating a record surplus. As a result, Bush had more flexibility on budget priorities than Clinton. Certainly, Bush's ability to cut income taxes significantly in 2001 was a direct result of the large budget surpluses. When Clinton assumed the presidency, the budget deficit was a central fact of life that limited what the federal government could do. New spending projects and tax cuts were taboo. With the deficit eliminated, it was possible to once again have a debate over whether the federal government should do more or cut taxes.[33] On this fundamental question, Bush set out the nation's course by making tax cuts a major priority of his administration. Thus, ironically, the main benefactor of the large federal government surpluses at the end of the Clinton presidency may have been George W. Bush.

Notes

1. Irene S. Rubin, *The Politics of Public Budgeting,* 5th ed. (Washington, DC: Congressional Quarterly, 2006), pp. 37–40.

2. Patrick Fisher, "Political Explanations for the Difficulties in Congressional Budgeting," *Social Science Journal* 36 (1999): 149–161.

3. Paul Johnson, Frances Lynch, and John Geoffrey Walker, "Income Tax and Elections in Britain," *Electoral Studies* 24 (2005): 393–408.

4. Richard Rose, "Maximizing Tax Revenue While Minimizing Political Costs," *Journal of Public Policy* 5 (1986): 289–320.

5. Ibid.

6. Allen Schick, *Congress and Money* (Washington, DC: AEI, 1980).

7. Junko Kato, *Regressive Taxation and the Welfare State* (New York: Cambridge University Press, 2003).

8. Scott J. Bassinger and Mark Hallerberg, "Remodeling the Competition for Capital: How Domestic Politics Erases the Race to the Bottom," *American Political Science Review* 98 (2004): 261–276.

9. Brandice Canes-Wrone, David W. Brady, and John F. Cogan, "Out of Step, Out of Office: Electoral Accountability and House Members' Voting," *American Political Science Review* 96 (2002): 127–140.

10. Congressional Quarterly, "Deficit Reduction Bill Has 'New Taxes,'" in *1990 Congressional Quarterly Almanac* (Washington, DC, 1991), pp. 167–172.

11. Gary C. Jacobson, "Deficit-Cutting Politics and Congressional Elections," *Political Science Quarterly* 108 (1993): 375–402.

12. Ibid.

13. Harris Poll (October 1990), national survey of 1,253 adults; 49 percent agreed with this statement and 49 percent disagreed, with 2 percent not sure.

14. USA Today Poll (October 1990), national survey of 760 adults.

15. Irene Rubin, *Balancing the Federal Budget* (New York: Chatham, 2003), p. 31.

16. Richard M. Pious, "The Limits of Rational Choice: Bush and Clinton Budget Summitry," *Presidential Studies Quarterly* 29 (1999): 617–637.

17. Andrei Cherny, "Obtuse Triangle," *The New Republic,* May 16, 2005, pp. 10–13.

18. David Mayhew, *America's Congress* (New Haven: Yale University Press, 2000), p. 239.

19. Harris Poll (January 1993), national survey of 1,224 adults. When asked, "Do you favor or oppose tax increases to cut the deficit?" 49 percent favored the increase, 48 percent opposed, and 3 percent were not sure.

20. Patrick Fisher, "The Prominence of Partisanship in the Congressional Budget Process," *Party Politics* 5 (1999): 225–236.

21. Robert Lee and Ronald Johnson, *Public Budgeting Systems,* 5th ed. (Gaithersburg, MD: Aspen, 1994), p. 205.

22. Rubin, *Balancing the Federal Budget,* p. 31.

23. Aaron Wildavsky and Naomi Caiden, *The New Politics of the Budgetary Process,* 5th ed. (New York: Longman, 2004), pp. 208–212.

24. Allen Schick, "A Surplus, If We Can Keep It," *Brookings Review* 18 (2000): 36–39.

25. Christopher Carroll, "Portfolios of the Rich," in Lugi Guiso, M. Haliassos, and Tullio Japelli, eds., *Household Portfolios* (Cambridge: Massachusetts Institute of Technology Press, 2002), p. 393.

26. Congressional Record, August 5, 1993.

27. David G. Levasseur, "The Role of Public Opinion in Policy Argument: An Examination of Public Opinion Rhetoric in the Federal Budget Process," *Argumentation and Advocacy* 41 (2005): 152–167.

28. Schick, "A Surplus, If We Can Keep It."

29. Robert J. Samuelson, "Candidate for the Status Quo," *Newsweek,* August 21, 2000, p. 50.

30. Carolyn Webber and Aaron Wildavsky, *A History of Taxation and Expenditure in the Western World* (New York: Simon and Schuster, 1986), p. 528.

31. Patrick Fisher, "The Success of the 1993 Budget Reconciliation Bill at Reducing the Federal Budget Deficit," *Review of Policy Research* 19 (2002): 30–43.

32. Susan Page and William M. Welch, "Poll: Don't Use Surplus to Cut Taxes," *USA Today,* January 16, 1998, pp. 1A, 6A.

33. E. J. Dionne, "Why Americans Hate Politics: A Reprise," *Brookings Review* 18 (2000): 8–11.

4

CUTTING TAXES

CUTTING TAXES HAS ENTIRELY DIFFERENT POLITICAL IMPLICA-
tions than raising taxes. Voters tend to dislike losses more than
they appreciate gains, and thus their resentment about tax increases
tends to be much greater than their excitement about tax cuts. At the
same time, voters often refuse to believe that they have received tax
cuts, even when they have. Evidence suggests that Americans do not
always hold opinions consistent with their own self-interest in regard
to tax policy.[1] Many do not know how much they pay in federal income taxes, and many do not notice the effects, because these effects
are partly offset by higher local taxes or Social Security payments.[2]
Public opinion on taxes is insensitive to some of the most important
implications of tax cuts and largely disconnected from general political beliefs and material interests.[3]

Tax cuts clearly have a generic appeal to Americans. When the
public is asked if they favor a "cut in federal income taxes," responses
are overwhelmingly positive. Americans also consistently say that
they pay too much in federal income taxes.[4] Furthermore, compared
to the citizens of other democracies, Americans are less concerned
about economic inequality.[5] Yet, at the same time, the popularity of
tax cuts can be considerably different when placed in context of "fair
shares." Americans may be generally opposed to taxes, but they also
tend to believe that upper-income earners pay too little in federal taxes
compared to lower- and middle-income earners.[6]

Knowledge about the tax code is sharply skewed by income.[7] At
the same time, raw policy-specific facts—such as the size of the federal budget deficit—have a significant influence on the public's political judgments. Rather than serving to dilute the influence of new

information, general knowledge appears to facilitate the incorporation of new policy-specific information into political judgments.[8]

The modern tax cut movement is often said to have started in 1978 with the passage of Proposition 13 in California, which dramatically lowered property taxes. Immediately after the success of Proposition 13, tax reduction referendums succeeded in a number of other states, including Illinois, Massachusetts, and Michigan. Proposition 13 succeeded in part due to the fact that dramatic increases in property tax occurred just prior to that issue coming onto the ballot. The California government did not increase tax rates, but the huge increases in property values in California had suddenly pushed property assessments much higher than they had previously been, creating the perception that the property tax in California was unfair. Flush with the success of Proposition 13 and other state tax reform measures, conservative attempts to reduce taxes were further aided by the election of Ronald Reagan as president in 1980. Reagan's tax cuts later served as the model for George W. Bush's tax cuts after he won the presidency in 2000.

The tax cuts of the past couple of decades have had a clear and marked impact on overall revenues. As a share of national income, federal taxes in 2004 amounted to 16.3 percent, the lowest in nearly half a century. In 2005, most households faced a lower overall tax burden than they did in 1980. Looking just at income taxes, a median family of four in 2005 paid a smaller share of its earnings in federal income taxes than in every year since 1957.[9]

The 1981 Reagan Tax Cuts

Ronald Reagan fulfilled his campaign promise to significantly cut taxes only eight months after he assumed office, with the passage of the sweeping Economic Recovery Tax Act. Among the significant features of the act: (1) tax cuts that ultimately equaled about 23 percent of tax brackets for personal income taxes were phased in over two years; (2) income tax brackets and exemptions were indexed for inflation, eliminating so-called bracket creep; (3) the top marginal tax bracket was reduced from 70 percent to 50 percent; and (4) a generous set of depreciation schedules (called the Accelerated Cost Recovery System) was initiated for businesses.[10]

The Reagan budget of 1981 was an era-defining legislative drive that, according to one political scientist, ranks only behind the Civil Rights Act of 1964 as the most significant legislative drive over the past half century.[11] The 1981 tax cuts were the largest in history at the time, at slightly more than 2 percent of GDP (George W. Bush's 2001 tax cuts, adjusted for inflation, were almost as large). Reagan's tax cuts were guided by an unusually coherent political-economic ideology. His philosophy regarding the size and scope of government has set the tone for budget politics to this day.[12]

Drafted under reconciliation rules created by the 1974 Congressional Budget Act as a means of forcing committees to comply with congressionally approved spending levels, the budget resolution consolidated in a single package the cuts sought by Reagan. The sweeping use of reconciliation to enact the president's economic program reflected a shift in power from the authorizing and appropriations committees to the budget committees. Once the reconciliation bill was enacted, the appropriations committees had little leeway in changing the levels of funding, since reconciliation had already set the spending ceilings. It also represented a shift in power from Congress to the White House.[13] By packaging the budget cuts together, and then forcing the House and Senate to vote on a single measure, Republicans hoped to prevent congressional committees and interest groups from chipping away at Reagan's budget plan. This strategy worked, far better than dismayed Democrats could have imagined. It is unlikely that the 1981 Reagan tax cuts, and their miscalculations, would have happened without a budget resolution. Reagan would have faced many hurdles in trying to enact his radical, supply-side economics under the pre-1974 budgetary process. Most likely his program would have been completely dismantled by successive committee actions. The budget resolution gave Reagan the centralizing vehicle he needed.[14]

That Reagan was able to succeed in his early effort to slash the budget in the Republican-controlled Senate was not surprising, but his victory in the Democratic-controlled House was not a forgone conclusion. Every House Republican stood behind the administration's budget, and a sizable group of conservative Democrats, dubbed "Boll Weevils," voted with the Republicans.[15] Reagan proved to be an adept legislative advocate. An analysis of the vote in Congress on the 1981 budget shows that Reagan's contacts with members of Congress succeeded in strengthening legislative support for his program. In particular, Reagan and his advisers were especially adroit at discerning those moments in the legislative process when the president's intervention would be most effective.[16]

The primary theoretical support for the Reagan tax cuts was provided by supply-side economic theory, to which early supporters of the Reagan plan strongly adhered. Supply-side economists argued

that in a market economy where productivity is based upon the incentives of the private sector, excessively high tax rates discourage
investment and innovation. Why work hard if the rewards are to be
taxed away? High taxes, according to supply-siders, arrest economic
growth, reducing the growth rate of income and thus the tax base. If
tax rates were cut, therefore, the economy would flourish and income
would grow, increasing tax revenues.

Using supply-side economic theory as a guide, Reagan argued that
economic stimulus resulting from a tax cut would result in an increase
of governmental revenues, even though economists overwhelmingly rejected this argument.[17] Reagan's tax revolution turned Franklin Roosevelt's New Deal on its head; instead of promising more benefits, the
strategy became to promise tax cuts and stay relatively silent on benefits.[18] Supply-side supporters of Reagan's radical program justified the
tax cuts by arguing that deficits would not be a problem; in fact, many
in the Reagan administration argued that deficits would even be reduced. A document released from the Executive Office of the President
in February 1981 showed a balanced budget by 1984 and a $30 billion
surplus in 1986.[19] While it is certainly true that tax cuts can aid economic growth, the economic growth that resulted from the Reagan tax
cuts was nowhere near enough to reduce the deficit. In fact, the opposite happened: deficits skyrocketed, from $74 billion in 1980 to more
than $200 billion by 1983.

The Reagan tax cuts reduced individual tax rates by 25 percent
over a thirty-three-month period.[20] It is estimated that as a result of
the Economic Recovery Tax Act, total revenues declined by $92 bil-
lion in 1983, and by $267 billion in 1986.[21] In 1980, with the econ-
omy in the grips of stagflation, the American public was in a mood to
accept the misleading promises of supply-side economics.[22] The result was a deficit that spiraled out of control as the 1980s progressed.
After 1981, budget politics became more contentious and more divi-
sive, and largely focused on the deficit.[23]

The Tax Reform Act of 1986

Another major tax initiative of the Reagan administration was the
Tax Reform Act of 1986, which made major changes to the federal tax
code. The main impetus for the act was a perception that tax deductions and exemptions had become unmanageable. Though the act was
officially "revenue-neutral" and did not increase overall tax levels, it
simplified the tax code, broadening the tax base and eliminating

many tax shelters and other preferences. The top income tax rate was reduced from 50 to 28 percent and the bottom rate was increased from 11 to 15 percent, the only time in the history of the United States that the top rate fell while the bottom rate simultaneously rose. Other reforms of the act included reducing the capital gains tax to the same tax rate as ordinary income as an incentive for investment, and increasing the home mortgage interest deduction as an incentive for home ownership. The act passed by a large bipartisan majority in Congress, in part because the measure was seen as revenue-neutral.

The origins of the act can be seen in a Democratic tax "reform" proposal first advanced in August 1982 by Senator Bill Bradley and Representative Richard A. Gephardt, and later in Reagan's call for tax reform in his January 1984 State of the Union address. As enacted, however, the legislation cut individual tax rates more than either the Reagan plan or the Bradley-Gephardt bill envisioned, but cut corporate taxes less than proposed. The law shifted tax liability from individuals to corporations, reversing a long trend of corporate taxes supplying a decreasing share of federal revenues.[24]

Enactment of the measure was accomplished through the perseverance of its chief backers in Congress over the objections of many special interest groups at risk of losing their favored status under the tax code. Public opinion was ambivalent; surveys reflected widespread doubt that whatever Congress did would result in real reform. Despite the nation being mired in a period of large budget deficits, Reagan refused to support any tax increases and as a result the bill neither raised nor reduced total federal tax collections over the five-year period following its enactment. As a result, the bill's adherents were ultimately able to turn back costly amendments in order to restore tax breaks, because offsetting revenues could not be produced.[25]

Though originally envisioned by Bradley and Gephardt as a way of eliminating all tax loopholes, the tax reform debate almost immediately focused on what loopholes, or "incentives," as members of Congress liked to call them, would be kept or added to the new tax bill. In a series of endless compromises, members of Congress, especially senators, went out of their way to protect their turf. In order to obtain the support of particular legislators, concessions often had to be made to benefit their constituencies. As a result, the 1986 tax bill was a hodgepodge reform effort, quite different from the pure proposals that come out of academia or think tanks.[26]

The Tax Reform Act of 1986 was a modern political miracle. Conventional wisdom held that significant tax reform would be nearly impossible, because there were simply too many entrenched special interests to make tax reform a realistic possibility. By 1986, however, the tax code had deteriorated to such an extent that members of Congress realized something had to be done. Since tax reform was seen to have salience among the public, members of Congress may have been more afraid of the displeasure of constituents than the displeasure of lobbyists. The public's desire for tax reform, as demonstrated by opinion polls, was perceived to be so strong that even the lobbyists themselves were afraid to be pinned as opponents of reform.[27] Political costs in the legislative process influence the likelihood and scale of tax reform.[28] For this particular legislation, the public's clamoring for tax reform reduced the political costs and thus increased the likelihood of tax reform.

Tax reform would never have been enacted were it not for the support of President Reagan. It was Reagan's tacit endorsement of tax reform that kept the bill alive at times when congressional abandonment seemed in order. The end result of the tax reform was certainly not entirely to the Reagan administration's liking. But throughout the creation of the bill, members of Congress met with the White House to ensure that particular compromises would be acceptable to the administration. Thus, in the end, it was the national perspective of the president that was enacted instead of the more distributional policy outcomes favored by Congress.[29]

The Tax Reform Act of 1986 was certainly not a defender of the status quo. Though the end result was far from the radical change Bradley and Gephardt originally advocated, it was still a considerable change from the previous policy. The fact that Congress passed serious tax reform was remarkable considering all the obstacles it faced. Since the 1986 tax reforms were enacted, however, Congress has made more than 14,000 changes to tax law, and few of these can be considered "reforms." Many of the loopholes and exceptions that were excised by the Tax Reform Act of 1986 have since essentially been restored.[30]

The 2001 Bush Tax Cuts

The surpluses that emerged in the final years of the Bill Clinton presidency offered an important opportunity to debate the nation's future budgetary priorities in the 2000 presidential election. After nearly thirty years of budget deficits, dealing with surpluses was a novelty for presidential candidates. Unleashed from the deficit burden, George

W. Bush and Al Gore relished the chance to be able to make popular promises. Both proposed spending hundreds of billions of dollars over the successive decade for purposes that were perceived to have been neglected. Despite the closeness of the 2000 presidential election and the disputed nature of Bush's victory, Bush followed through with his campaign promise to make cutting taxes the number one priority of his new administration after he was inaugurated. The passage of significant tax cuts in 2001 was the culmination of years of debate over whether the nation could afford a substantial tax reduction at a time of large and growing federal budget surpluses. The 2001 tax cuts represented a dramatic change in US tax policy and fundamentally reshaped the nation's fiscal landscape.[31]

The manner in which a president articulates his budgetary priorities can set the agenda and the tone of the national debate. Both Bush and Gore promised billions for what their core supporters wanted most. While Bush advocated tax cuts, Gore called for higher levels of domestic spending. Yet it was not as simple as whether or not the nation should spend the surplus or cut taxes. Reducing the national debt was also an important factor, and Bush and Gore accused the other of trying to break the bank.

There was one important area of agreement between Gore's and Bush's proposals: both called for protecting the Social Security trust fund in a so-called lockbox. Besides putting Social Security off limits, however, Bush and Gore found little common ground and each was critical of the other's proposals. Gore argued that the combination of Bush's Social Security privatization plan and tax cut would eliminate the projected surplus along with any hope of paying down the national debt, which Gore favored. Bush, on the other hand, argued that Gore was planning on returning to the days of "tax and spend" policies and "big government."

Gore's proposed budgetary policies differed little from those pursued by the Clinton administration. Gore hoped that Americans would support the status quo by rejecting Bush's tax cut proposals as threatening, unfair, and unnecessary. Gore may have articulated populist themes at times during the campaign, but his main goal was to instill anxiety that Bush's "risky schemes" would spoil America's current prosperity. Bush, on the other hand, proposed much larger tax cuts than Gore and did not believe that reducing the national debt should be a priority.

Bush's victory in 2000, therefore, had major budgetary consequences. Bush's emphasis on tax cuts over deficit reduction was a radical departure from the budgetary strategy of Clinton. After the 2000 elections, Republicans controlled both the White House and Congress for the first time since the Dwight Eisenhower administration and were free to dictate the budget process. Despite the popularity of Ronald Reagan as president, the political as well as policy success of supply-side economics was still much in doubt until the election of George W. Bush. When Bob Dole proposed a major tax reduction after winning the Republican presidential nomination in 1996, for example, his proposals were met with general skepticism and failed to help propel him to victory. One potential reason for this was that the proposed tax cuts were linked to the tax cuts of 1981 and the massive budget deficits the latter helped to create.[32] With the election of George W. Bush, however, the Republicans once again embraced supply-side economics as a justification for lowering taxes.

President Bush argued that his plan to cut taxes would restrain the growth of government spending and provide the money needed to address issues he considered priorities. At the same time, he contended that the projected federal surplus of $5.6 trillion over the successive decade justified his $1.6 trillion tax cut in the same period as affordable. "The surplus is not the government's money," claimed Bush in a speech in Omaha on the first day of a trip to sell his tax cut and budget plan. "The surplus is the people's money. And I'm here to ask you to join me in making that case to any federal official you can find."[33] Bush also sold the tax cut as a way to bolster the economy, which was showing signs of slowing. Thus, not only was the tax cut a means to return to people their own money, but it was also anti-recession insurance.

Congressional Democrats, no longer able to rely on a veto from the White House to back them up, criticized the plan as a boon to the wealthy and argued that they would press for a considerably smaller tax cut, with benefits primarily directed to low- and middle-income households. Democrats also argued that Bush's plan relied on money that was supposed to be off limits: $526 billion over the successive decade in temporary surpluses from one division of the Medicare system. Not all Democrats, however, dismissed the Bush plan. The plan was cosponsored in the Senate by Senator Zell Miller of Georgia. Republicans hoped that getting a Democratic senator to cosponsor the legislation would ease its passage.

Republican leaders in the House moved quickly to give Bush's tax plan political momentum and, with unanimous support from House Republicans, passed a budget resolution with a $1.6 trillion tax cut one month after Bush sent his budget blueprint to Congress. The budget that was approved by the House left Bush's proposed budget mostly intact; only minor changes were made. The debate in the Senate was much more contentious. After the House passed the budget resolution, it became clear that in a Senate equally divided between the two political parties there would be insufficient votes to approve a $1.6 trillion tax reduction. Eventually the Senate approved a budget measure to allow a $1.2 trillion tax reduction and the White House and congressional Republicans proclaimed victory for the Bush plan.

Since the House and Senate passed budgets with different tax cut amounts, the measure went to a conference committee to hammer out the differences. Despite threats by some senators that any tax cut total greater than the Senate's version would not be passed, the conference committee decided on a tax reduction of $1.35 trillion. After days of intense negotiations over how to apportion the tax cut, it was decided that instead of the top federal income tax rate of 33.0 percent that Bush wanted, the top rate would be 35.0 percent, but this was still a reduction of the top rate of 39.6 percent that had been in effect since 1993; the bottom rate was reduced to 10.0 percent, compared to 15.0 percent since 1993 (see Table 4.1). At $875 billion through 2011, the income tax cuts were by far the most expensive part of the bill, accounting for 65 percent of its total cost.[34]

Republican leaders moved the so-called Economic Growth and Tax Relief Reconciliation Act of 2001 quickly through both the House and the Senate. It passed the House by a vote of 240 to 154, with 28 Democrats joining all Republicans in support of the bill. The Senate then passed it by a vote of 58 to 33, with 12 Democrats joining 46 Republicans in support, and 2 Republicans voting against. The 2001 tax cuts were a major legislative victory for Bush. The administration

Table 4.1 Change in Individual Income Tax Rates After Passage of 1993 and 2001 Budget Reconciliation Bills (percentage)

1993		2001	
15	($0–22,100)	10	($0–7,000)
28	($22,100-53,500)	15	($7,000–29,000)
31	($53,500–115,000)	25	($29,000–70,000)
36	($115,000–$250,000)	28	($70,000–145,000)
39.6	($250,000+)	33	($145,000–315,000)
		35	($315,000+)

Source: Internal Revenue Service.

compromised only enough to gain the support of wavering members of Congress and achieved most of what it had initially proposed.[35]

Democrats criticized the bill for being unfairly tilted toward the wealthy. In 2006, for example, the tax cuts were equivalent to 0.3 percent of after-tax income for the bottom quintile of the income distribution, 2.5 percent of income for the middle quintile, and 4.1 percent of income for the top quintile.[36] Democrats also claimed that the United States would come to regret the day the legislation was enacted because the tax cuts left too little money for other purposes and risked a return to the budget deficits that had plagued the federal government after Reagan's large 1981 tax cuts, deficits that would arrive just as the government would need to begin confronting the costs of paying Social Security and Medicare to an aging population. According to Senate Democratic leader Tom Daschle, the tax cuts were "good short-term politics" but "disastrous long-term policy." Congress, Daschle predicted, would ultimately have to "make corrections" to the tax policy.

Even though the plan approved by Congress was smaller than the $1.6 trillion plan Bush had originally proposed, the president signed the bill with enthusiasm. He had made a large tax cut his first legislative priority and was now able to declare victory. Not only was passage of the bill a victory for Bush, but it was also a victory for Republicans in Congress, who had been thwarted in their tax-cutting efforts while Clinton was in the White House.

An extraordinary provision in the 2001 tax cut package was the final one slated to take effect: the repeal of the entire measure at the end of 2010. Much of the 2001 tax cut package was not set to take effect until the second half of the decade—after the 2004 presidential election. That made budget forecasts—which historically have been profoundly unreliable even when revenue outlook is relatively stable—even more uncertain than usual.

The sunset provisions were necessary for the legislation to comply with the 2001 budget resolution, which limited the cost of the tax cuts to $1.35 trillion through 2011. The 2001 reconciliation ceiling was too low to accommodate everything the administration wanted, which totaled $1.78 trillion. A vote by sixty senators could have raised that ceiling, but the package's supporters concluded early that they could not muster a supermajority. The Bush administration, however, was confident that the sunset provisions would never take effect, because it believed that a future Congress would agree to extend the provisions of the 2001 law; to do otherwise could be politically portrayed as "raising

taxes." Three-fifths of the package's cost came after 2006. To critics, the measure's back-loaded nature and limited duration allowed
Bush and congressional Republicans to grossly underestimate the
true cost of the tax cuts.[37]

The fact that the tax cuts would officially end in 2011 created
room for some interesting budgetary maneuvering. Revenue projections rest on the assumption that current tax laws will remain unchanged by future legislation. If the provisions were made permanent
rather than allowed to expire, however, future revenue would be significantly lower. As a result of the sunset provisions, revenues were
projected to increase sharply in 2011, when statutory tax rates would
rise. Individual income tax revenues were projected to rise steadily
until 2010, at which point they were projected to increase substantially, reaching close to 10 percent of GDP in 2012.[38] Under the assumption that current laws and policies would remain the same, it
was projected that income tax revenues would reach nearly 20 percent of GDP in 2016, a level that had been exceeded only five times
since the end of World War II.[39]

After Bush won reelection in November 2004, he quickly an-
nounced that his reelection was a "mandate" from the public that Congress make his 2001 tax cuts permanent. It is debatable whether Bush's
victory truly reflected public opinion in regard to tax policy. Taxes received relatively little attention in the 2004 presidential campaign
compared to issues such as the war in Iraq and gay marriage. Also,
Bush's victory by 3 percentage points, though arguably decisive, was
not overwhelming, making any claim of a "mandate" potentially problematic. Regardless, Bush's proposal to make the tax cuts permanent
would have had major implications for projected long-term deficit levels. If all the tax provisions that are set to expire in 2011 were extended, the budget outlook for 2016 would change from a surplus of
$67 billion to a deficit of $584 billion.[40] Overall, projected revenues
would be reduced by about $2.64 trillion from 2011 to 2016 if the tax
cuts were made permanent.[41]

Along with income taxes, the 2001 tax cuts included a reduction
in the federal estate tax. Since the estate tax is only imposed on an estate after the owner has died, critics refer to this tax as a "death tax."
The estate tax, however, is only imposed on estates valued in the mil-
lions. Before the cut in 2001, the estate tax was imposed on only those
estates valued at more than $1 million; in 2006, this figure was to be
increased to $2 million, and then to $3.5 million in 2009. The tax was
then to disappear in 2010, but reappear in 2011 at its 2001 level. In

2001, the top estate tax rate was 50 percent, but was scheduled to drop to 45 percent in 2009 before returning to a top rate of 50 percent in 2011. Prior to the 2001 cuts, the estate tax raised $30 billion a year for the federal government. By 2011, the cost of the repeal was projected to reach $60 billion.[42]

Advocates of reducing the estate tax argue that this will increase economic growth by encouraging savings and increasing capital stock. Proponents of the estate tax, on the other hand, argue that it is an important source of revenue for the federal government that has merit in a system of progressive taxation, since it only affects estates of considerable size and provides numerous credits that allow a significant portion of estates to escape taxation. Proponents also argue that the high effective transfer tax rate encourages billions of dollars in charitable donations each year, since donations substantially reduce the tax on large estates.

Despite its political contentiousness, the estate tax affects remarkably few households. Fewer than 2 percent of estates paid federal estate taxes before the reductions in 2001.[43] In 2003, nearly 2.5 million Americans died, but only about 30,000 decedents left behind substantial enough estates to owe the federal estate tax in 2004 (when returns would have been generally due). Thus, taxable estate tax returns in 2004 represented just 1.2 percent of all Americans who died in 2003, for a total of $21.6 billion in federal estate taxes. As Table 4.2 demonstrates, most of this amount was paid by a small number of the largest estates. The 520 taxable estates worth over $20 million paid more than a quarter of the 2004 estate taxes, and the 3,500 taxable estates worth over $5 million—0.1 percent of decedents—paid 62 percent of all federal estate taxes. For all estates larger than $1

Table 4.2 Federal Estate Taxes, 2004

Size of Estate	Total No. of Decedents	No. with Estate Tax	Average Net Estate ($)	Average Federal Estate Tax (all) ($)
< $1 million	2,385,570	0	0	0
$1–2.5 million	45,974	21,152	1,466,000	80,000
$2.5–5 million	10,887	5,630	3,326,000	427,600
$5–10 million	3,806	2,166	6,765,000	1,148,600
$10–20 million	1,315	808	13,494,000	2,466,800
>$20 million	736	520	55,016,000	7,715,100
Total	2,448,288	30,276	—	8,800

Sources: Internal Revenue Service and National Center for Health Statistics, with calculations by Citizens for Tax Justice, April 2006.

million, only 11.5 percent of the net estate after expenses went to federal estate taxes and about 3.4 percent went to state taxes. Most of the estates (85.1 percent) went to family, friends, and charity.[44] Thus, even when the top rate was 50 percent, the effective rate of the estate tax was only 17 percent.[45] Bush's attempt to defend the cut by referring to the estate tax as a "death tax" was made easier by the fact that, even though only 2 percent of families would ever pay it, nearly half the public believed that it applied to "most families." As a result, the administration's rhetoric about saving the family farm or small business from the estate tax received relatively little skepticism among a misinformed public.[46]

Federal revenues dropped significantly after the 2001 tax cuts were enacted; in four years the federal government went from producing its largest surplus to producing its largest deficit. In January 2001 the Congressional Budget Office projected that the surpluses for 2002–2011 would total $3.1 trillion. By January 2002 the predicted cumulative ten-year budget surplus had dropped by a staggering $4 trillion. After deficits returned in 2002, the Bush administration adopted a policy of deliberate deficit spending, reversing its aspiration to reduce deficits and the debt that had been accepted since the mid-1980s. Just two years after record surpluses, the administration did not even pretend that it was trying to balance the budget.[47] Tax cuts, the "war on terror" after September 11, 2001, and a stagnant economy wiped out projected surpluses faster than most could have imagined.

Despite the Bush administration's denials that the tax cuts led to the large deficits, econometric estimates show that the tax cuts led to a considerable drop in revenue. Figure 4.1 compares actual federal revenues in the four years after the tax cuts were passed to projected revenues had the tax cuts never been enacted. Without question, the tax cuts led to considerably lower revenue levels. In 2004, for example, revenues after the tax cuts were $385 billion lower than they would have been had the tax cuts not been passed, accounting for more than 90 percent of the entire deficit that year. Without the tax cuts, instead of a record deficit of $412 billion in 2004, it would have been only about $27 billion; in other words, the budget would have been nearly balanced. In 2001, the CBO projected that the federal government would be running a surplus greater than $700 billion in 2011; in 2003, the Concord Coalition predicted a budget deficit of more than $500 billion in 2011. Nearly half of this difference was related directly to the Bush tax cuts.[48]

Figure 4.1 Revenue Consequences of the 2001 Tax Cuts

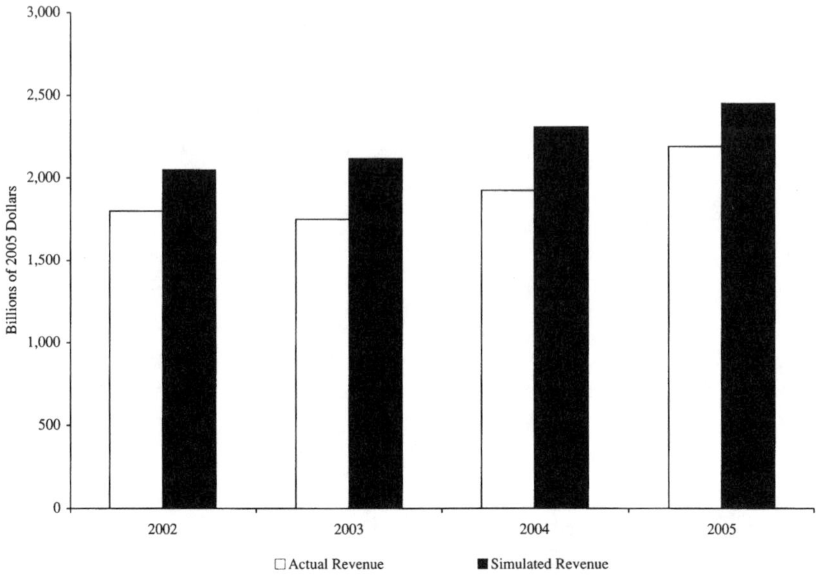

□ Actual Revenue   ■ Simulated Revenue

Sources: Isabel Sawhill, "Why Worry About the Deficit? (And What We Can Do About It)," Brookings Institution; Concord Coalition, "Fiscal Wake-Up Tour," University of Nebraska, April 4, 2006; US Department of Treasury; Bureau of Economic Analysis, "Current and 'Real' Gross Domestic Product," February 28, 2006.

Note: Simulated revenue assumes tax levels continued at 2001 level (19.7 percent of GDP).

The government's overall fiscal health clearly deteriorated after the Bush tax cuts were enacted. Before Bush was elected, the government had run surpluses in four consecutive years and forecasters were predicting trillions of dollars in surpluses over the coming decade. By 2006, however, the government was predicting deficits of more than $100 billion a year through 2011 and more than $1 trillion of new debt in the successive decade.[49] As Robert L. Bixby, executive director of the Concord Coalition, contended, the Bush approach represented "a significant retreat from the bipartisan balanced budget goal that existed only a few years ago."[50] Bush's budget policies, along with his positions on Iraq and social issues, contributed to making him the most polarizing president since the advent of polling.[51]

To critics, the Bush administration offered dubious justification for the tax cuts by manipulating traditional budget projection norms. From its creation in 1974 until 2003, the CBO calculated the effects of tax cuts and estimated growth using consensus-minded econometric models. To aid Bush's tax cut efforts, conservatives in Congress were able to persuade the CBO to use a "dynamic" model that assumes, as supply-siders do, that cutting top marginal tax rates will spur higher growth rates. To critics, the CBO's tradition of neutrality was compromised. While the CBO had historically calculated the economic effects of government revenue lost from tax cuts, it steered clear of both Keynesian and supply-side models, leaving much less room for individual economists to impose their own ideological agendas. The economy's performance during the Bush administration demonstrated that the CBO's old methods predict economic performance far more accurately than does dynamic scoring.[52]

Another controversial feature of the Bush tax cuts was their distribution. The Bush tax cuts, like the Reagan tax cuts, disproportionately benefited the wealthy. Due to the Bush tax cuts, combined federal, state, and local taxes took in only a slightly higher income of the richest Americans than the average for all other income groups. The combined federal, state, and local taxes on the wealthiest 1 percent of Americans equaled 32.8 percent of income in 2004, while for other groups these combined taxes averaged 29.4 percent of income. The tax cuts enacted under Bush lowered the overall federal, state, and local taxation of the wealthiest 1 percent of taxpayers by 12 percent. For the poorest 20 percent of taxpayers, on the other hand, the Bush tax cuts reduced overall taxes by only 3 percent.[53] By 2010, 52 percent of the total tax cuts would go to the richest 1 percent, whose average 2010 income would be an estimated $1.5 million. Of the estimated $234 billion in tax cuts scheduled for 2010, $121 billion would go to just 1.4 million taxpayers.[54] The regressive nature of the Bush tax cuts is demonstrated in Table 4.3. While the wealthiest 20 percent averaged a tax cut of $4,890, nearly 60 percent of the tax cut

Table 4.3 Distribution of the 2001 Bush Tax Cuts

Income Group	Average Income ($)	Average Tax Cut ($)	Share of Tax Cut (%)	Percentage Change in After-Tax Income
Lowest 20%	16,600	230	2.8	1.5
Second 20%	38,100	720	8.3	2.2
Middle 20%	57,400	980	11.5	2.0
Fourth 20%	84,300	1,520	17.7	2.3
Highest 20%	203,700	4,890	59.9	3.3
All	80,100	1,680	—	2.7

Source: David Kamin and Isaac Shapiro, "Studies Shed New Light on Effects of Administration's Tax Cuts," Center on Budget and Policy Priorities, September 13, 2004, p. 5.

share, the poorest 20 percent averaged a tax cut of $230, less than 3 percent of the tax cut share. The change in after-tax income for the wealthiest quintile was 3.3 percent, more than twice that for the lowest quintile.

This reinforced a trend, which had begun in the 1970s, in which the wealthiest Americans increasingly receive a larger percentage of all income in the nation. The top 10 percent of all income tax filers, for example, increased their share of the national income from 30.6 percent in 1960 to 41.7 percent in 2002.[55] About 72 percent of the total tax reduction went to the top 20 percent of taxpayers, and 45 percent went to the top 1 percent of taxpayers.[56] Bush, however, defended the tax cuts by arguing that they were not regressive. According to Bush, the tax cuts offered "the greatest help for those most in need" because "the highest percentage tax cuts go to the lowest income Americans." This is true, but only because the lowest-income groups already pay so little; reducing tax liabilities for the poor represents a large percentage cut, but a small substantive benefit for the taxpayer.[57]

The regressive nature of the 2001 tax cuts was reinforced by the 2003 tax act that lowered the top rate of corporate stock dividends from 35 to 15 percent, and reduced the top capital gains tax rate from 20 to 15 percent. As a result of those changes, the size of the Bush tax cuts for those with adjusted gross incomes greater than $10 million a year increased from an average of $522,000 in 2001 to $1,020,000 in 2003—a 95 percent increase. On the other hand, the 71 percent of taxpayers with adjusted gross incomes of less than $50,000 saved an average of only $10 each from capital gains and dividend tax cuts, adding only 2 percent to their $425 average tax reduction in 2003. Altogether, almost 43 percent of the capital gains and dividend tax cuts in 2003 went to the 181,000 filers with adjusted gross incomes greater than $1 million, representing only 0.1 percent of all tax returns.[58]

There were three potential risks for the Bush presidency in this "tax cuts at any cost" approach. First, it was only a matter of time before enduring deficits would divide the administration's support among congressional Republicans. Second, large deficits handed the Democrats a potential issue in future elections. Third, large deficits put at risk spending prospects for other policies the Bush administration advocated.[59]

After dramatically increasing from 2002 to 2004, the budget deficit dropped from a record $412 billion in 2004 to $248 billion by 2006. The drop was largely the result of a robust growth of federal revenues, which increased by $526 billion (28 percent) from 2004 to 2006. Revenues as a share of GDP rose for the first time since 2000.[60] In his 2004 reelection campaign, Bush promised to cut the deficit in half by 2009 and the drop in the deficit seemed to vindicate his pledge. Bush argued that the deficit reduction was the result of the tax cuts he had consistently promoted throughout his presidency: "Some in Washington say we had to choose between cutting taxes and cutting the deficit . . . that was a false choice. The economic growth fueled by tax relief has helped send our tax revenues soaring."[61]

To critics of Bush's tax cuts, the drop in deficit levels after 2004 by no means justified the cuts. The growth in revenue originated from a low baseline. In 2004, income tax revenue fell to its lowest level as a share of the economy since World War II. As *The New Republic* argued, "The fact that the deficit is going to drop to somewhere around $300 billion a year, with the economy red-hot, is not good news. It is a sign that our tax and spending policies are producing a large structural deficit. And when the business cycle cools down again, the deficit is going to explode."[62] Detractors contended that Bush was unduly optimistic about the nation's fiscal condition, especially over the long run. As Robert L. Bixby, executive director of the Concord Coalition, argued, "The real news here is that even into our fifth year of economic recovery and with two years of strong revenue growth, we still have a deficit this year [2006] of almost $300 billion. Interest on the debt has become the fastest growing category of federal spending. Moreover, the deficit for next year is projected to go up and the Administration's projections beyond 2007 do not include the likely costs of important policies such as the war in Iraq and Alternative Minimum Tax relief."[63]

Even with the deficit decreasing, it still approached 2 percent of GDP, meaning that the United States was still borrowing 2 percent of total economic output to finance its deficit. At the peak of the last business cycle in 2000, the government was running a surplus of 2.4 percent of GDP.[64] Revenues increased in 2005–2006, but only in comparison with how low they had plunged in the early 2000s. Adjusted for inflation, revenue from individual income taxes, the largest component of federal revenue, was far lower in 2006 than in 2000.[65]

Not only were deficit levels still high, but it is also dubious to make a connection—as Bush did—among tax cuts, economic growth, and higher taxes. For example, in the five years following the tax increases of 1993, annual real economic growth averaged 3.8 percent, while in the five years after the tax cuts of 2001, annual real economic growth averaged 3.1 percent. Furthermore, in the five years after the 1993 tax increases, annual revenue growth averaged 8.3 percent, while in the five years after the 2001 tax cuts, annual revenue growth averaged 4.0 percent.[66] The performance of the economy during the Clinton administration compared to that during the George W. Bush administration, therefore, does not lend support to the claim that tax cuts are always better for the economy than tax increases.

The more than $600 billion swing in the federal government's surplus/deficit levels from 2000, the last year of the Clinton administration, to 2004 indicates the importance of the president's tax policies on deficit levels. There were major differences between the Clinton and Bush tax policies, and these differences played an important role in determining the degree to which the federal government would produce a surplus or deficit. The Clinton administration decided that deficit reduction should be a priority, and thus raised taxes significantly. Coupled with a strong economy, this resulted in record-breaking surpluses at the end of the twentieth century. The Bush administration, on the other hand, decided that tax reduction was a higher priority than deficit reduction, a tax policy that contributed to record deficits at the start of the twenty-first century.

Evolving Public Opinion on Tax Cuts

The Reagan tax cuts in 1981 were clearly in tune with public opinion of the time. Effective tax rates rose to politically unacceptable levels in the late 1970s (partially due to "bracket creep" that occurred because inflation was pushing income levels to higher tax brackets) and the public was eager to support politicians like Reagan who were advocating tax cuts. What made the Reagan tax cuts problematic was the size of the resulting budget deficits, which were easily the largest in US history. In regard to deficit spending, however, it can be argued that the actions of the Reagan administration were consistent with public opinion. By the late 1970s, there was clearly a strong demand for tax cuts, regardless of deficit levels. A 1977 poll, for example, showed that there was strong support for cutting income taxes even if that meant a larger budget deficit (see Figure 4.2). It may thus be said that the large deficits that plagued the federal government throughout the Reagan administration were reasonably in accord with public preferences.

The public's lack of concern toward federal government deficits in the 1980s can be seen in their political responses. President Reagan

Figure 4.2 Public Opinion on Taxes and the Deficit, 1977

"Are you in favor of a cut in federal income taxes, or not?"

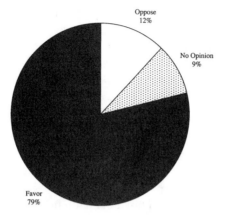

Asked of those who favored a tax cut: "Would you still favor a cut in federal income taxes even if that meant a larger government deficit?"

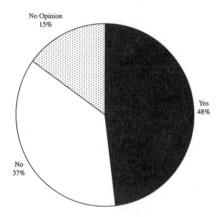

Source: Gallup Poll (January 14–17, 1977), national survey of 918 adults.

became the classic example of the politician who is not punished for large deficits. In a 1984 poll, voters were asked, "Regardless of your own political views, what would you give as the best reason for voting against President Reagan?" The deficit ranked ninth (4 percent), far behind foreign policy (21 percent) and fairness (18 percent).[67] Thus, even though deficits skyrocketed during his administration, Reagan was easily able to win reelection. While a large majority of citizens may have favored a balanced budget in the abstract, they did not want higher taxes and they did not want spending cuts for most programs.[68]

What made the tax cuts of the George W. Bush administration especially noteworthy is the fact that they appeared to contradict public opinion. Unlike the Reagan tax cuts, the Bush tax cuts proved a hard sell with the public, with majorities in polls preferring much smaller cuts and many opposed to any cuts at all.[69] When Reagan advocated major tax cuts after being elected president, public opinion at the time was overwhelmingly supportive of tax cuts, even if that meant larger budget deficits. Reagan's policies were therefore consistent with strong public demand for lower taxes. When George H. W. Bush and Bill Clinton raised taxes in their respective administrations in the name of deficit reduction, the public, though not enamored with tax increases, clearly believed that large budget deficits were a problem and became more supportive of tax increases than was the case during the Reagan years. George W. Bush's tax initiatives, however, were not the result of public demand, but the result of economic policies that placed a premium upon tax cuts above all else. This represented a fundamental change in the nature of presidential tax policy. Pursuing tax cuts even in the face of large budget deficits was a radical departure from the actions of previous presidents, even Reagan.[70] Though tax cuts were consistently advocated by the White House and congressional Republicans after Bush was elected president, there was relatively little grassroots support for the concept. In fact, the substance of the Bush tax cuts was sharply at odds with public preferences.

Why the continued emphasis on tax cuts even though it flew in the face of traditional economic policy and seemingly contradicted public opinion? One theory is that the central tenet of the George W. Bush presidency was to complete the conservative ideological agenda of Reagan, replacing liberal conceptions about the proper role of government with a conservative regime of supply-side economics.[71] It has been argued that Bush's tax cuts were successful politically, even though they were sharply at odds with public preferences, because tax policy was pulled off center by the increasing incentives of political elites to cater to their partisan and ideological base and by the increasing capacity of politicians to abandon the middle to escape political retribution.[72] Traditional electoral theories have suggested that as candidates move toward their political base, they should be more vulnerable in general elections.[73] Yet with the Bush tax cuts this was definitely not the case. Even though the tax cuts appeared to contradict public opinion and were an overt attempt to appeal to the conservative base of the Republican Party, congressional Republicans who supported the tax cuts, as well as President Bush, did not pay a price at the polls (at least, not an immediate price).[74]

Ironically, despite the fact that the Bush administration staked a lot of political capital on selling the desirability of tax cuts and claimed a major political victory when they passed, many Americans refused to believe that their taxes had indeed been reduced. In May 2004, for example, one poll found that only about one in ten said they were paying less in federal taxes than had been the case before the cuts.[75] In another poll taken in March 2004, only 22 percent reported lower taxes, 46 percent reported no change, and 25 percent even reported higher taxes.[76]

Respondents from higher-income families were significantly less supportive of the 2001 tax cuts than those from lower-income families, other things being equal. Since those with higher incomes received more benefits with the tax cuts, this suggests that real material interests cannot have been the overriding determinant of respondents' policy preferences.[77] At the same time, support for the Bush administration's tax cuts was largely due to the detachment between inequality and public policy. While most people believed that the difference between the wealthy and the poor had increased over the preceding twenty years and that this was a bad thing, most people still supported the regressive 2001 tax cuts. Support for the Bush tax cuts was strongly shaped by people's attitudes toward their own tax burdens, not their attitudes about the tax burden of the rich. This was even the case with the estate tax, which only affects the wealthiest taxpayers.[78]

The regressive nature of the Bush tax cuts probably undermined their popularity. Part of the lack of support for the tax cuts may be derived from the fact that Americans tend to believe that upper-income earners pay too little in federal taxes compared to lower- and middle-income earners. According to a 1999 poll, while 51 percent of Americans believed that lower-income earners paid "too much" in federal taxes and 59 percent believed the same of middle-income earners, only 10 percent felt the same for upper-income earners. On the other hand, nearly two-thirds of respondents believed that upper-income earners contributed "too little" in income taxes (see Table 4.4). Americans are not indifferent to economic inequality, but to a large degree they fail to connect inequality and tax policy.[79]

As Figure 4.3 displays, an American public who overwhelmingly supported tax cuts in the late 1970s became much more ambivalent about them twenty years later. In 1979, 62 percent of Americans agreed that "the government ought to cut taxes even if it means putting

Table 4.4 "Fair Share" of Taxes by Income Group, 1999 (percentage)

"As I read off some different groups, please tell me if you think they are paying their fair share in federal taxes, paying too much, or paying too little."

	Fair Share	Too Much	Too Little	No Opinion
Lower-income people	34	51	11	4
Middle-income people	35	59	4	2
Upper-income people	19	10	66	5

Source: Gallup Poll (April 6–7, 1999), national survey of 1,055 adults.

Figure 4.3 Change of Public Opinion on Tax Cuts, 1979 vs. 1999

"The government ought to cut taxes even if it means putting off some important things that need to be done."

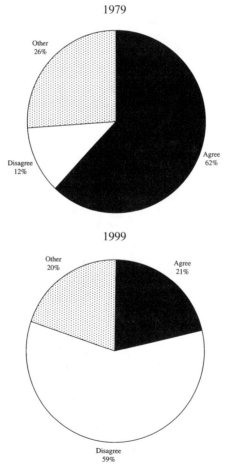

Sources: Gallup Poll (August 16–18, 1999), national survey of 1,028 adults; Gallup Poll (January 16, 1979), national survey of 2,651 adults.

off some important things that need to be done"; twenty years later, only 21 percent agreed. The fact that tax cuts appeared to be a less salient issue in 1999 than two decades earlier demonstrates an important change in public opinion. By the late 1990s, public opinion potentially presented an opportunity for the federal government to continue producing surpluses and reduce the national debt.

Why has public opinion on taxes changed since the 1970s? One obvious reason is that Americans pay lower taxes than they did in the 1970s, so the demand for cutting taxes has been fulfilled to some degree. Also, the surpluses at the end of the Clinton administration ironically may have changed the context of tax cuts. It is possible that the tax cut demands of the 1970s and 1980s were to some degree encouraged by the large budget deficits of the era, which symbolized government's failings. Americans today have more confidence in how government spends their tax money than was the case in the 1970s and 1980s, and this makes current levels of taxation more acceptable. When Ronald Reagan was elected president in 1980, for example, nearly 80 percent of Americans thought that government wastes "a lot" of tax money; by 2004, this figure had been reduced to about 60 percent (see Figure 4.4). Taxes are simply more palatable

Figure 4.4 Public Opinion on Government Waste, 1958–2004

"Do you think that people in the government waste a lot of money we pay in taxes, waste some of it, or don't waste very much of it?"

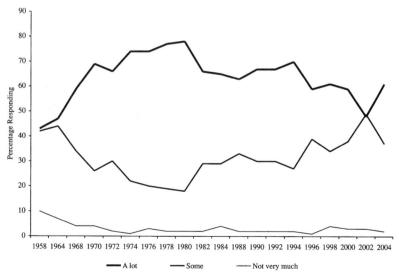

Source: American National Election Studies.

if the public believes that the revenues garnered through taxation are not being wasted, which is relatively more the case today than it was in the 1970s and 1980s.

To some degree, therefore, the contradictions of citizen demands on taxing and spending priorities were mitigated, at least temporarily, and the public became more supportive of deficit and debt reduction. The federal government was able to produce budgetary surpluses from 1998 to 2001 mainly because of an unexpected windfall of revenues. But a changed climate in public opinion also aided the federal government in this endeavor. This was especially true when it came to public opinion on taxation.[80] Once large deficits returned to the scene during the George W. Bush administration, tax cuts were further marginalized as a priority. Right after Bush won reelection in November 2004, Americans were asked whether tax cuts or reducing the deficit should be a higher budget priority. Respondents overwhelmingly argued for reducing the deficit, by a 67 percent to 28 percent margin.[81] Despite the public hostility to further tax cuts at a time of record budget deficits, however, Bush continually pressed for tax cuts. The Bush administration's emphasis on tax cuts helped to create a pessimistic mood about future deficit levels. At Bush's second inauguration, in January 2005, 66 percent of Americans believed that the federal budget deficit would be bigger at the end of his second term in office and only 8 percent believed that it would be smaller.[82]

Conservatives and Tax Cuts

Historically, the Republican Party has been regarded as the party that puts a higher emphasis on balancing the budget. Conservatives have strongly favored balanced budgets going back to 1798, when Thomas Jefferson proposed a balanced budget amendment to the Constitution. Once Franklin Roosevelt endorsed the Keynesian concept of short-term deficit spending in order to stimulate the economy after he was elected president in 1932, the Democrats became the party associated with Keynesian economic principles, which justified short-term deficits, and the Republicans largely reaffirmed their historical belief in balanced budgets. The election of Reagan as president marks the beginning of the modern conservative drive to stress tax cuts above all other budgetary considerations. Prior to Reagan, Republicans had historically pushed for tax cuts, but not at the expense of large budget deficits. Regardless of the political motivations, it is clear that the policy implications of implementing supply-side economic theory have been enormous. It has been estimated, for example, that the Economic Recovery Tax Act of 1981 cost the federal government more than $2 trillion in lost revenue over the period 1982–1991.[83]

The George W. Bush administration's acceptance of large deficits demonstrates the degree to which the supply-side dogma of the Reagan era has come to dominate the tax philosophy of the Republican Party. Today, many conservatives like George W. Bush are tax-cutters first and budget-balancers second.[84] Ever since George H. W. Bush abandoned his "no new taxes" pledge in 1990, not a single Republican has voted in Congress for a major tax increase. Tax-cutters have redefined the Republican Party. An example of this can be seen in Bob Dole's presidential run in 1996. Before 1996, Dole had been viewed as a committed deficit hawk. But in order to rally the Republican conservative base behind him in 1996, Dole advocated significant supply-side tax cuts.

Conservative justification for cutting taxes, even in the face of large deficits, tends to be based on one of two premises. One argument is that tax cuts can be so liberating that they will actually pay for themselves by inspiring new economic activity. The other argument is that if you want smaller government, you have to "starve the beast." Larger deficits, according to this second school of thought, increase the pressure for spending cuts. Deficits, therefore, can be seen as a useful political tool.[85]

For many conservatives, therefore, reducing the deficit is simply not as important as cutting taxes and limiting the size of government. Tax cuts can be regarded as conservative in that they are a means to reduce the power of the state, even if that means larger deficits.[86] As conservative strategist Grover Norquist put it: "If we had a little teeny government and a big deficit, I wouldn't care. It's the size of the government we're focused on."[87] Similarly, Representative Sue Myrick, chair of the Republican Study Committee, a group of fiscally conservative House members who had been ardent opponents of deficit spending in the 1990s, argued that "anything that will help us stop spending money, I'm in favor of . . . if there's a deficit, that may help us."[88] This approach, however, is certainly controversial: even some Republicans have argued that Congress's embrace of tax cuts is excessive, especially when tax cuts are presented as patriotic.[89] According to Peter Peterson, former Treasury secretary during the Richard Nixon administration, "so-called conservatives are outpandering LBJ. They must have it all: guns, butter, and tax cuts."[90]

Since the 1970s, it is clear that the Republican political base has shifted geographically to the south and ideologically in a more

conservative direction. One argument for the Republican Party's conversion on taxes and deficits is that pressure from the Sunbelt states
led the party to adopt supply-side tax policies.[91] Another argument
is that the adoption of supply-side economics resulted from increasingly vocal public opinion about tax burdens and policies.[92] Both of
these theories imply that it was Washington elites who responded to
pressure outside the capital. The Reagan tax cuts were clearly influenced by public opinion at the time, with polls in the late 1970s and
early 1980s showing strong support for cutting income taxes even if
that meant a larger budget deficit. Even though many representatives
believed they enacted Reaganomics because of constituent support,
however, there is persuasive evidence indicating that partisanship
and conservatism were more important factors. For legislators who
were undecided, the unity of the activist response was so overwhelming that it at least temporarily convinced many of them to support
Reagan's budget package.[93] Ultimately, the Republican Party's pro-
motion of large, across-the-board tax cuts from 1977 to 1981 was the
result of calculated and coordinated decisions by elites within the
party that changed what "conservative" economic principles were.[94]

By making taxes a central issue, the Republicans highlight the
class-related differences between the parties.[95] Recent federal tax
changes, particularly the repeal of the estate tax and the reduction in
capital gains tax rates, have exacerbated cross-sectional wealth disparities.[96] Conservatives justify cutting taxes for the wealthy by arguing that the economy is changing, with the greater growth of higher
incomes rewarding desired talents. Critics of the current tax system
point out that the top 1 percent of the wealth spectrum pay rates
about ten times those of the bottom half. Since the affluent carry the
bulk of the income tax obligation, conservatives argue that they are
most deserving of tax cuts.[97] Support for tax breaks for the wealthy
in an era of increasing economic inequality can be said to be a product of the American culture. Americans embrace an ideology of opportunity that sees economic inequality as natural and unobjection-
able.[98] Compared to citizens of other democracies, Americans are
less worried about inequality, and this can be seen in the changes in
the nation's tax policies since 1980.

Notes

1. Jeffrey M. Stonecash, *Class and Party in American Politics* (Boulder:
Westview, 2000).

2. "If You Don't Hear It Fall, Is It a Tax Cut?" *New York Times,* May 2, 2004, p. R3.

3. Larry Bartels, "Homer Gets a Tax Cut: Inequality and Public Policy in the American Mind," *Perspectives on Politics* 3 (2005): 15–31.

4. Frank Newport, "Tax Cuts Have Generic Appeal, but Are Not Voters' Highest Priority," Gallup Organization, June 27, 1999, http://www.gallup.com/releases/pr990626.asp.

5. Nathan Glazer, "On Americans and Inequality," *Daedalus* 132 (2003): 111–115.

6. Stonecash, *Class and Party in American Politics.*

7. Jacob S. Hacker and Paul Pierson, "Abandoning the Middle: The Bush Tax Cuts and the Limits of Democratic Control," *Perspectives on Politics* 3 (2005): 33–53.

8. Martin Gilens, "Political Ignorance and Collective Policy Preferences," *American Political Science Review* 95 (2001): 379–396.

9. Office for Social Justice, Archdiocese of St. Paul and Minneapolis, May 24, 2006, http://www.osjspm.org/101_taxes.htm.

10. Gary R. Evans, *Red Ink* (San Diego: Academic Press, 1997), pp. 36–38.

11. David Mayhew, *America's Congress* (New Haven: Yale University Press, 2000), p. 79.

12. M. Stephen Weatherford and Lorraine M. McDonnell, "Ronald Reagan as Legislative Advocate: Passing the Reagan Revolution's Budgets in 1981 and 1982," *Congress and the Presidency* 32 (2005): 1–29.

13. Congressional Quarterly, "Budget and Appropriations," in *1981 Congressional Quarterly Almanac* (Washington, DC, 1982), pp. 245–246.

14. Louis Fisher, *Constitutional Conflicts Between Congress and the President,* 4th ed. (Lawrence: University Press of Kansas, 1997), p. 209.

15. Congressional Quarterly, "Budget and Appropriations."

16. Weatherford and McDonnell, "Ronald Reagan as Legislative Advocate."

17. Howard E. Shuman, *Politics and the Budget,* 2nd ed. (Englewood Cliffs, NJ: Prentice Hall, 1988), p. 104.

18. Peter G. Peterson, *Running on Empty* (New York: Farrar, Straus and Giroux, 2004), p. 135.

19. Evans, *Red Ink,* p. 38.

20. Weatherford and McDonnell, "Ronald Reagan as Legislative Advocate."

21. Irene Rubin, *Balancing the Federal Budget* (New York: Chatham, 2003), p. 31.

22. Daniel Franklin, *Making Ends Meet* (Washington, DC: Congressional Quarterly, 1993), p. 235.

23. David W. Brady and Craig Volden, *Revolving Deadlock,* 2nd ed. (Boulder: Westview, 2006).

24. Congressional Quarterly, "Congress Enacts Sweeping Overhaul of Tax Law," in *1986 Congressional Quarterly Almanac* (Washington, DC, 1987), p. 491.

25. Ibid.

26. Jefferey H. Birnbaum and Alan S. Murray, *Showdown at Gucci Gulch* (New York: Random, 1987), p. 289.

27. Ibid., p. 9.

28. Scott J. Bassinger and Mark Hallerberg, "Remodeling the Competition for Capital: How Domestic Politics Erases the Race to the Bottom," *American Political Science Review* 98 (2004): 261–276.

29. Birnbaum and Murray, *Showdown at Gucci Gulch,* p. 347.

30. Jeffrey H. Birnbaum, "Oregon Senator Wants to Take on the Burden of Fixing the Tax Code," *Washington Post,* July 24, 2006, p. D1.

31. Hacker and Pierson, "Abandoning the Middle."

32. Rubin, *Balancing the Federal Budget,* p. 34.

33. Richard W. Stevenson, "The President's Budget: The Proposal; President Unveils $1.96 Trillion Plan That Trims Taxes," *New York Times,* March 1, 2001.

34. Daniel J. Parks and Bill Swindle, "Tax Debate Assured a Long Life as Bush, GOP Press for New Cuts," *Congressional Quarterly Weekly,* June 2, 2001, pp. 1304–1309.

35. John C. Fortier and Norman J. Ornstein, "President Bush: Legislative Stategist," in Fred I. Greenstein, ed., *The George W. Bush Presidency: An Early Assessment* (Baltimore: Johns Hopkins University Press, 2003), pp. 147–151.

36. Urban Institute and Brookings Institution Tax Policy Center, "The Distribution of the 2001–2006 Tax Cuts," November 15, 2006, http://www .taxpolicycenter.org/publications.

37. Parks and Swindle, "Tax Debate Assured a Long Life."

38. Congressional Budget Office, *The Fiscal and Economic Outlook: Fiscal Years 2007 to 2016* (Washington, DC, 2006), p. 84.

39. Ibid., p. 79.

40. Ibid., p. 3.

41. Ibid., p. 101.

42. Office for Social Justice, http://www.osjspm.org/101_taxes.htm.

43. Ibid.

44. Citizens for Tax Justice, "Who Pays the Federal Estate Tax?" April 4, 2006.

45. Office for Social Justice, http://www.osjspm.org/101_taxes.htm.

46. Gary C. Jacobson, *A Divider, Not a Uniter: George Bush and the American People* (New York: Longman, 2007), p. 244.

47. Aaron Wildavsky and Naomi Caiden, *The New Politics of the Budgetary Process,* 5th ed. (New York: Longman, 2004), pp. 212–219.

48. Concord Coalition, "How Budget Projections Have Changed, 2002–2011," September 29, 2003.

49. Edmund L. Andrews, "White House Forecasts Drop in Deficit," *New York Times,* July 12, 2006, p. A21.

50. Concord Coalition, "Concord Coalition Warns Against Fiscal Euphoria," July 11, 2006.

51. Jacobson, *A Divider, Not a Uniter.*

52. Franklin Foer, "The Closing of the Presidential Mind," *New Republic,* July 5, 2004, pp. 17–20.

53. Citizens for Tax Justice, "Overall Tax Rates Have Flattened Sharply Under Bush," April 13, 2004.

54. Citizens for Tax Justice, "Year-by-Year Analysis of the Bush Tax Cuts Shows Growing Tilt to the Very Rich," June 12, 2002.

55. Mark D. Brewer and Jeffrey M. Stonecash, *Split: Class and Cultural Divides in American Politics* (Washington, DC: Congressional Quarterly, 2007), pp. 48–49.

56. Ben Fritz, Bryan Keefer, and Brendan Nyhan, *All the President's Spin: George W. Bush, the Media, and the Truth* (New York: Simon and Schuster, 2004), pp. 75–78.

57. Jacobson, *A Divider, Not a Uniter,* p. 75.

58. Citizens for Tax Justice, "Tax Cuts on Capital Gains and Dividends Doubled Bush Income Tax Cuts for the Wealthiest in 2003," April 5, 2006.

59. Steven E. Schier, "George W. Bush's Presidential Project and Its Prospects," *The Forum* 1 (2003): Article 2, Issue 4 (online edition).

60. Congressional Budget Office, *The Fiscal and Economic Outlook,* p. 4.

61. Andrews, "White House Forecasts Drop in Deficit."

62. "Laughter Curve," *New Republic,* July 3, 2006, p. 7.

63. Concord Coalition, "Concord Coalition Warns Against Fiscal Euphoria."

64. "Laughter Curve," *New Republic.*

65. Edmund L. Andrews, "Those Wild Budget Swings," *New York Times,* July 16, 2006, p. WK4.

66. Concord Coalition, "Concord Coalition Warns Against Fiscal Euphoria."

67. Joseph White and Aaron Wildavsky, *The Deficit and the Public Interest* (Berkeley: University of California Press, 1989), pp. 427–428.

68. Wildavsky and Caiden, *The New Politics of the Budgetary Process.*

69. *Washington Post,* March 28, 2003, p. A1; *Los Angeles Times,* April 4, 2003, p. A1.

70. Peterson, *Running on Empty,* p. 146.

71. Schier, "George W. Bush's Presidential Project and Its Prospects."

72. Hacker and Pierson, "Abandoning the Middle."

73. Anthony Downs, *An Economic Theory of Democracy* (New York: Harper and Row, 1957).

74. Hacker and Pierson, "Abandoning the Middle."

75. "If You Don't Hear It Fall, Is It a Tax Cut?" *New York Times.*

76. Ibid.

77. Bartels, "Homer Gets a Tax Cut."

78. Ibid.

79. Ibid.

80. Patrick Fisher, *Congressional Budgeting: A Representational Perspective* (Lanham, MD: University Press of America, 2005), chap. 6.

81. New York Times/CBS News Poll (November 18–21, 2004), national survey of 885 adults.

82. New York Times/CBS News Poll (January 14–18, 2005), national survey of 1,118 adults.

83. John Cranford, *Budgeting for America,* 2nd ed. (Washington, DC: Congressional Quarterly, 1989).

84. John W. Burns and Andrew Taylor, "The Mythical Causes of the Republican Supply-Side Economics Revolution," *Party Politics* 6 (2000): 419–440.

85. Michael Kinsley, "A Beast of an Idea," *Time,* January 12, 2004, p. 84.

86. Julian E. Zelizer, *Taxing America: Wilbur D. Mills, Congress, and the State, 1945–1975* (New York: Cambridge University Press, 1998).

87. Robin Toner, "A $304 Billion Deficit That Republicans Can Embrace," *New York Times,* February 9, 2003, p. WR3.

88. David Firestone, "Conservatives Now See Deficits as a Tool to Fight Spending," *New York Times,* February 11, 2003, p. A24.

89. Peterson, *Running on Empty,* p. 146.

90. Ibid., p. xxv.

91. Michael S. Berkman, *The State Roots of National Politics: Congress and the Tax Agenda, 1978–1986* (Pittsburgh: University of Pittsburgh Press, 1993).

92. E. J. Dionne, *Why Americans Hate Politics* (New York: Simon and Schuster, 1991).

93. Darrell West, "Activists and Economic Policymaking in Congress," *American Journal of Political Science* 32 (1988): 662–680.

94. Burns and Taylor, "The Mythical Causes of the Republican Supply-Side Economics Revolution."

95. Brewer and Stonecash, *Split,* p. 45.

96. Jenny B. Wahl, "From Riches to Riches: Intergenerational Transfers and the Evidence from Estate Tax Returns," *Social Science Quarterly* 84 (2003): 278–296.

97. Brewer and Stonecash, *Split,* pp. 47–48.

98. Glazer, "On Americans and Inequality."

5

THE POLITICS OF SPENDING

THE SIZE AND COMPLEXITY OF US GOVERNMENT SPENDING ARE truly awe-inspiring. Total annual expenditures for the federal government now exceed $2.5 trillion. With such a tremendous amount of money at stake, it is important to study how and why this money is being spent. Given the intricacies of the federal budget process, spending decisions are largely disconnected from and much different than taxing decisions. Yet even with this disconnection, there are limits to how much government can spend. Ultimately, the politics of spending is the politics of choice, because there is simply not enough money to go around. Budgets, simply put, make choices between expenditures.

The federal budget can be divided into five categories of roughly equivalent expenditures: Social Security, health care (Medicare and Medicaid), domestic discretionary spending, defense, and other mandatory spending and interest on the national debt (see Figure 5.1). The largest component of federal spending is a broad category of human resources, or entitlements. This includes Social Security benefits, health care, assistance for the poor, and education. The growth of the federal role in human resource programs has increased the number of people and groups with an interest in federal budgetary decisions and has thus increased the political pressure on budgetary decisionmakers.[1]

Entitlements

More than half the federal budget is devoted to entitlement spending. Entitlements are benefits extended to those who qualify under the

Figure 5.1 Major Components of Spending, Fiscal Year 2007

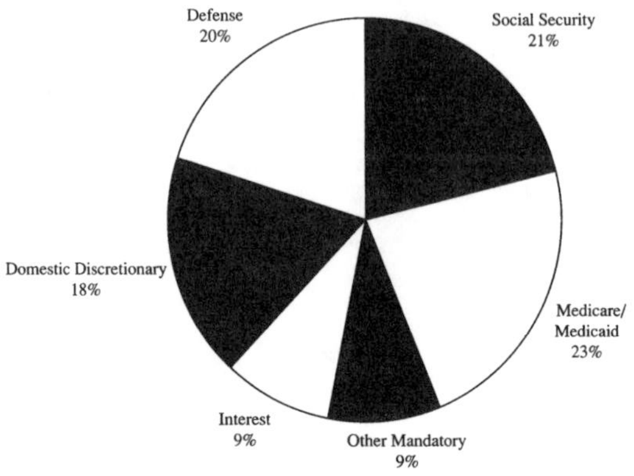

Source: Congressional Budget Office.

provisions of law. If a recipient meets the criteria, he or she is "enti-tled" to the money. Federal entitlement programs range from the enormous, such as Social Security and Medicare, to the tiny, such as an indemnity program for dairy farmers whose milk is contaminated by chemicals. While most entitlements go to people, some also go to other units of government. The Title XX Social Services block grant, for instance, goes to states based on population. Entitlement pay-ments are legal obligations of the federal government; their manda-tory nature is what distinguishes them from the other major types of congressional spending. The only way an entitlement can be changed is by amending the authorizing legislation that extends the benefit.

Entitlement programs can be grouped into roughly four categories: retirement (Social Security and other such benefits, including federal pensions), medical care (Medicare, the federal health insurance for the elderly and disabled, and Medicaid, the joint federal-state health pro-gram for the poor), unemployment, and need-based entitlements. Though some of the costs of entitlements (such as for Medicaid) are covered by the states, the federal government finances the bulk of these programs. The three largest entitlement programs—Social Secu-rity, Medicare, and Medicaid—dominate federal spending and are re-sponsible for more than 80 percent of all mandatory spending.[2]

The term "entitlements" means different things to different peo-ple. The psychological "entitlements" that many criticize are different from the legalistic "entitlements" that others support.[3] Entitlements thus pose a philosophic quandary for policymakers. Does "entitled to" mean the same as "deserving of"? This is of course a political question. Who should give or take how much from whom? Entitlements not only benefit some people, but they also represent costs to others. At the same time, politicians across the political spectrum have reason to be critical of entitlement spending. Conservatives fear that the dramatic increase in entitlement spending will lead to much higher taxes in the future, while liberals fear that entitlements will squeeze out other programs.[4]

Critics often label entitlements as "uncontrollable" spending, because they are difficult to curtail once created. Labeling them as such, however, is somewhat misleading. While Congress cannot control levels of eligibility in the population through the appropriations process, it can control such levels under the law (cost-of-living adjustments, for example). However, it would be accurate to say that, politically, entitlements are relatively uncontrollable. Entitlements are subject to a vote, but only if Congress decides to arrange one. Since the clientele of entitlements includes not only direct beneficiaries but also service providers whose livelihood depends on the recipients, the budget process is much less insulated than it was before the rise of entitlement spending.[5]

Another criticism of entitlements is that they largely fund what has been called "middle-class welfare." The middle classes are the major benefactors of entitlements because benefits are dispensed largely on the basis of means other than income. Most entitlement spending does not go to the needy. Entitlements are also criticized for disproportionately benefiting the elderly. More than 60 percent of all entitlement spending goes to the elderly, even though the group who is now at greatest risk of poverty is children. It be argued that the elderly bias is not only unfair, but also poses serious long-term budgeting problems.

Spending growth for the federal government in general has been driven by entitlement spending. As a share of the federal budget, entitlement spending has increased from less than one-third in the mid-1960s to more than one-half today; as a percentage of GDP, entitlement spending has more than doubled since the mid-1960s (see Figure 5.2). The transition to large and chronic deficits beginning in the 1960s was partly a result of nondefense spending growth due to the expansion of entitlement benefits. While spending levels began increasing substantially in the 1960s, revenue levels did not, leading to large deficits.[6]

Entitlements are the fastest-growing part of the budget, and the largest entitlement programs are projected to grow rapidly as the nation's population gets older. As Figure 5.3 displays, Social Security,

Figure 5.2 Growth of Entitlement Spending, 1965–2007

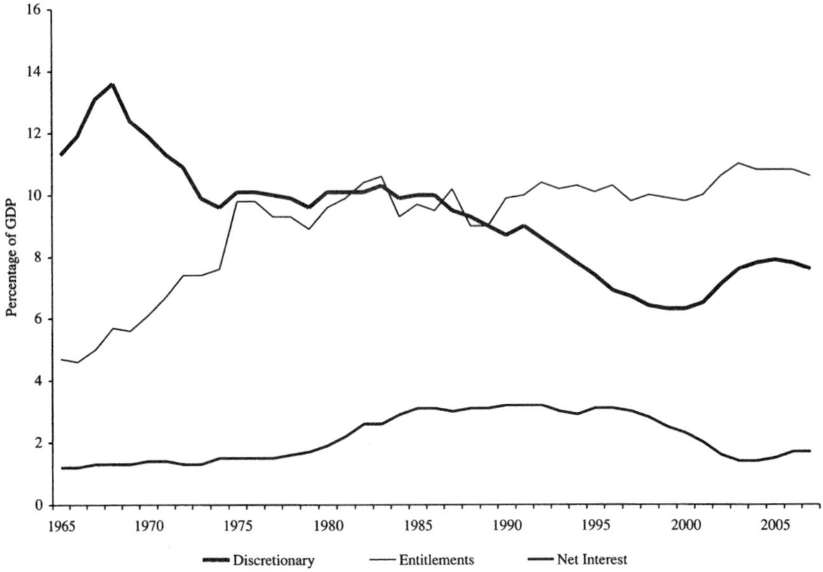

Source: Congressional Budget Office.

Medicare, and Medicaid combined are expected to double their 2000 level (as a percentage of GDP) by 2030. Entitlement spending is now greater than $1 trillion annually and is projected to continue climbing faster than the economy—5.8 percent each year—up to 2016, meaning it will double in size over the next decade.[7] Thus, long-term projections suggest that, as the American population ages, entitlement spending for the elderly (specifically Social Security and Medicare) risks overwhelming the budget.

The increase in mandatory spending is driven not only by increases in the number of people receiving benefits, but also by cost-of-living and other automatic adjustments. When an entitlement benefit is tied to measures of price changes, such as the Consumer Price Index, the benefit is said to be "indexed." The Congressional Budget Office has estimated that cost-of-living adjustments will increase by 2.2 percent each year through 2016. Social Security and Medicare, among other entitlements, are all adjusted annually for price changes. Cost-of-living adjustments are projected to add an annual $214 billion to entitlement spending by 2016, accounting for 18 percent of growth over the preceding decade.[8]

Figure 5.3 Projected Federal Spending for Social Security, Medicare, and Medicaid

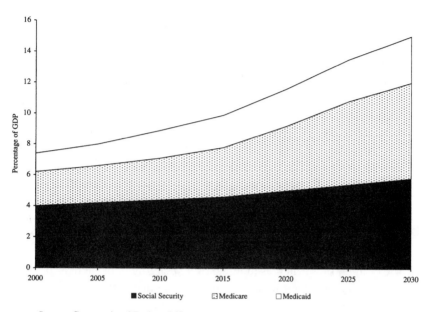

Source: Congressional Budget Office.

Social Security and Medicare's long-term financial problems are the result of changing demographics. The baby boomers—the generation born between 1946 and 1964—are nearing retirement. This is problematic because they had much fewer children than their parents. As a result, the number of workers available to support the baby boomers' retirement costs will grow at a slower rate. Also, people are living longer. In 1940, the average sixty-five-year-old lived about another fourteen years; today that person lives another eighteen years. Continued improvements in health care, furthermore, are expected to allow people to live even longer in coming decades, increasing the number of beneficiaries. Due to these trends, there will be fewer workers to support each retiree—and the burden on each worker will grow. By the middle of the twenty-first century, it is projected that spending on the elderly will account for 40 percent of the entire economy.[9] Thus the financing of these programs in the long run is extremely dubious. Given current law, the long-term costs of Social Security and Medicare potentially jeopardize the financial integrity of the overall budget. The problem of future entitlement spending is a subject that has extremely important political implications for the nation but has been largely ignored by the public and the nation's policymakers.

The generational equity position attributes Social Security and Medicare's political strength to elderly Americans' willingness to support spending on themselves to the exclusion of spending on others. The elderly, for example, still receive a disproportionate amount of entitlement benefits even though they are not the group most likely to be living in poverty (as was the case during the Great Depression, when Social Security was created). The generational equity model assumes that elderly self-interest will be expressed as an increase in support for programs benefiting the elderly, such as Social Security and Medicare, and a decrease in support for programs that disproportionately benefit other age groups, such as education. Despite the perception that the elderly behave in this manner, empirical evidence suggests otherwise. Elderly Americans have been found to support increased spending on programs that invest in the health and welfare of other age groups. A greater percentage of elderly citizens, for example, favor increased education spending over increased Social Security spending. It has also been found that younger Americans have historically expressed equivalent support for Social Security spending compared to elderly citizens.[10] Surveys now show, however, that as the intergenerational competition for scarce resources intensifies, older generations will likely push for greater spending while younger generations will push for reductions.[11] This reversal could have a major impact on budgetary policy in the future.

Social Security

Social Security is the single most expensive federal program. Social Security provides pensions for retired workers as well as benefits to a variety of other citizens, including disabled workers as well as children of workers who die before retirement. Social Security spending, with outlays greater than $500 billion annually, has exceeded defense spending since 1992. Administrative costs amount to less than 1 percent of Social Security outlays; the vast amount of these outlays goes directly to the recipients of the program. Besides Social Security, the federal government is responsible for benefit payments to federal civilian and military retirees that total about $150 billion annually, about 10 percent of mandatory spending. Payments to government retirees and veterans are currently projected to grow at a rate of 3.5 percent annually, reaching $216 billion by 2016.[12]

Social Security is a product of the environment in which it was created—the Great Depression. It was the most important piece of legislation of Franklin Roosevelt's New Deal, a conscious attempt by the federal government to develop rational programs to achieve societal goals, such as the reduction of poverty. The Great Depression convinced the national leadership that destitution could result from forces over which the individual had no control, such as loss of job, old age, death of the family breadwinner, or physical disability. Social Security was based on the same notions as private insurance: sharing risks and setting aside money for times of need.

Social Security has always been an overwhelmingly popular program. In fact, it has been called "the third rail of American politics"—touch it and die. The program reaches beyond direct beneficiaries; their families, who are relieved of the burden of support, also benefit, as do their service providers, who derive some of their own livelihood from Social Security beneficiaries. In addition, most Americans expect to one day themselves reach the age of sixty-five and thus expect to receive Social Security benefits. Finally, Social Security is a redistributive program that to some degree skews benefits toward those more in need, reducing disparities between rich and poor.[13]

From its beginning, Social Security has been financed by a flat-rate payroll tax. Since 1990, employers and employees have each paid 7.65 percent of their earned income to finance Social Security and Medicare: 6.20 percent for Social Security and 1.45 percent for Medicare. Self-employed individuals pay both shares, or 15.3 percent. Workers do not pay Social Security taxes on wages over $97,500, but they do pay the health insurance tax on all wages.

Social Security is deemed a "pay as you go" program, with current workers paying for existing retirees—an unavoidable actuality given that the government made retired workers eligible for Social Security as soon as the program was created in 1935. This means that Social Security obligations in any given year must be met by revenues in the same year. The current surpluses in the Social Security trust have provided a way to borrow from the future to pay for the present. In other words, the intended use of the Social Security surplus—saving to pay for future retirees—has been subverted to finance consumption today. Thus, Social Security, even though it is designed to be insulated from budgetary politics, has produced subtle accounting changes that significantly affect the budget.[14]

Social Security has clearly succeeded at its goal of reducing the number of elderly living in poverty. During the Great Depression, the elderly were the poorest segment of the population; today, they are the least likely to be living in poverty. Due to its success, Social Security has been a remarkably stable program since it was created. The few changes to the program have generally been to extend benefits. In 1956, benefits were extended to the disabled, and in 1972, Social Security became automatically indexed for inflation. By indexing Social Security, policymakers hoped to protect its benefits from inflation while also insulating the program from election-year maneuvers. At the time, the costs of indexing did not seem excessive, but policymakers picked the wrong time, from a budgetary point of view. Soon after Social Security became indexed, inflation jumped dramatically and benefit payments escalated. The decision to index Social Security therefore set the stage for large automatic increases in spending.[15]

Despite the program's success and popularity, Social Security faces long-term funding problems. In 1940, only 7 percent of the population was aged sixty-five and older; the elderly segment today is twice as large, and by 2050 is projected to comprise one-fifth of the population. In the 1960s there were five workers supporting each retiree, compared to three workers today and a projected two workers by 2030. The $500 billion that was allocated to Social Security in 2005 is projected to escalate to more than $900 billion in 2015. How to continue financing the system remains a fundamental problem that today's politicians do not want to address. Ironically, concern for Social Security to some degree stems from its predictability—we can calculate changing demographic trends.

It is questionable whether or not the nation's long-term fiscal health can be maintained without curbing Social Security spending. Defenders of the status quo insist that Social Security should remain unchanged because it is self-financed by the payroll tax, which is currently running a huge surplus. A problem with this argument is that it leaves the mistaken impression that the biggest program in the budget does not affect the rest of the budget. To critics, the sheer size of Social Security makes it a must for any sizable budget cuts.

Due to the impending funding problems for Social Security as the baby boom generation retires, a number of reforms to the program have been proposed through the years. The Greenspan Commission in the 1980s proposed raising contributions and reducing benefits. When the federal government was producing surpluses in the late 1990s, the Clinton administration proposed enlarging the trust fund and paying down the national debt. This strategy sought to improve the financial position of the federal government over the long term to meet the Social Security crunch due to retirement of the baby boomers. It has also been suggested that Social Security should be privatized, either fully or partially. Advocates of privatization argue that Social Security should promote individual savings and investment, wealth accumulation, and legal ownership of benefits.

Advocating Social Security reform, however, has historically proven to be politically unpopular. Despite the calls for reform, among the public there appears to be a bipartisan consensus that Social Security should basically be left in its current form. Majorities of Democrats, Republicans, and Independents oppose increasing the Social Security tax rate, raising the retirement age for receiving full benefits, reducing benefits for future retirees, or changing the formula for calculating benefits to reduce their rate of growth.[16] About two-thirds, however, support raising the amount of income that is subject to Social Security taxes.[17]

The political difficulties of reforming Social Security can be seen in the Ronald Reagan administration's failed attempt. Reagan had long advocated eliminating Social Security, but when he ran for president in 1980 he switched positions and promised not to make significant changes to the program. The large deficits that materialized after the 1981 tax cuts, however, led the Reagan administration to propose reducing Social Security benefits for persons retiring before age sixty-five, tightening eligibility requirements for the program, and reducing cost-of-living increases. Senior citizens strongly opposed the proposal, however, and handed President Reagan one of the worst defeats of his administration. Reagan's failed attempt to reform Social Security firmly established the political principle that Republicans could not suggest reducing entitlements.[18]

Social Security has been remarkably successful at reducing poverty among the elderly. Since the 1930s, however, it is children who have become the demographic group at greatest risk of poverty. Thus the nation's entitlement priorities can be critiqued as misguided. Older generations will increasingly have an advantage in influencing spending choices as the baby boom generation moves toward retirement age.[19] If the baby boom generation desires to hold on to the tax and benefit promises extended to today's elderly, the costs to future generations could be excessive.[20]

Medicare and Medicaid

The United States is the only industrialized democracy not to have some sort of national health insurance; as a result, about one in six Americans has no health insurance. Government, however, still plays an important role in providing health insurance—about one in five Americans gets their health insurance through the federal or their state government. Together, Medicare and Medicaid are now more expensive than Social Security. Since Medicare and Medicaid are currently and by far the fastest-growing entitlements, their combined cost will soon surpass that of Social Security. Medicare and Medicaid have been growing at tremendous rates because of both demographics and technology. It is projected that Medicare and Medicaid will account for 55 percent of the total growth in entitlement spending through 2040.[21]

Health care in the United States is extremely expensive and absorbs a disproportionate share of national production when compared to that of other nations. Total spending on health care is about one-sixth of GDP, more than 50 percent greater, on a per capita basis, than in any other country. Two factors that are often critiqued as important reasons for this large differential are supply constraints that create waiting lists in other countries, and the level of malpractice litigation in the United States. Services that typically have queues in other countries, however, account for only 3 percent of US health spending, and the cost of defending malpractice claims is less than 0.5 percent of total health spending. Rather than lack of supply constraints and malpractice, the two most important reasons for US spending appear to be higher incomes and higher medical care prices.[22] The United States has more doctors and hospitals per capita than any other nation in the world. Those doctors and hospitals have access to the most sophisticated medicines and technical equipment. Americans receive the best medical care in the world—if they can afford it.

It can be argued, however, that the costs of health care in the United States have become excessive. US businesses are struggling to cope with escalating health care costs. General Motors, for one, has blamed its near-bankrupt status on the US health care system. As the largest private provider of health care in the United States, General Motors spent $5.6 billion in 2006 to provide health insurance coverage for about 750,000 workers and retirees, as well as their family members.[23] The problems associated with escalating health care costs can also be seen in the Defense Department. The military health benefit program, Tricare, accounts for 8 percent of the total defense budget, and, according to Defense Department projections, is expected to reach 12 percent by 2015. In other words, the Pentagon spends more on health care than it does on new jets for the Air Force or new ships for the Navy.[24]

Medicare is the most important legacy of Lyndon Johnson's Great Society. Today, over 30 million people receive Medicare benefits. When Medicare was created in 1965, only about half of the elderly had health care insurance and their incomes were highly vulnerable to medical emergencies. The creation of Medicare, however, was not without controversy. Liberals saw it as an incremental step toward the goal of universal health insurance, a goal liberals had been promoting at least since Harry Truman ran for reelection in 1948 on a universal health care pledge. Conservatives, on the other hand, opposed Medicare as an expensive program that extended too much government control over medical care. The medical establishment was particularly hostile to the program, though medical providers have clearly profited from it.

Medicare is divided into two parts, hospital insurance and medical insurance. Aside from the Medicare payroll tax, there are premiums of $88.50 for the medical insurance (there are no premiums for the hospital insurance). Medicare is financed by a tax earmarked through the payroll tax (approximately 55 percent of outlays), by the premiums paid for the medical insurance (15 percent), and by general revenues (30 percent). The special tax dedicated to Medicare (technically to the hospital fund only) is the 1.45 percent component of the 7.65 percent federal payroll tax. Unlike the Social Security component of the payroll tax, however, the Medicare tax is not capped.

Medicare operates simultaneously on three different groups of people: the elderly, who contribute modestly to the program; workers, who finance most of the program through payroll taxes; and the medical community, who are responsible to the federal government, through a complex set of regulations, for the cost and quality of care. Since asking the elderly to shoulder more of the costs of Medicare has proven to be a tough sell politically, workers and the medical establishment have been responsible for much of the burden of the increase in Medicare spending.[25]

The implementation of Medicare is completely controlled by the providers of health care services, including physicians, hospitals, and insurance companies. Most of the implementation of Medicare is done by private agencies and individuals, not government agencies. Thus, although Medicare was established to improve the health of the elderly, it has been implemented in a way that increases the income of providers, thus increasing the cost of services. Nonetheless, Medicare is a popular program and any effort to alter Medicare benefits has met stiff resistance.

Medicare is one of the most rapidly growing federal programs, increasing from 3.5 percent of all federal spending in 1970 to 13.5 percent in 2005. Medicare has thus been growing at twice the rate of Social Security. By the 1990s, Medicare was averaging a 10 percent growth each year; the growth of the program is forecast to continue rising much faster than the growth of the economy as the baby boomers retire.[26] The growth in Medicare is partly due to the fact that more people have become eligible for the program. A bigger factor, however, is the escalating costs of health expenditures, which have grown much faster than general prices, since payment rates in the fee-for-service sector (covering about 85 percent of participants) are subject to automatic updates based on prices. Also, since Medicare was designed to be an open-ended entitlement, with certain provisions for deductibles and copayments, beneficiaries may choose to use the entitlement as much as they want. Neither health service providers nor Medicare recipients have any incentive to restrict usage, because the bills are paid by the government.[27] Another source of increased costs for Medicare has been fraud. In 1997, for example, the General Accounting Office estimated that more than $20 billion of Medicare fee-for-service payments (11 percent of total costs) were improper, mostly due to fraudulent health administrator claims.[28]

The costs of Medicare are also expected to increase because of newly created prescription drug benefits. Medicare began subsidizing outpatient prescription drugs under a new part of the program in 2006 that furnishes coverage through a combination of private prescription drug plans available to all Medicare enrollees, managed health care plans, and employer or union-sponsored plans. Enrollment in this part of the program is voluntary, and enrollees are charged premiums to pay for benefits not subsidized by Medicare. The program also provides federal subsidies to help cover the cost of drugs for low-income beneficiaries. In 2007, the program's first full year, the costs of outpatient prescription drug subsidization were $70 billion; by 2016, spending for the program is estimated to be $202 billion.[29]

The growth of Medicare costs displays the distribution biases of beneficiaries of federal health programs. There is a problem of equity between generations—today's retirees and today's workers. While elderly Americans are covered by Medicare, many Americans of working age have no health insurance. And the program that benefits the poor—Medicaid—is much less generous than Medicare.

Medicaid, like Medicare, is a Great Society program, created in 1965 in order to help the poor cover the costs of health care. Medicaid is primarily oriented toward needy children and their mothers, pregnant women, and the disabled. Like other need-based programs, therefore, Medicaid is conspicuous for whom it omits. Single individuals, unless disabled, are not entitled to Medicaid benefits. As a result, federal coverage of health benefits ranges from generous for the elderly, to adequate for needy mothers and their children, to nothing at all for poor young men.[30]

The enactment of Medicaid was an outgrowth of a decade-spanning gradual involvement of government in health care. As early as the 1790s, the federal government provided medical care for the armed forces, and later it provided health care coverage for veterans and Native Americans. The Federal Relief Act of 1933 constituted the first federal attempt to provide health care for the poor. Under this act, funds were made available to states to help pay for the medical care of the unemployed. Though this program lasted less than three years, it set a precedent for the federal government to finance medical care for the needy.[31]

Medicaid is a state fund matching program in which the states determine the amount of coverage available. Each state designs its own program, which the federal government must approve. The federal government sets minimum standards for coverage, but the states can extend eligibility and benefits. States must pay no less than 17 percent and no more than 50 percent of total program costs. As a result, implementation varies from state to state; some have very liberal benefits, whereas others do not. The Medicaid program, aside from the financial contribution made by the states, is financed through general tax revenues; unlike Medicare, there is no special tax or earmark for Medicaid.

Like Medicare, Medicaid has become much more expensive since it was created. In 1970 the federal government's share of Medicare spending was less than $3 billion; by 1990 that figure had jumped to $41 billion and in 2005 it was $182 billion. One reason for Medicaid's dramatic growth is its evolution to embrace new categories of eligible beneficiaries, such as the elderly in nursing homes. The joint funding of the program has also contributed to increased costs. Since states have an incentive to maximize federal reimbursement, many states, especially in the South, have expanded eligibility. The states have become adept at exploiting loopholes in the federal matching reimbursement mechanisms to increase funding. Also, higher health care prices, including for prescription drugs, and rising enrollment have driven Medicaid costs upward.[32]

A common criticism of Medicaid is the uneven distribution of benefits across the country. Some states spend more than four times as much as others to provide health care to the disadvantaged. Socioeconomic and partisan factors explain much of this spending-level difference.[33] The costs of Medicaid have become so large that state governments are increasingly pursuing reductions, abandoning efforts popular in the 1990s to cover more individuals who do not have health insurance. Medicaid's strain on the states has increasingly led them to lobby for greater financial help from the federal government.

Need-Based Entitlements

Other than Medicaid, need-based entitlements—those entitlement programs that recipients qualify for based on income level—comprise a relatively small portion of all federal entitlement spending. Historically, the most important need-based entitlement other than Medicaid was Aid to Families with Dependent Children (AFDC). From 1935 until 1996, AFDC was the primary cash support program for impoverished families with children. AFDC was an entitlement program, but its qualifications and benefits, unlike those for Social Security and Medicare, were determined in part at the state level, which resulted in considerable variation from state to state. In 1993, for example, average monthly family cash benefits ranged from $121 in Mississippi to $751 in Alaska.[34]

AFDC was created as part of the Social Security Act of 1935 and was originally intended to aid widows with children. It was not originally intended to be a means-tested entitlement. By the early 1960s, however, it was clear the purpose and nature of AFDC had changed; instead of aiding widows, the benefits were going disproportionately to broken families in urban areas. The costs of the program exploded and welfare reform became a goal for every president from Richard Nixon to Bill Clinton. Despite its longevity, by the 1960s AFDC was politically unpopular; policymakers simply could not agree on how to replace it. During his presidential campaign, Clinton pledged to "end welfare as we know it"; despite some delays, he finally made good on his promise once the Republicans took control of Congress after the 1994 elections. Even at its peak, however, AFDC was never a comparatively expensive program. In 1994 the program's cost represented only about 2 percent of federal expenditures, and from 1970 to 1994 AFDC benefits declined by 50 percent when accounting for inflation.[35]

AFDC was eliminated in 1996 with the establishment of the Temporary Assistance for Needy Families (TANF) program, which made welfare the responsibility of the states. While AFDC was an entitlement program, TANF is not, at least not at the federal level.

TANF is a block grant program subject to annual appropriations and a budgetary cap. TANF also placed restrictions on receiving aid that AFDC did not have; TANF benefits are discontinued after sixty months, and adult parents who qualify for TANF benefits are required to find work after receiving benefits for two years.

While social insurance entitlements such as Social Security and Medicare are politically popular and enjoy the support of large numbers of active beneficiaries, public assistance programs that aid the poor are far less popular. As a result, benefits for participants in public assistance programs are not projected to grow nearly as rapidly as Social Security and Medicare benefits. Spending for family support programs is projected to remain flat for the next decade, rising from $24 billion in 2006 to $25 billion in 2016. TANF is capped by law at $17 billion per year and thus its costs are declining when accounting for inflation. Not all public assistance programs are waning like TANF, however. Outlays for the food stamp program—which currently costs about $35 billion annually—have grown in recent years, largely as a result of steady growth in participation; food stamp caseloads rose from 17.3 million people in 2001 to 25.7 million in 2005.[36]

Discretionary Spending

Discretionary spending is so named because Congress has, legally speaking, absolute discretion in deciding whether or not to spend such monies through the annual legislative appropriations process. Discretionary spending, unlike entitlement spending, is good for only one year. Essentially, policymakers decide each year how many dollars to provide and to which activities. Discretionary spending represents the money Congress appropriates each year for everything from battleships to Head Start education. Most of what the federal government does domestically—under the Federal Bureau of Investigation (FBI), the National Park Service, the Weather Bureau, and the Bureau of Citizenship and Immigration Services, for example—falls into the catchall category of discretionary spending.

Congress has two distinct processes for establishing and funding federal programs and agencies: authorizing legislation, which establishes the legal foundation for operating these agencies and programs, and appropriation of money, which allows these agencies and programs to assume obligations and expenditures. Every discretionary program has the potential for duplication of effort in Congress and friction between the authorizing and appropriations committees. Duplication and conflict tend to be modest for entitlement programs that have permanent authorizations, but can be significant for those that are reauthorized annually.[37]

Discretionary spending includes spending on programs for highway infrastructure, highway and motor carrier safety, public transit, and airport infrastructure. Many transportation programs receive mandatory budget authority, but each year the annual appropriations acts control spending for those programs by limiting how much of the budget authority the Department of Transportation can obligate. These limitations, known as obligation limitations, are treated as a measure of discretionary resources, and the resulting outlays are considered discretionary spending.[38]

Unlike entitlement spending, the sector of government that Congress can readily access from one year to another is no longer expanding; in fact, since the 1990s, discretionary spending has actually shrunk in real terms. Spending for nondefense discretionary programs has remained relatively steady, ranging between 3.2 and 3.9 percent of GDP annually since the 1980s.[39] In 2007, nondefense discretionary spending actually decreased by $3 billion from the previous year. Including defense, discretionary outlays are projected to shrink as a percentage of GDP, from 7.6 percent in 2006 to 5.9 percent in 2016.[40]

Discretionary spending has remained relatively flat since limits on appropriations were enacted in the 1990 Budget Enforcement Act. This means that the money to cover the same services the government now provides, let alone to expand them, is decreasing. Though some discretionary spending programs have undoubtedly outlived their usefulness, critics of cutting discretionary spending argue that limiting these funds will sacrifice the capacity of Congress to build new programs appropriate to national needs.[41] Nondefense discretionary spending is not the primary source of growth in federal government spending. Rather, it is entitlement spending. Due to the low growth of domestic discretionary spending, however, the annual growth in nondefense spending (including both entitlement and discretionary spending) has actually decreased considerably since the Lyndon Johnson and Richard Nixon administrations (see Figure 5.4).

Defense

The defense budget officially comprises not only the activities of the Department of Defense but also the nuclear weapon programs of the

Figure 5.4 Growth in Nondefense Spending
by Presidential Administration

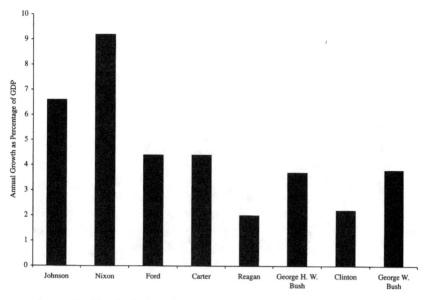

Source: Brookings Institution calculations from Budget of the United States Government,
Fiscal Year 2007, tabs. 1.3, 4.1, 8.2.
Note: Data for George W. Bush administration through fiscal year 2007.

Department of Energy and other security activities under other agencies. In 2006, the Department of Defense was allocated over $500 billion for the first time, representing one-fifth of all federal expenditures. There are about 1.4 million active uniformed service personnel and approximately 1 million civilian employees. More than 80 percent of federal employees work for the Department of Defense.[42] Despite the large number of defense workers, however, only one-fourth of defense spending is allocated to personnel.[43]

Annual defense budgets have fluctuated from 9.5 percent to as low as 3.0 percent of GDP ($300–500 billion in constant 2006 dollars) since the Vietnam War era (see Figure 5.5). From 1965 to 2007, the United States spent on average about 5.3 percent of GDP annually on defense ($400 billion in constant 2006 dollars). Despite decreasing since the 1960s as a percentage of GDP, in constant dollars defense spending is now higher than it has been at any time since the Korean War. Also, since the end of the Cold War, defense spending has decreased globally, with the United States now accounting for

Figure 5.5 Defense Spending, 1965–2007

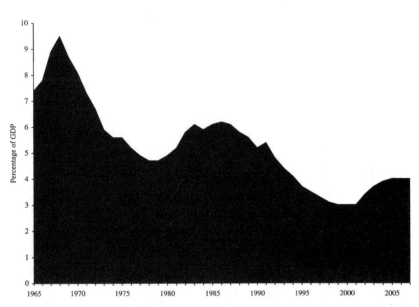

Source: Congressional Budget Office.

about half of all defense expenditures in the world.[44] Despite the increase in defense spending during the George W. Bush administration, however, domestic spending (mainly on entitlements) has increased far more rapidly than defense spending over the past four decades.

How much should the nation spend on defense? Economic research supports the contention that the United States can afford whatever level of military outlays it deems necessary.[45] Economists disagree, however, as to whether increases in military spending come primarily from resources that would otherwise go to investment or consumption. Since investment contributes much more directly to economic growth, the cost of lost opportunities is higher when military spending is pulled from investment resources than when taken from money that would otherwise go toward current consumption. Studies have found, however, that on the whole, defense spending has not drained investment funds from the civilian economy.[46]

Debates over how much to spend on defense relative to domestic programs—the so-called guns versus butter dilemma—are as old as the United States. Prior to the nation's entry into World War II, Americans were reluctant to finance a large standing military and were suspicious of those who profited from the military's business. The Japanese attacks on Pearl Harbor on December 7, 1941, and the advent of the Cold War radically changed the historical tendency of the United States to spend relatively little on defense. By 1960, defense spending had become so large that President Dwight Eisenhower, in his presidential farewell address, warned of a military-industrial complex that risked overwhelming the budget.

After declining in the 1970s due to the end of the Vietnam War, defense spending enjoyed a surge in budgetary importance after Ronald Reagan was elected president. Defense spending rose to record peacetime levels in the 1980s, reaching 6.2 percent of GDP in 1986. The Reagan defense buildup was distinct because other significant increases in defense spending had occurred during wartime. In the Reagan years, however, the increases in defense spending were a result of the administration's contention that US military preparedness needed to be strengthened. Only by bargaining from strength, it was argued, could the nation hope to face down the Soviet Union and other adversaries. Such increases in peacetime were unprecedented and critics of the Reagan administration's plans argued that the defense budget needed to be both reduced and smartened.[47] Congress began to put a halt to Reagan's defense buildup at its peak in 1986, in order to address the soaring budget deficit and shortchanged domestic needs. The breakdown of communism in the Soviet Union and Eastern Europe in the early 1990s made defense cuts politically more palatable to both Congress and the American public.

In part because of domestic political realities and in part because of changing international conditions, deep cuts in the Pentagon's conventional forces became inevitable after the end of the Cold War. Generally, the Defense Department and defense advocates try to obtain as much as they can, as fast as they can, as long as they can. The strongest argument for defense spending is war, and the Cold War had provided justification for a large defense budget. The end of the Cold War, however, changed the rationale. As a result, defense spending was cut regularly throughout the 1990s, and its share of the budget declined from one-fourth to one-sixth by the end of the decade.[48]

From the end of World War II until 1990, defense budgets reflected Cold War ideas of deterrence and containment, with forces worldwide ready to confront a single enemy. But with the collapse of the Soviet Union, the Pentagon almost overnight had to redefine its mission. After forty years of maintaining a heavily armed ground force in Europe and a massive retaliatory force around the world, the United

States now faced drastically different problems demanding new tactics.[49] The Gulf War in 1991 demonstrated the need for rapid deployment of forces for regional wars around the world, as well as the increased significance of high-tech weapons. With the end of the Cold War, the new standard became the ability to fight two major regional conflicts at once.

   As the nation's first post–Cold War presidents, George H. W. Bush and Bill Clinton were able to consistently cut the defense budget during their administrations. After the terrorist attacks of September 11, 2001, however, President George W. Bush argued that the nation needed to strengthen its defense and proposed the largest increase in defense spending since the Reagan administration. Defense outlays rose 14 percent in 2002, in part due to military operations in Afghanistan, and continued to rise as military operations began in Iraq, increasing by an additional 16 percent in 2003 and 12 percent in 2004. As Figure 5.6 demonstrates, defense spending rose much more dramatically under the George W. Bush administration than under any of the preceding seven administrations. In fact, the rate of growth in defense spending under Bush was over 80 percent higher than under

Figure 5.6 Growth in Defense Spending by Presidential Administration

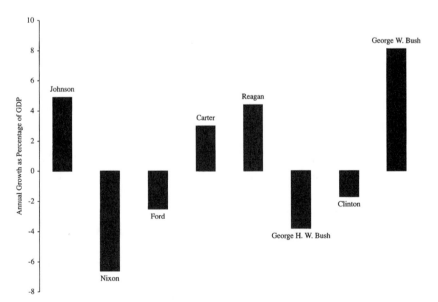

Source: Brookings Institution calculations from Budget of the United States Government, Fiscal Year 2007, tab. 8.2.
Note: Data for George W. Bush administration through fiscal year 2007.

Reagan, and 65 percent higher than under Johnson. From 2000 to 2005, defense spending increased from 3 to 4 percent of GDP.

Since the Vietnam War there have been strong partisan differences in defense policy. Republicans generally advocate for stronger defense and accuse Democrats of weakening national security by cutting defense spending. Democrats counter that Republicans increase defense spending excessively relative to other budget priorities. Spending on defense, however, has not consistently increased under Republican presidencies relative to Democratic presidencies. Defense spending increased during the Johnson administration and decreased during the Nixon and Ford administrations, for example. On the other hand, defense spending increased dramatically during the Reagan and George W. Bush administrations and decreased during the Clinton administration.

Part of the defense budget—unlike the rest of the federal budget—is secret. This is the so-called black budget, consisting of highly classified projects. The black budget is currently about $30 billion. This obviously poses some problems. Though there may be good reasons to classify part of the defense budget for security purposes, accountability becomes a problem. A detailed line-item budget is a means by which citizens can keep government accountable—it allows taxpayers to know exactly where their taxes are going. But restricted access to classified funding means that the Department of Defense and Congress typically exercise less oversight for such funding. This lower level of scrutiny has possibly contributed to performance problems and escalating costs in a number of programs, such as the Navy's ill-fated A-12 attack aircraft program.[50]

Another remarkable characteristic of the defense budget is that it does not make any provision for fighting wars. Wars are simply treated as "supplementals" to the budget. Wartime budgeting, therefore, becomes problematic from an accountability perspective, as uncertainty about war costs makes advance appropriation onerous. US military actions since September 11, 2001, have thus included significant costs that are outside the official defense budget. From 2001 to 2006, Congress appropriated more than $500 billion in ten "emergency supplementals" for military operations in Iraq and Afghanistan. By comparison, for the Korean and Vietnam Wars, there were only seven such emergency bills.[51] Determining exactly how much is being spent is difficult, because the Treasury Department does not distinguish between outlays from regular appropriations and those from supplemental appropriations, nor does it distinguish between spending for peacetime operations and spending associated with the "war on terror."[52] Not only has the irregular pattern of funding for military activities in Iraq and Afghanistan made budget projections more difficult, but keeping track of all the money being spent on these activities and on related efforts such as rebuilding has proven problematic as well. The US Agency for International Development (part of the State Department), for example, which was in charge of $1.4 billion in reconstruction money in Iraq, was found to have hidden cost overruns and knowingly withheld information from Congress.[53]

Interest on the National Debt

Interest on the national debt is a significant expense for the federal government, which borrows a considerable amount of money to finance its programs. The interest payments on that borrowed money have exceeded the cost of all but a few of the largest federal programs.[54] From 1980 to 2005, the portion of the national debt held by the public ballooned from $712 billion to $4.6 trillion.

The federal government's debt falls into two main categories: debt that is held by the public in the form of Treasury securities, and debt that is held by government accounts. Debt held by the public is the more meaningful measure, because it represents debt that the Treasury issues to raise cash to fund operations and pay off the maturing liabilities of the federal government. In 2007 the US government owned 44 percent of the debt, the American public owned 30 percent (55 percent of the publicly held debt), and foreigners owned 26 percent (45 percent of the publicly held debt). Debt held by the public equaled nearly 50 percent of GDP in 1993, fell to 33 percent by 2001, and is currently about 37 percent of GDP.[55] Securities issued by the Treasury to various accounts of the federal government totaled about $3.8 trillion as of 2007. The largest balance among government accounts is held in the Social Security trust funds, which total more than $1.8 trillion.[56]

All of the US Treasury's bills and bonds are issued at full faith and credit, meaning that the federal government is legally required to redeem them at full value when they mature. This requirement makes them a safe investment, but also makes interest costs a relatively uncontrollable item in the federal budget, at least in the short term. As federal budget deficits and the debt ballooned in the 1980s and early 1990s, interest costs grew to become one of the largest items in the federal budget.[57]

Generally, the amount of debt that the Treasury borrows is roughly equal to the annual budget deficit or surplus. A number of factors, however, also affect the government's need to borrow money from the public. The Congressional Budget Office projects that debt held by the public will increase more than the cumulative deficit from 2006 to 2016, because changes in other means of financing will increase the Treasury's borrowing needs.[58]

Net interest is determined by the size and composition of the government's debt, annual budget deficits or surpluses, and market interest rates. In 2006, interest costs totaled $217 billion, $33 billion more than in 2005. About half of that increase was attributable to an increase in interest rates and the other half of the increase stemmed from the accumulating debt that financed previous deficits. Interest costs are expected to grow significantly faster than noninterest spending. The CBO projects that interest costs will increase more than 50 percent from 2006 to 2010. The increase in interest payments is attributable to accumulating debt as well as rising interest rates.[59]

The Treasury's authority to go into debt is restricted by a statutory ceiling. This ceiling, for political purposes, is symbolic—Congress regularly raises the debt ceiling when the debt approaches the maximum allowed under the law. In recent years, when the Treasury's borrowing has reached the debt ceiling, the department has been able to use accounting mechanisms to remain below the limit for a couple of months.[60] As the intricacies of interest payments demonstrate, keeping track of federal expenditures is an extremely complex process.

Notes

1. David Nice, *Public Budgeting* (Belmont, CA: Wadsworth, 2002), p. 24.

2. Congressional Budget Office, *The Fiscal and Economic Outlook: Fiscal Years 2007 to 2016* (Washington, DC, 2006), p. 55.

3. David A. Super, "The Political Economy of Entitlement," *Columbia Law Review* 104 (2004): 633–729.

4. Aaron Wildavsky and Naomi Caiden, *The New Politics of the Budgetary Process,* 5th ed. (New York: Longman, 2004), pp. 124–128.

5. Eric Patashnik, "Budgeting More, Deciding Less," *Public Interest* 138 (2000): 65–79.

6. Dennis S. Ippolito, *Why Budgets Matter: Budget Policy and American Politics* (University Park: Pennsylvania State University Press, 2003), p. 312.

7. Congressional Budget Office, *The Fiscal and Economic Outlook,* p. 55.

8. Ibid.

9. Donald F. Kettl, *Deficit Politics,* 2nd ed. (New York: Longman, 2003), pp. 60–63.

10. Debra Street and Jeralynn Sittig Cossman, "Greatest Generation or Greedy Geezers? Social Spending Preferences and the Elderly," *Social Problems* 53 (2006): 75–96.

11. Susan A. MacManus, "Taxing and Spending Politics: A Generational Perspective," *Journal of Politics* 57 (1995): 607–629.

12. Congressional Budget Office, *The Fiscal and Economic Outlook,* p. 63.

13. Wildavsky and Caiden, *The New Politics of the Budgetary Process,* pp. 136–138.

14. Kettl, *Deficit Politics,* pp. 56–57.

15. Ibid., p. 64.

16. Gary C. Jacobson, *A Divider, Not a Uniter: George Bush and the American People* (New York: Longman, 2007), p. 217; ABC News/Washington Post Poll (March 10–13, 2005), national survey of 1,001 adults.

17. New York Times/CBS News Poll (February 24–28, 2005), national survey of 1,111 adults.

18. Kettl, *Deficit Politics,* pp. 55–56.

19. MacManus, "Taxing and Spending Politics."

20. Peter G. Peterson, *Running on Empty* (Farrar, Straus and Giroux: New York, 2004), p. 48.

21. Ibid., p. 72.

22. Gerald F. Anderson, Peter S. Hussey, Bianca K. Frogner, and Hugh R. Waters, "Health Spending in the United States and the Rest of the Industrialized World," *Health Affairs* 24 (2005): 903–914.

23. Paul Webster, "US Big Businesses Struggle to Cope with Health-Care Costs," *Lancet* 367 (2006): 101–102.

24. Richard Jackson, "A Hasty Retreat on Military Health Care," *Facing Facts Quarterly: A Report About Entitlements and the Budget from the Concord Coalition* 2 (October 2006): 2–3.

25. Kettl, *Deficit Politics,* pp. 57–59.

26. General Accounting Office, "Medicare Reform: Ensuring Fiscal Sustainability While Modernizing the Program Will Be Challenging," Statement of David M. Walker, Comptroller General of the United States, September 22, 1999.

27. Wildavsky and Caiden, *The New Politics of the Budgetary Process,* pp. 138–140.

28. General Accounting Office, *Medicare, Health Care Fraud, and Abuse Control Program Financial Report for Fiscal Year 1997* (Washington, DC, June 1998), p. 4.

29. Congressional Budget Office, *The Fiscal and Economic Outlook,* pp. 58–59.

30. Gary R. Evans, *Red Ink* (San Diego: Academic Press, 1997), pp. 127–128.

31. Margaret Greenfield, *Medicare and Medicaid: The 1965 and 1967 Social Security Amendments* (Westport: Greenwood, 1968).

32. Wildavsky and Caiden, *The New Politics of the Budgetary Process,* pp. 141–142.

33. Thad Kousser, "The Politics of Discretionary Medicaid Spending, 1980–1993," *Journal of Health Politics, Policy, and Law* 27 (2002): 639–671.

34. Evans, *Red Ink,* pp. 114–116.

35. Daniel Patrick Moynihan, "The Devolution Revolution," *New York Times,* May 6, 1995, p. E15.

36. Congressional Budget Office, *The Fiscal and Economic Outlook,* p. 62.

37. Allen Schick, *The Federal Budget: Politics, Policy, Process* (Washington, DC: Brookings Institution, 1995), pp. 110–164.

38. Congressional Budget Office, *The Fiscal and Economic Outlook,* p. 54.

39. Ibid., p. 69.

40. Ibid., p. 72.

41. Kettl, *Deficit Politics,* pp. 52–54.

42. Wildavsky and Caiden, *The New Politics of the Budgetary Process,* pp. 153–154.

43. Evans, *Red Ink,* pp. 83–84.

44. William Hudson, *American Democracy in Peril,* 5th ed. (Washington, DC: Congressional Quarterly, 2006), chap. 8.

45. Murray Weidenbaum, "How Much Defense Spending Can We Afford?" *Public Interest* (Spring 2003): 52–61.

46. Ibid.

47. Kettl, *Deficit Politics,* pp. 48–49.

48. Wildavsky and Caiden, *The New Politics of the Budgetary Process,* pp. 155–156.

49. Kettl, *Deficit Politics,* p. 49.

50. Defensetech.org, "Pentagon Budget Goes Black," July 24, 2006, http://www.defensetech.org/archives/001489.

51. Neil Howe, "Election Year Paralysis," *Facing Facts Quarterly: A Report About Entitlements and the Budget from the Concord Coalition* 2 (October 2006): 1.

52. Congressional Budget Office, *The Fiscal and Economic Outlook,* p. 6.

53. James Glanz, "Audit Finds U.S. Hid Actual Cost of Iraq Projects," *New York Times,* July 30, 2006, p. A1.

54. Nice, *Public Budgeting,* pp. 24–25.

55. Congressional Budget Office, *The Fiscal and Economic Outlook,* pp. 17–18.

56. Ibid., p. 19.

57. Nice, *Public Budgeting,* p. 130.

58. Congressional Budget Office, *The Fiscal and Economic Outlook,* p. 18.

59. Ibid., p. 75.

60. Ibid., pp. 20–21.

6

THE GROWTH OF GOVERNMENT SPENDING

FEDERAL EXPENDITURES HAVE INCREASED DRAMATICALLY AS THE scope of US government has expanded over the past century. Only 3.4 percent of GDP in 1930, federal expenditures nearly tripled during the New Deal era before skyrocketing during World War II, reaching a record 43.6 percent of GDP in 1944 (see Figure 6.1). After World War II, expenditures decreased considerably but remained much higher than they were before the war; spending as a percentage of GDP in the 1950s was about twice what it was in the 1930s. After another period of growth in the late 1960s, spending levels have remained relatively stable at about 20 percent of GDP since the 1970s.

The fiscal dimension of government is at the heart of key battles over the size and role of the federal government. Looking at budgeting from a historical perspective illustrates how dramatically the role of government in the United States has changed since the nation was founded. Determining the appropriate size of government is a common feature of budget policy development in the United States. As the US government has grown, the federal budget process has become more complex and conflicted.[1]

Due to the prevailing consensus that a powerful central government should be avoided, the Founding Fathers designed a relatively limited role for the federal government and throughout the nineteenth century government spending was minimal. Federal activities were restricted to traditional public good functions; prior to the 1930s, three-fourths of federal peacetime expenditures were directly related to the military, veterans, and interest on war-related debt. In 1902, all

Figure 6.1 Federal Expenditures as Share of GDP, 1930–2007

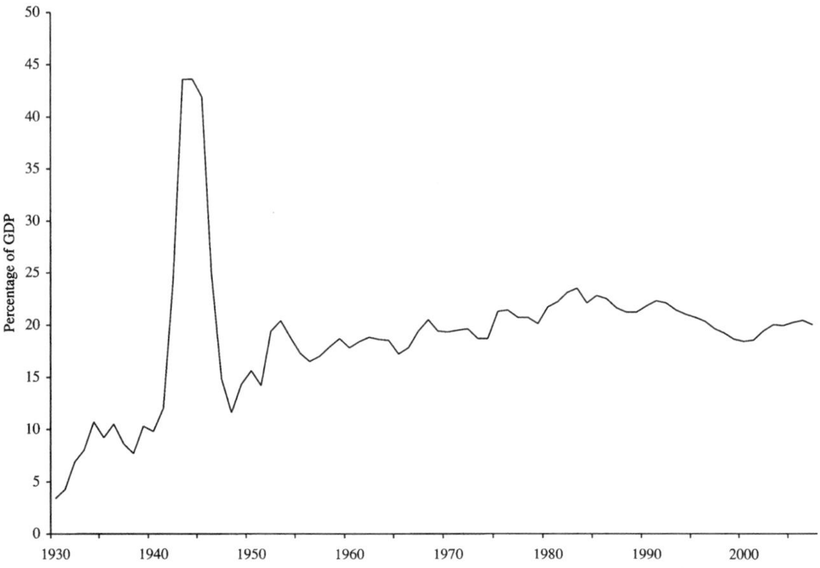

Source: Office of Management and Budget.

levels of government combined spent $1.6 billion, with more than half of this money being spent at the local level and only a third at the federal level.[2] A hundred years later, total government spending was more than $3 trillion, with a majority of this spending at the federal level and less than a fifth at the local level.[3]

As a consequence of its restricted role, the federal government consumed only a small and fairly constant share of the economy until the Civil War. Demobilization after the Civil War ended led federal expenditures to drop quickly to a level that was maintained until World War I. Though expenditures rose dramatically with World War I, government spending declined sharply after the war as military expenses were cut back, as had been the case with the post–Civil War period.[4]

The turning point in federal government spending occurred during the 1930s and 1940s, as the nation turned to massive federal programs to pull the economy out of the Great Depression at the same time it was becoming a world military power. In all three broad categories of spending—entitlement spending, discretionary spending, and defense spending—the role of the federal government was redefined in a manner that increased expenditures.

The New Deal era saw the advent of significant entitlement programs for the first time; particularly important was the creation of

Social Security, the nation's most expensive government program. In the early days of the United States, the concept of entitlement did not exist and there were no such programs. The first entitlement program in the United States was a pension program provided for veterans of the Civil War and their widows. The modern era of entitlements began with the New Deal response to the Great Depression. The Social Security Act of 1935 created a number of entitlement programs, including Social Security, unemployment insurance, and aid to dependent children.

In regard to discretionary spending, Franklin Roosevelt and New Dealers initiated one program after another to provide jobs and income assistance to those in need. The New Deal also promoted the federal government's redistribution of income from one group of Americans to another, from one region to another, and from one set of institutions to another. Egalitarian measures promoted spending as a means to "level the playing field," offering the underprivileged more opportunity to compete in a marketplace too subject to chance. For the first time, federal officials began to influence the distribution of wealth significantly. The redistribution of income was made easier by the adoption of Keynesian economic policy, which provided theoretical justification for deficit spending and the abandonment of the balanced budget tradition.

Keynesian economics contended that government should engage in deficit spending to pump money into a flagging economy and run surpluses during boom times. Keynesianism maintained that government can alter its behavior to affect the business cycle. Thus, if the economy is in a recession and suffering from lack of demand compared to supply, government should stimulate demand by increasing spending, cutting taxes, or cutting interest rates. Or, if the economy is growing fast and inflationary, government should reduce demand by decreasing spending, increasing taxes, or increasing interest rates. To smooth out the business cycle, the government should act in a countercyclical fashion. Contradicting laissez-faire sentiment, Keynesianism assumes that government should moderate the fluctuations of the market system if capitalism is to flourish.[5] Thus, Keynesian theory promoted a mixed economy in which both the state and the private sector had important roles. Macroeconomic trends, Keynesians held, can overwhelm the micro-level behavior of individuals. By acting to smooth out the business cycle and stabilize the economy, the ultimate goal was to prevent future depressions from occurring. In this regard, Keynesian economic policy has been remarkably successful. As Figure 6.2 demonstrates, since the federal government began active intervention in the 1930s, the economy has been remarkably stable. Prior to the New Deal era, the economy went through major booms and busts and, in 1932, the last year before the New Deal, the nation's GDP shrank a staggering 23 percent. Since 1950, however, the economy has grown every year and over the past five decades GDP growth rates have been extraordinarily stable from a historical perspective, ranging from 3 to 12 percent annually.

Finally, World War II pushed military spending to new levels. Even though military spending declined sharply at the end of the war, it remained considerably above prewar levels and has remained a sizable portion of the budget ever since. In 1940, defense spending was 1.7 percent of GDP. Since the advent of World War II, defense spending has never been lower than 3 percent of GDP (its 1999–2001 level).

Responsive Government as an Explanation for Spending Growth

Why have government expenditures risen so dramatically the past century? Government may simply be responding to new citizen demands.

Figure 6.2 Economic Stabilization After the Great Depression

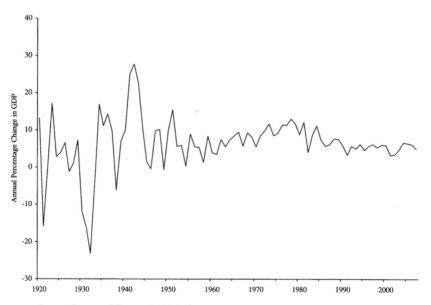

Source: Bureau of Economic Analysis.

Since federal expenditures are not tethered to revenues, public officials can appease citizens who want more spending without paying the political consequences of increasing taxes. Responsive-government explanations for growth view government as reacting to external demands for public sector activity. The institutions of government are thus seen as neutral with respect to choice outcomes, and affect the size of the public sector only to the extent that they faithfully reflect the external demands of the population.

One responsive-government explanation is Wagner's Law, which suggests that the rise of government expenditures is largely driven by changes in society, particularly those of industrialization and urbanization. As a nation's economy shifts from being largely agricultural to industrial and high-tech, demands on transportation systems, law enforcement, fire protection, and sanitation systems all increase.[6] Furthermore, as a society becomes more urbanized, changes in societal norms (i.e., society becomes much more impersonal) lead to the greater potential for conflict and inequality, which in turn causes government to take on more responsibilities. As Wagner's Law suggests, public expenditures are driven to a large degree by major economic forces. A relatively wealthy nation, for example, will spend more than a country where almost everyone is poor, regardless of the preferences of public officials. Similarly, a rapidly growing economy will produce more revenues for expansion of programs, while a declining economy will force cuts in programs.[7]

Under many circumstances it may be desirable for legislators to seek political credit via public spending. It has been argued that this leads to a relative oversupply of public goods and services and thus to artificially high levels of taxation.[8] The problem with this argument, however, is that taxing and spending decisions are not made in tandem. Voters would like more benefits for the same or lower taxes. This obviously poses a quandary for policymakers if the budget is to be balanced. Officials favor structures that reduce the probability of conflict, promote the routine resolution of disputes, and put distance between themselves and whatever conflicts arise. As a result, policymakers have strong incentives to do what voters want and to take entrepreneurial action in representing group interests.[9] The end result is a budget whose expenditures are generally considerably higher than its revenues.

Policymakers are also sensitive to the fact that the public may notice and respond to budgetary policy change. Though the public is not very well informed about the structure of appropriations, changes in budget preferences have been found to be negatively related to spending decisions: the public prefers less spending downward when appropriations increase, and prefers increased spending when appropriations decrease.[10] Such public responsiveness implies that people acquire and process fairly accurate information about budgetary policy. For example, it has been found that as Democratic presidents obtain relatively fewer defense appropriations, public support for more defense spending tends to increase, while as Republican presidents obtain more defense appropriations, public support tends to decrease. In fact, the change in defense appropriations is about $11 billion higher under Republican presidents than under Democratic presidents, given public preferences.[11] Thus both public opinion and the party of the president structure appropriations, but in different directions.

Parochialism

When producing the budget, members of Congress address state and local interests as well as promote broad national or public interests. As a result, Congress is often criticized for being too concerned with local, or parochial, interests. Without doubt, legislators experience significant pressure from their constituents on budgetary matters. As a result, members of Congress are caught between conflicting demands. Since members must appease the desires of their constituencies in order to win reelection, national budgetary interests may be given lower priority than local interests. In fact, local and national interests are sometimes in direct conflict.

The parochial nature of Congress, therefore, may be a cause for the nation's budgetary woes. Congress is a diverse group of 535 members who represent approximately 480 different constituencies. Since these constituencies have different interests and needs, it should be expected that members of Congress will have numerous views on spending policy. Parochial interests make it difficult to keep the nation's collective good in mind.

The fiscal concerns of members of Congress are the natural outcome of the job. One duty of members of Congress is to represent their constituencies, which they do well, particularly in defending existing programs. The public may want a balance between representing constituency interests and representing national interests, but there are limits to what the public will support in order to obtain this balance—and their representatives act accordingly. By failing to reduce expenditures, members of Congress can satisfy the demands of many particular groups (and obtain the political benefits of doing so). Deficit spending can thereby be regarded as a reflection of the public's contrary demands, and the desire of Congress to try to accommodate them.[12]

The emphasis of Congress on individuals, because of the nature in which legislators are elected (in separate single-member constituencies in a system of relatively weak political party cohesion), has made it difficult for Congress to balance the budget in an era when much is expected from the government. Furthermore, many of the problems that comprehensive budget proposals face within Congress stem from the nature of Congress as an institution and the place of Congress in the separation of powers framework of the Constitution. The organizational requirements for fiscal policy are quite different from those of representation that are characteristic of Congress. Since budgeting is not the sole mission of Congress, the criteria by which to evaluate the performance of congressional budgeting are not obvious.[13]

Congress is responsive to public opinion, attentive to constituency concerns, and highly accessible to a broad diversity of groups and interests. Its members are also very much aware of their accountability to voters. Every member's definition of the fiscal good arises in reference to concrete political and institutional circumstances. The result is ambivalence in supporting proposals to balance the budget by reducing spending. The budget process as it is now organized tends to serve the political interests of individual members well, but not necessarily the interests of the institution as a whole.[14] Congress lacks the will to cut spending—this "will" problem is inherent in a representative institution such as Congress, which wields real budgeting powers.[15]

Macroeconomic theories focus on the aggregate amounts of government spending, taxing, and borrowing. Microeconomic theories, on the other hand, look more closely at individual programs, such as targeted public works jobs, or subsidies to wheat farmers.[16] Congress is designed to be a much better microbudgeter than macrobudgeter. Where the federal budget is concerned, however, macro and micro concerns often collide. For example, a representative from Iowa may favor reducing the deficit, but not through reduced agricultural subsidies to Iowa farmers. Similarly, job training programs are seen as important in urban districts, often even by those representatives who publicly call themselves fiscal conservatives. Budgeting in Congress, therefore, is not the same as budgeting in the executive branch. While it is the weaker branch dealing with the totals, Congress dominates the microbudget. This may result in political pressure to inflate overall spending levels. The parochial nature of congressional representation, therefore, may to some degree explain why members of Congress behave as they do in regard to expenditure legislation.

Due to its power to appropriate funds and its unique status as a representative body, Congress can still be considered the "first branch of government" that the constitutional framers had in mind.[17] Of course, Congress by no means produces budgets in isolation, and is heavily influenced by the budgetary preferences of the executive branch. In fact, since the Budget and Accounting Act of 1921, Congress has consistently delegated budgetary power to the presidency. The contemporary shift of spending powers from Congress to the president goes against the core belief of the constitutional framers that each branch of government would protect its own prerogatives. This shift of budgetary power toward the president, however, means that he must share responsibility for large deficits.[18] Presidents, in the end, are as capable as Congress in promoting programs, and proposals for expensive programs are as likely to come from the White House as from Congress.[19]

Pork Barreling

Parochialism is perhaps nowhere as obvious as in the much criticized practice of pork barreling, the process by which legislators try to earmark special projects and funds for their districts. When members of Congress refer to public preferences, they generally refer to the public in a broad sense—the "American people," "Americans," or "the people." Members of Congress much less frequently invoke specific groups who desire specific spending programs.[20] Pork barreling, however, is targeted directly to particular geographic groups. Even though it can be argued that "pork" can often comprise legitimate public goods, and that pork barrel spending has only a small impact on the federal deficit, critics claim that legislators' attempts to obtain special projects or funds for their districts are detrimental to the budget as a whole. A major reason why economically unsound projects seem politically attractive is that they represent a return for the tax dollar. Each project looks worthwhile in isolation to its proponents and beneficiaries. Collectively, however, the nation's taxpayers are underwriting many projects that will not pay for themselves. Though the beneficiaries of pork barrel projects are minority groups of taxpayers, the practice of "logrolling"—voting for other legislators' interests with the understanding that the latter will return the favor—tends to make pork barreling a politically attractive option. Ironically, despite the widely held belief that incumbent members of Congress are rewarded by the electorate for bringing federal dollars to their districts, the empirical evidence supporting this belief is generally weak.[21] Generally, supporting increased spending (both in general and within the representative's district) does not appear to help an officeholder.

Defenders of pork barreling argue that it aids valuable local projects that might otherwise go unfunded. Critics of pork barrel politics, however, hold not only that pork barreling is economically inefficient, but also that it sometimes fuels corruption. Former representative Randy "Duke" Cunningham, for example, pleaded guilty to accepting $2.4 million in bribes to earmark funds to defense contractors.[22] Opponents of earmarks also argue that money is allocated based not on need, but on how much power a particular member of Congress wields. Local projects can thus take funds away from national needs. Yet it can be argued that the Founding Fathers recognized that parochial interests would collide with national interests and that there would inevitably be an instinct to steer money toward local projects, even at the expense of the greater public good. "Congress is exerting power it has had since 1789," according to Don Ritchie, associate historian of the Senate. "It's not doing anything new."[23]

Pork barreling would be less of a concern if approximately equivalent federal funds were earmarked to all jurisdictions. The problem of inequitable distribution, however, is inherent to the way Congress distributes pork. Since members of Congress attempt to allocate resources strategically to the areas that provide the best return in terms of votes, areas within congressional districts that vote at higher rates will be privileged over areas that vote at lower rates.[24]

Appropriations committee and subcommittee chairs are in an especially good position to ensure that their districts receive considerable shares of federal funding. For example, in the fiscal 1993 transportation bill, William Lehman (D-FL), chair of the House Transportation Appropriations Subcommittee until his retirement at the end of the 102nd Congress, managed to secure Florida $72.5 million in federal transportation projects. In the 1994 appropriations bill, created after Lehman retired, Florida secured only five projects worth a combined total of $19.5 million.[25] And any discussion of the unequal distribution of pork barrel spending must mention the exploits of Senators Robert Byrd (D-WV) and Ted Stevens (R-AK). As the ranking Democrat on the Senate Appropriations Committee, Byrd was able to move large Washington bureaucracies, such as the Coast Guard's national computer operations center, a NASA research center, and an FBI unit that stores over 190 million fingerprints, to West Virginia.[26] Similarly, as the ranking Republican on the Senate Appropriations Committee, Stevens was able to direct billions of dollars in spending toward Alaska. In fact, in every year from 2000 to 2006, Stevens was able to direct more pork barrel spending, on a per capita basis, to Alaska ($645 million in 2005 alone) than any other senators were able to direct to their respective states.[27]

The number of projects passed by Congress that can be considered pork increased dramatically after the Republicans took control of the House in the 1994 elections. Pork barrel projects accounted for $10 billion in federal spending in 1995, and increased steadily to a record $29 billion by 2006 (see Figure 6.3). The latter amount included nearly 10,000 projects in the thirteen appropriations bills that constituted the discretionary portion of the federal budget. In 2006, Alaska led the nation with $489 of pork barrel legislation per capita ($325 million total), followed by Hawaii with $378 per capita ($482 million total) and the District of Columbia with $182 per capita ($100 million total).[28] After increasing during the first six years of the George W. Bush administration, pork barrel spending decreased

Figure 6.3 Pork Barrel Spending, 1995–2007

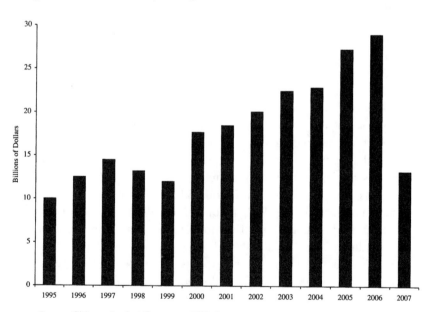

Source: Citizens Against Government Waste.

markedly in 2007, to $13.2 billion, after the Democrats won control of Congress. This reduction in pork can be partly attributed to a moratorium on earmarks enacted by the chairmen of the House and Senate appropriations committees as well as to new budgeting standards adopted by congressional Democrats.[29]

Excessive Government as an Explanation for Spending Growth

Some hold that growth of government spending is not a response to citizen demands but rather a result of excessive government. Excessive-government theories view the choices that government institutions make as fundamental to understanding growth of the public sector. In other words, the demand for expansion is conceived as internal to government through a variety of mechanisms such as public-employee block voting or "fiscal illusions" that mislead the public into underestimating the costs of public services. Government, therefore, generates its own growth internally.

How can government get away with such expansion if it contradicts public demand? The disconnection between taxing and spending may make an expansion of government spending easier because the piecemeal federal budget process makes budgetary accountability difficult to ascertain. It has been argued that citizens fail to properly estimate their true tax costs. As a result, taxpayers do not realize how much they pay relative to the governmental services they receive.[30] Also, since it is generally perceived as desirable for policymakers to seek political credit via public spending, this leads to a relative oversupply of public goods and services and thus to artificially high levels of taxation.[31] Since decisions about how money will be spent are made not by those providing the money but instead by elected representatives, government expenditures are inflated.[32] The marked increase over the past four decades in the number of persons receiving direct financial benefits from the government, therefore, may not be a symptom of policymakers following the public's wishes as much as it is a mechanism to insulate policymakers from political retribution.

The lack of a linkage between spending decisions and public desires can also be seen in the budgetary claims made by policymakers, whose assertions are usually unaccompanied by evidence. Polls, for example, do not play an important role in the debate over budget policy in Congress. Of 226 policy arguments on the budget in Congress from 1998 to 2000, only 5 cited polling data.[33] Concerns about a lack of public understanding are sometimes voiced during budget debates. In these circumstances, policymakers will thus defend their own positions or attack their opponents' positions by alluding to the public's misconceptions. This is not necessarily the case in other countries. The British public, possibly because they are prodded to do so through the strong party system in the House of Commons, appear to notice and respond to changes in public spending in particular domains more than does the US public. British policymakers represent these preferences in spending.[34]

Critics of excessive federal spending also point to the development of the welfare state as a cause. A welfare state is a liberal democratic state in which the government actively intervenes in economic matters with the objective of better equalizing life opportunities through income redistribution and the provision of an extensive network of basic social services. In today's world there is wide variation in types of welfare states, the comprehensiveness of their programs, the way in which they operate, and how they are perceived by the citizenry.

The birth of the US welfare state is often associated with the Social Security Act of 1935. This legislation was the first of many enacted during the middle to late 1930s in a variety of areas, from old-age pensions and welfare benefits to expanded agricultural subsidies. The New Deal was the most effective period of social policy exploration and implementation in US history. Efforts have been made, most notably as part of Lyndon Johnson's Great Society program, to expand and complete the New Deal's welfare state agenda, but the impact of such programs has generally been limited compared to the New Deal.

The welfare state is now well institutionalized in all industrialized democracies. Social programs constitute the largest public expenditures in most of these countries, accounting for about a third of such monies.[35] The United States, however, ranks at the bottom among industrialized democracies on virtually all measures relating to its commitment to provide social services to its citizenry, and is the only industrialized democracy that does not offer universal health care and family benefits.

Americans are not totally comfortable with the ideological conception of the welfare state; it contrasts sharply with a cultural emphasis on individualism and the desirability of limited government. Opponents of the welfare state argue that welfare programs cost too much and that citizens are being asked to shoulder excessive tax burdens to fund them, and these demands are likely to become even greater in the future. Critics also argue that the programs are ineffective, not reaching the groups in need with the services promised. Furthermore, the delivery capabilities of government are seen as being limited and inefficient, thus causing programs to fail to achieve their intended objectives. Another criticism of the welfare state is the question of fairness. The balance between spending on children and spending on the elderly is one important measure in evaluating the allocation of public welfare spending. During the 1990s, the gap in per capita welfare spending between these two groups grew 20 percent, increasing the imbalance in public spending toward the elderly relative to children.[36]

Due to the development of the welfare state, budgeting is often regarded as an incremental, largely uncontrollable process. The proportion of uncontrollable federal expenditures has been increasing as discretionary spending has been reduced. This is not unique to the United States—for most governments in industrialized democracies, only a very small percentage of the budget can be touched in any budget year.[37] The largest determining factor of this year's spending is last year's. Long-term commitments have been made, and these commitments limit the government's spending options.[38]

Yet, however intense the criticism, welfare state policies have consistently enjoyed a strong base of support in the United States. The popularity of the New Deal established the Democrats as the majority party in the electorate for more than a generation, and Americans still overwhelmingly support Social Security, the most important New Deal program. Today, nearly 80 percent of Americans believe that it should be the government's responsibility to provide a decent standard of living for the elderly.[39] Americans are also reluctant to alter Social Security at all: only about one in five Americans favors establishing personal retirement accounts if this would result in a reduction of guaranteed Social Security benefits.[40]

Republican presidents since Ronald Reagan have tried to dismantle parts of the welfare state and return the United States to a purer form of a laissez-faire market economy, similar to that of the pre–New Deal 1920s. In the budgetary wars since the 1980s, however, Democrats have vigorously defended middle-class entitlements such as Social Security and Medicare. As a result, efforts to reduce the scope of the welfare state have enjoyed little success—cutting taxes has proved much easier than cutting spending. The failure of the Reagan and both Bush administrations to fundamentally alter welfare state policies shows the strength and intensity of the public's commitment to the continuation of entitlement programs.

Spending Levels Since the 1960s

The expansion of federal government spending continued for more than three decades after the New Dealers came to power. Since the 1960s, however, congressional policymaking has shifted from an environment in which new programs were added and existing programs were expanded to an environment in which spending is constrained by large budget deficits. Despite public perception to the contrary, the growth of federal spending since the mid-1960s has slowed considerably. Since 1965, federal spending as a share of GDP has remained remarkably stable at about 20 percent, ranging from 17.2 percent (1965) to 23.5 percent (1983).

Despite the fact that Republicans won control of Congress in 1994 in part on a platform of promised spending reductions, and even though they may have influenced the content of domestic public policy from 1995 to 2006, they were unable to significantly alter the politics of domestic spending.[41] Evidence suggests that Republican control produced a partial shift in the interests that were rewarded by federal spending, but that overall levels of spending did decrease; in fact, spending levels increased. Spending decreased as a percentage of GDP during the Bill Clinton administration, but increased significantly after George W. Bush was elected president, by 7.8 percent in 2005 alone. Federal expenditures now exceed $20,000 per household (in 2002 dollars), for the first time since World War II.[42] Much of this increase is due to entitlement spending, which is now at an all-time high. Defense and the "war on terror" accounted for less than half of all new spending during the Bush administration.

Part of the increase in spending during the Bush administration was due to a dramatic increase in supplemental and additional appropriations. From less than $20 billion in 2000, supplemental and additional appropriations provided by Congress skyrocketed to nearly $160 billion by 2005 (see Figure 6.4). This circumvention of the traditional expenditure process demonstrates the deterioration of traditional budgetary norms that were put in place to control spending. The 2006 baseline budget, for example, omitted a significant amount of spending that occurred to finance military activities in Iraq and Afghanistan and to pay flood insurance claims resulting from Hurricane Katrina. These additional outlays totaled more than $20 billion.[43]

Many critics of increased spending since 2000 place the primary blame on President Bush. For example, Bush was criticized for not vetoing any bills during his first term, for the first time since the

Figure 6.4 Budget Authority Provided Through Supplemental
and Additional Appropriations

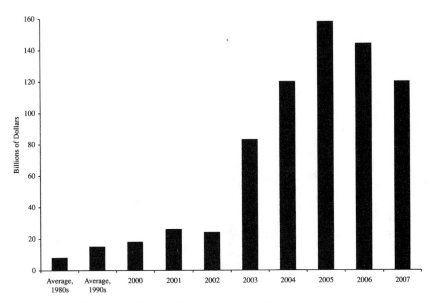

Sources: Congressional Budget Office; Congressional Research Service.

presidency of John Quincy Adams, including unnecessary pork barreling.[44] Bush was also criticized for allowing the "pay-go" rule—a
set of restrictions under the Budget Enforcement Act of 1990 that
limited spending levels—to expire. While proposing no significant
outlay reduction in major entitlement programs, Bush allowed welfare spending to increase. When Bush was inaugurated president in
2001, the money that the federal government spent on health care,
housing, food, and income support for the poor constituted 15.3 percent of the budget. By 2006, this figure reached 16.0 percent.[45] Overall, government expenditures during the George W. Bush administration rose faster as a percentage of GDP than during any presidential
administration since that of Lyndon Johnson (see Figure 6.5). Annual
growth of spending during the Clinton administration, on the other
hand, was the lowest over this time period. Though some of Clinton's
major economic policy initiatives promoted more spending, his legislation broke with liberal orthodoxy. Reagan's terms as president
aside, mean annual percentage increases in discretionary domestic
spending under Clinton were smaller than those of Republican presidents since 1960.[46]

Figure 6.5 Spending Growth by Presidential Administration

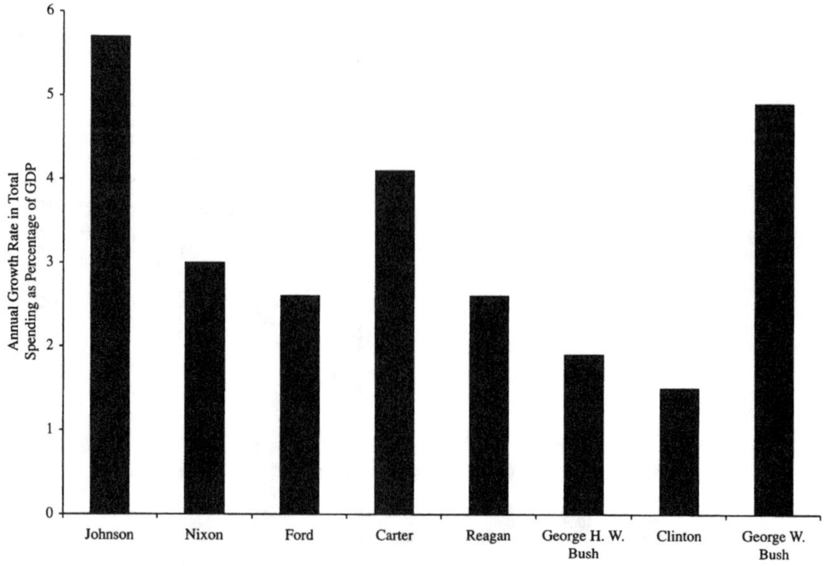

Sources: Isabel Sawhill, "Why Worry About the Deficit? (And What We Can Do About It)," Brookings Institution; Concord Coalition, "Fiscal Wake-Up Tour," University of Nebraska, April 4, 2006.

Controlling expenditures in the future will be a colossal political task. It is questionable whether current levels of federal spending can be maintained. The percentage of the population aged sixty-five and older is projected to increase from 14 percent in 2016 to more than 19 percent in 2030. At the same time, there is no evidence that growth in health care costs, which have risen faster than GDP over the past four decades, will slow significantly in the near future. As a result, spending for Social Security, Medicare, and Medicaid under current law is expected to claim a larger share of total outlays. If these trends are maintained over the long term, the escalating demands of these programs will exert such pressure on the budget as to make current fiscal policy unsustainable.[47] Over the next three decades, spending on federal programs is projected to increase by 50 percent as a share of the economy. If revenues remain at their historical level, the resulting deficits would be ten times larger than today's deficits.[48] Given such scenarios, the expenditures for some programs—at least given current revenue levels—will undoubtedly need to be curtailed.

The budget process has poorly managed the trade-offs among entitlements, discretionary spending, revenue declines, and balanced budget concerns. The current disconnection between taxing and spending decisions has left the United States vulnerable to future demands. Though spending cuts for some programs are inevitable, there are good policy reasons to increase future spending for other programs. A considerable number of Americans, for example, are now receptive to the idea of the federal government providing universal health care. The long-term decline in nondefense discretionary spending may also prove problematic if there are not enough funds to support future policy priorities, such as the environment and transportation. All told, the recent era of spending politics has left the United States ill-prepared for future growth and development.

Notes

1. Soumaya M. Tohamy, Hashem Dezbakhsh, and Peter H. Aranson, "A New Theory of the Budgetary Process," *Economics and Politics* 18 (2006): 47–70.

2. David Nice, *Public Budgeting* (Belmont, CA: Wadsworth, 2002), p. 21.

3. Office of Management and Budget, *Budget of the United States Government: Fiscal Year 2005* (Washington, DC, 2005), tab. 15.2, http://www.whitehouse.gov/omb/budget/fy2005/hist.html.

4. Donald Ogilvie, "Constitutional Limits and the Federal Budget," in Rudolph Penner, ed., *The Congressional Budget Process After Five Years* (Washington, DC: AEI, 1981), pp. 101–134.

5. David C. Barker and Stephanie T. Muraca, "'We're All Keynesians Now'? Understanding Public Attitudes Toward the Federal Budget," *American Politics Research* 31 (2003): 485–519.

6. Nice, *Public Budgeting,* p. 22.

7. Ibid., p. 9.

8. Craig Volden, "Intergovernmental Political Competition in American Federalism," *American Journal of Political Science* 49 (2005): 327–342.

9. R. Douglas Arnold, *The Logic of Congressional Action* (New Haven: Yale University Press, 1990).

10. Christopher Wlezien, "The Public as Thermostat: Dynamics of Preferences for Spending," *American Journal of Political Science* 39 (1995): 981–1000.

11. Ibid.

12. Patrick Fisher, *Congressional Budgeting: A Representational Perspective* (Lanham: University Press of America, 2005), chap. 7.

13. Mark Kamlet and David Mowery, "The First Decade of the Congressional Budget Act: Legislative Imitation and Adaptation in Budgeting," in Albert Hyde, ed., *Government Budgeting* (Pacific Grove, CA: Brooks Cole, 1992), pp. 118–138.

14. Richard Fenno, *The Emergence of a Senate Leader: Pete Domenici and the Reagan Budget* (Washington, DC: Congressional Quarterly, 1991).

15. Jasmine Farrier, *Passing the Buck: Congress, the Budget, and Deficits* (Lexington: University Press of Kentucky, 2004).

16. John Cranford, *Budgeting for America*, 2nd ed. (Washington, DC: Congressional Quarterly, 1989).

17. Louis Fisher, *Constitutional Conflicts Between Congress and the President,* 4th ed. (Lawrence: University Press of Kansas, 1997).

18. Farrier, *Passing the Buck.*

19. Louis Fisher, *Congressional Abdication on War and Spending* (College Station: Texas A&M Press, 2000).

20. David G. Levasseur, "The Role of Public Opinion in Policy Argument: An Examination of Public Opinion Rhetoric in the Federal Budget Process," *Argumentation and Advocacy* 41 (2005): 152–167.

21. Steven D. Levitt and James M. Snyder, "The Impact of Federal Spending on House Election Outcomes," *Journal of Political Economy* 105 (1997): 30–53.

22. Marcia Clemmitt, "Bringing Home the Bacon," *Congressional Quarterly Researcher* 16 (2006): 538–540.

23. Sheryl Gay Stolberg, "What's Wrong with a Healthy Helping of Pork?" *New York Times,* May 28, 2006, p. W4.

24. Paul S. Martin, "Voting's Rewards: Voter Turnout, Attentive Publics, and Congressional Allocation of Federal Money," *American Journal of Political Science* 47 (2003): 110–127.

25. Jon Healey, "The States' Pipeline," *Congressional Quarterly,* December 11, 1993, pp. 12–14.

26. Martin L. Gross, *The Government Racket* (New York: Bantam, 1992), pp. 183–185.

27. Citizens Against Government Waste, "Senator Ted Stevens' Pork Tally," February 27, 2008, http://www.cagw.org.

28. Citizens Against Government Waste, "2006 Congressional Pig Book Summary," October 15, 2006, http://www.cagw.org.

29. Citizens Against Government Waste, "2007 Congressional Pig Book Summary," March 17, 2007, http://www.cagw.org.

30. James Buchanan, "Why Does Government Grow?" in Thomas Borcherding, ed., *Budgets and Bureaucrats: The Sources of Government Growth* (Durham: Duke University Press, 1977), pp. 3–18.

31. Craig Volden, "Intergovernmental Political Competition in American Federalism."

32. Irene S. Rubin, *The Politics of Public Budgeting,* 5th ed. (Washington, DC: Congressional Quarterly, 2006), pp. 17–20.

33. Levasseur, "The Role of Public Opinion in Policy Argument."

34. Stuart N. Soroka and Christopher Wlezien, "Opinion-Policy Dynamics: Public Preferences and Public Expenditure in the United Kingdom," *British Journal of Political Science* 35 (2005): 665–689.

35. B. Guy Peters, *The Politics of Taxation* (Cambridge: Blackwell, 1991), pp. 82–83.

36. Susmita Pati, Ron Keren, Evaline Alessandrini, and Donald Schwarz, "Generational Differences in U.S. Public Spending, 1980–2000," *Health Affairs* 23 (2004): 131–141.

37. Peters, *The Politics of Taxation,* pp. 101–102.

38. Aaron Wildavsky and Naomi Caiden, *The New Politics of the Budgetary Process,* 5th ed. (New York: Longman, 2004), p. 46.

39. New York Times/CBS News Poll (February 24–28, 2005), national survey of 1,111 adults.

40. Ibid.

41. Kenneth Bickers and Robert Stein, "The Congressional Pork Barrel in a Republican Era," *Journal of Politics* 62 (2000): 1070–1086.

42. Brian Riedal, "$20,000 per Household: The Highest Level of Federal Spending Since World War II," December 3, 2003, http://www.heritage.org/research/budget/bg1710.cfm.

43. Congressional Budget Office, *The Fiscal and Economic Outlook: Fiscal Years 2007 to 2016* (Washington, DC, 2006), p. 1.

44. Peter G. Peterson, *Running on Empty* (New York: Farrar, Straus and Giroux, 2004), pp. 16–17.

45. Jesse Walker, "Welfare as We Know It," *Reason* 38 (2006): 16.

46. John W. Burns and Andrew J. Taylor, "A New Democrat? The Economic Performance of the Clinton Presidency," *Independent Review* 5 (2001): 387–408.

47. Congressional Budget Office, *The Fiscal and Economic Outlook,* p. 3.

48. Bob Kerrey and Warren Rudman, "Securing Future Fiscal Health," *Washington Post,* August 28, 2006, p. A15.

7

REDUCING SPENDING

DEMOCRACY COMPLICATES BUDGETING BECAUSE IT IS WIDELY held that spending money helps one win election, while imposing costs through higher taxes is politically harmful. The ideal world for policymakers is one in which they can make everyone happy and alienate no one.[1] Revenue levels do not appear to provide any leverage in the battle to reduce spending. Even though some conservatives hope that revenue shortfalls will provide such leverage, there is no evidence that reducing taxes has much of an impact on spending in any consistent way. The incentives for policymakers to cut spending are weak partly due to the perception that cuts alienate voters, and partly due to the inability of policymakers to agree on what programs should be eliminated. Politicians often talk about cutting spending without mentioning what programs they would cut. This is simply a convenient mechanism to avoid making difficult choices. Vague calls to eliminate "waste," "pork," or "fraud" are unlikely to result in a real reduction of spending.

Theoretically, policymakers should be able to reduce budgets in the same way that they have increased them. Formulas could simply be adjusted downward. Subtracting, however, is not the same as adding. In order to reduce spending, it is necessary to establish mechanisms that will force consideration of automatic decisions, set binding ceilings that limit permissible claims, and make choices that will prevent budget circumvention. Spending cuts eat into the established base of what agencies expect to receive, leading to greater conflict as more and more existing commitments are attacked.[2] Without the ability to significantly reduce or eliminate individual spending programs, it is unlikely that policymakers can meaningfully and stably reduce spending. Politicians, therefore, tend to overestimate their ability to make significant budget cuts. Even Ronald Reagan, who achieved an impressive victory in 1980 campaigning on a platform of cutting expenditures, found it excruciatingly difficult to reduce federal spending. After Reagan was elected president, reductions were made in federal spending, but at levels much below what was claimed at the time. It has been estimated that fiscal 1986 outlays were $52 billion below what they would have been without the 1981 budget cuts, which were much lower than the Reagan administration advertised.[3]

The parochial nature of budgeting is a substantial obstacle in cutting spending. Legislators take care of parochial interests as well as promote national public interests when making decisions on spending priorities. Since members of Congress desire to be reelected, constituency pressures impose meaningful constraints on their ability to support spending cuts.[4] Members of Congress tend to be extremely sensitive to public opinion in their districts, which has been found to have a major impact on legislative behavior even when congressional actions seem to contradict public opinion. Electoral risk is by far the best predictor of whether or not a member of Congress will vote against controversial spending legislation.[5]

A potential tool—one that has been used in the past—to reduce spending levels is impoundment. The president can use the 1974 Impoundment Control Act to propose the rescission or deferral of funds. When the president dominates the executive-legislative relationship, Congress tends to accept the impoundments; otherwise, it usually rejects them. In 1981 and 1982, Reagan used the impoundment power to control spending, but use of this power is more the exception than the rule. The loss of impoundment power has subtracted from presidential power and, some have argued, made it more difficult to control federal spending.[6]

Budgets are difficult to cut not only because of the rigidities of the decisionmaking process, but also because they often constitute long-term commitments to key individuals and groups. The result is that not all areas of the budget are equally susceptible to cuts. In practice, budget cutting tends to concentrate on the controllable parts of the budget and to inflict losses on the politically weaker sections of society (food stamps, welfare programs, foreign aid, etc.). Ultimately, the politics of subtraction is limited by its social and economic consequences.[7]

Since the advantages of budget cuts lie in accumulating them to make a substantial impact on the deficit, compromise is required.[8] Because compromise is difficult to bring about, few programs are completely eliminated because of resistance by Congress, the White House, interest groups, and administrative agencies. As well, because the budget process is so decentralized, a program usually needs only one important ally to avoid significant cuts. And because Congress has found itself unable to make specific cuts in areas that are widely acknowledged as needing them (such as military base closures), it has found itself delegating authority to independent commissions to make these when it lacks the political courage to do so.

As a result of the political obstacles to reducing spending, government has turned to innovative means, including tax legislation. Tax legislation to control spending is conventionally based on the belief that spending will increase to consume all revenue—the more government has, the more it spends. So by reducing the Treasury's resources, the theory goes, spending must decrease. The problem with this strategy is that, since it is much easier to reduce taxes than to cut spending, tax revenues will drop much more than spending will be limited, creating large deficits.

The ability to cut spending is also closely related to economic conditions. Since World War II, the transformation of federal budgeting from a process oriented toward control to one oriented toward spending growth has upset the relationship between available resources and demands on the budget. Claims on the budget became stronger when budgeting was an expansionary process, and it has not been easy for politicians to reverse course as the climate has become more constrained. To cut spending, therefore, expectations have to be changed.[9] The budget process cannot be conducted the same way and produce the same results when resources are scarce as when they are plentiful. The assumptions on which the budget's prescriptions are based all lie at the mercy of national economic conditions. Politics and economics combine to shape the varying patterns of activity for policymakers working on the budget.[10] On the one hand, economic goal-setting has often been a frivolous exercise in symbolic politics in the absence of realistic means to achieve goals. As economic conditions change, so do priorities; policymakers need to maintain their ability to respond accordingly.

Cutting spending, of course, suggests that the level of spending is too high. But is this really the case? One could also argue that, given the important societal needs currently unmet, spending should actually be increased. It may be that spending produces benefits that are not fully appreciated by voters. A major portion of government benefits are remote compared with taxes and private benefits. Thus, citizens fail to realize all the government benefits they are receiving. The actual budget will therefore be smaller than the "correct" budget, because even indirect taxation is much more apparent than many remote government benefits.[11] Spending therefore should not be cut, but actually increased to fit public preferences. This may also help to explain the levels of economic inequality in the United States.

Cutting spending, of course, is politically easier when the public is supportive. And generally speaking, cutting spending is usually a difficult sell. As Figure 7.1 displays, since the Reagan administration, Americans have tended to be more supportive of increased rather than decreased services and spending. Only in the early parts of the Reagan and Clinton administrations was support for cutting services and spending greater than support for increasing services and spending.

Figure 7.1 Support for Government Services and Spending, 1982–2004

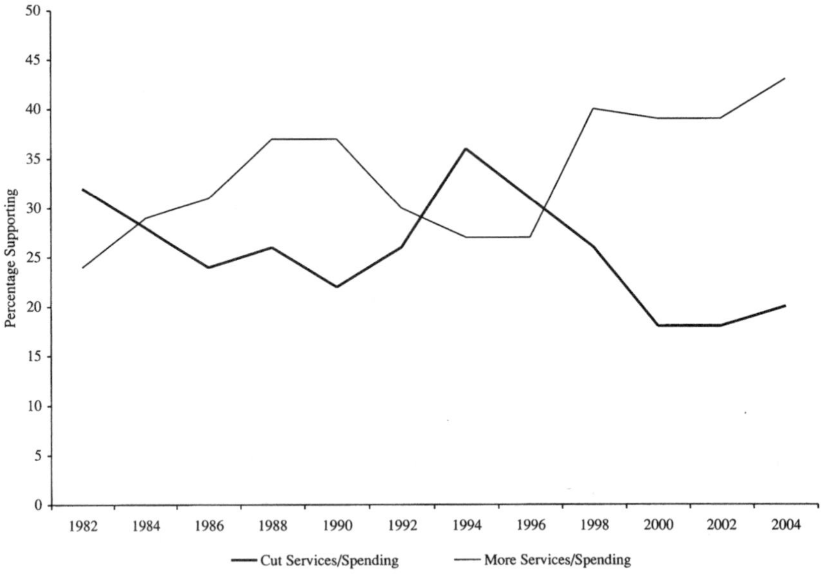

Legend: Cut Services/Spending — More Services/Spending

Source: American National Elections Studies.

Notes: Question text: "Some people think that government should provide fewer services, even in areas such as health and education, in order to reduce spending. Other people feel that it is important for the government to provide many more services if it means an increase in spending. Where would you place yourself on this scale, or haven't you thought much about this?" Seven-point scale shown to respondent; responses 1–3 coded as support for cutting services and spending, responses 5–7 coded as support for more services and spending.

Since Clinton's election to a second term in 1996, the American public has shifted strongly toward preferring more services and spending. In 2004, 43 percent of voters supported increased services and spending, more than twice the number who desired that the government cut services and spending. In particular, Americans tend to strongly support increased spending for health care, welfare assistance, the environment, and education.[12]

What Should Be Cut?

If budget cuts are deemed necessary, the political problem becomes what should be cut. On this point, policymakers are strongly divided. Theoretically, all government spending could be cut almost immediately. Governments create programs and governments can abolish those programs. Politically, however, it is safe to say that few programs are targets for complete elimination. The parts of the budget that are easiest to control have been cut to the point where few obvious cuts remain.[13] Yet it is also obvious that, since the late 1970s, policymaking has shifted from an environment in which new programs were added and existing programs were expanded to an environment in which budgetary policy, due to large deficits, constrains all policymaking.[14]

There are three broad areas of the budget in which Congress can reduce spending: (1) entitlements, which include the largest programs in the federal budget—Social Security, Medicare, and Medicaid; (2) domestic discretionary spending; and (3) defense. Although governments in all industrialized nations now spend heavily for social services, health care, education, and defense, there are significant differences in the relative amounts they spend. France, for example, spends twice as much as a percentage of all expenditures for social welfare as Australia; defense spending in the United States is about 20 percent of total expenditures, but in Italy is only 2 percent. In addition to variances in spending priorities, there are marked differences in the manner in which governments spend. Some countries are very centralized and others rely heavily on subnational governments to provide programs.[15]

Entitlements

The bulk of the US budget today is spent on entitlements, which, unlike discretionary spending, cannot be controlled by presidential and appropriations review. Despite cuts in some entitlement programs, overall entitlement spending continues to increase due to the proliferation of these programs. Entitlements are important in maintaining political transparency—the scope, benefits, and eligibility requirements of entitlement programs are relatively easy for voters to comprehend. Voters, however, tend to assume that most programs are entitlements, overestimating the support available to target populations.[16]

Entitlement programs are so large that any real reductions in federal spending would almost certainly have to include entitlements, including the popular Social Security program. Social Security is by far the largest item in the budget and is growing rapidly. In 1990, Social Security cost less than $250 billion; by 2005, it cost more than $500 billion. Critics of Social Security argue that times have changed since 1935, when it first became law; there are now fewer workers per retired person, and life expectancy has increased dramatically. Social Security now takes 6.2 percent of workers' paychecks. If benefits are not cut or if other financial methods to generate Social Security revenue are not devised, payroll taxes will need to be increased dramatically. Proposals for cutting Social Security costs include reducing the indexing of benefits to cost of living, increasing taxes on Social Security income, and raising the age of retirement. Advocating any of these, however, has proven to be politically unpopular and members of Congress, even conservative Republicans, have usually shied away from introducing measures that would change the nature of Social Security benefits dramatically.

Some conservatives, however, argue that such steps do not go nearly far enough and propose transferring Social Security (either in whole or in part) to private retirement accounts. Privatization on its own would not necessarily affect Social Security spending. Yet many Social Security reformists like the idea of privatization because private retirement accounts offer the possibility of a high return rate for investors, though at the same time they carry much greater risk.[17] Individual accounts could potentially be an important component of a comprehensive reform plan, but the money to fund the reform must come from somewhere. If the money comes from the current payroll tax, the deficit will increase, perhaps dramatically. Individual accounts alone, therefore, will not solve the long-term funding problems of Social Security. This problem was evident in the Social Security reform proposals that George W. Bush pushed after winning reelection in 2004. Bush's proposals included no measure to address what he himself argued was the real problem: the growing future gap between program revenues and expenditures. Bush's proposal to create debt-financed personal accounts would have vastly increased the size of the national debt and thus was criticized as potentially undermining the long-term solvency of Social Security.[18]

The size of Medicare suggests that it too would need to be cut if the federal government is to significantly cut spending. In 1995 the new Republican majority in Congress passed a large cut in Medicare, but it was vetoed by President Clinton. Two years later, the 1997 Balanced Budget Act made extensive cuts in Medicare by reducing payments to medical providers. Many of these cuts, however, have been restored, due largely to lobbying by the American Medical Association.[19]

The major revision of welfare in the United States with the elimination of Aid to Families with Dependent Children shows that cuts in major entitlement programs, though difficult, are possible. Since AFDC was replaced by Temporary Assistance for Needy Families in 1997, the number of Americans receiving welfare benefits has decreased dramatically (see Figure 7.2). After peaking at 5.5 percent in

Figure 7.2 Percentage of the Population Receiving Welfare, 1960–2007

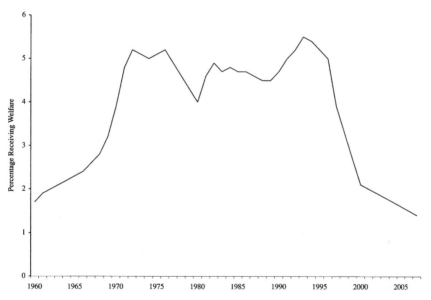

Sources: Michael J. O'Grady, Assistant Secretary for Planning and Evaluation, "Indicators of Welfare Dependence," July 2005; Office of Family Assistance, "TANF Families and Households."

Note: Figures represent percentage of the population receiving either AFDC or TANF benefits.

1993, the proportion of Americans receiving welfare benefits dropped to less than 2.0 percent by 2002, the lowest since 1961. AFDC's demise, therefore, did have a noteworthy budgetary impact. The decline of the number of Americans receiving welfare benefits indicates that, under the right political conditions, even previously well-entrenched spending can be cut.

Domestic Discretionary Spending

Rather than tackling popular entitlement programs, policymakers usually look toward domestic discretionary spending when seeking cuts. Since Congress has absolute discretion to spend or not spend discretionary funds each year through the legislative appropriations process, these funds are the easiest part of the budget to cut. The Reagan spending cuts of 1981, for example, were about equally divided between entitlement programs and discretionary domestic spending, but since discretionary spending comprises a much smaller part of the budget, it was cut disproportionately compared to entitlement spending.[20] From the mid-1960s to mid-2000s, domestic discretionary spending decreased by more than 40 percent as a share of GDP. The problem for policymakers, however, is how much further domestic discretionary spending can realistically be reduced. Much domestic discretionary spending goes to popular programs that would be difficult to cut. At the same time, it can be argued that the long-term decline of discretionary spending has been detrimental, because important societal needs are going unmet in current spending patterns. Certainly the American public is receptive to increased discretionary spending for many programs, both existing and proposed. The logic for choosing areas to cut in domestic discretionary spending has consistently avoided any real prioritization.[21] While entitlement spending is projected to grow by about 6 percent per year until 2016, faster than the economy as a whole, domestic discretionary spending is projected to increase only about 2 percent per year, simply keeping pace with inflation.

Cutting nondefense discretionary spending can sometimes be justified on the grounds that a program is a luxury that can no longer be afforded—a want rather than a need. A number of discretionary programs have seen their funding levels decrease in recent years. At the extreme, Project BioShield is an example of a program for which Congress voted to terminate funding because it was seen as being simply too expensive for its perceived benefits in an era of budget constraints. Project BioShield was a comprehensive effort to develop and distribute drugs and vaccines to protect against attack by biological and chemical weapons. The program received an appropriation of $2.5 billion in 2005 but did not receive any funding in 2006. Other entities that saw a significant reduction of funding (more than $500 million) in 2006 compared to 2005 included the Office of Elementary and Secondary Education, the Federal Bureau of Investigation, and the Employment and Training Administration.[22] The largest cuts (approximately $29 billion), a result of the Deficit Reduction Act of 2005, targeted federal obligations for college student loan programs.[23]

A part of discretionary spending that might prove politically attractive for federal policymakers to cut is grants to state and local governments. It might be tempting for a federal government that is running large deficits to simply allow state and local governments to assume greater financial responsibilities. The practice of reducing aid to lower levels of government has already been tried in Canada and Australia as a means of reducing the national deficit. In both countries, there was a reduction of expenditures at the national level, but at the expense of an increase in deficits of the lower levels of government.[24] Thus, such a maneuver simply transfers federal budget problems to lower levels of government. Since almost all US states have balanced budget requirements, they are forced to do the actual cutting of government jobs and services.

Defense

The third area of the budget that could be cut is defense. From the end of the Cold War in 1990 until the terrorist attacks of September 11, 2001, defense had been the easiest part of the budget to cut, with defense spending declining from $320 billion in 1991 to $276 billion in 1999. This reduction reflected public opinion; the end of the Cold War produced marked changes in the defense spending preferences of politically informed Americans.[25] Since 2001, however, spending on defense has increased dramatically, from $306 billion in 2001 to $520 billion in 2006. Military spending is now greater in real terms than during any year since the end of World War II, with the exception of the Korean War years in 1952 and 1953.[26]

Critics of defense spending argue that it is excessive in an era when no other nation comes anywhere near the United States in terms of military might. With the demise of the Soviet Union, the United States no longer faces a serious military challenger in the traditional sense. The United States, for example, now spends about as much as the rest of the world combined on defense.[27] Defense spending has increased dramatically since September 11, 2001, but it is not necessarily clear that the "war on terror" is to be fought by the traditional military.[28] Regardless, the end of the Cold War and September 11 aside, public opinion has tended to strongly support defense spending, making significant cuts in defense politically problematic.[29] Public opinion, therefore, is an important factor in determining overall levels of defense spending. One study found that legislators' votes on a series of defense budget roll calls in the first year of the Reagan administration were related to constituency opinions on defense spending during the 1980 election campaign. For example, the strong aggregate constituency demand for increased military spending in 1980 is estimated to have resulted in the addition of almost $17 billion (about 10 percent) to the total fiscal 1982 Pentagon appropriation.[30] Thus, though the United States could potentially afford to devote a substantially larger share of its resources to military purposes, this amount is determined fundamentally through the political process and on the basis of national security.[31]

Defense spending today is the result of decisions made years ago. Pentagon officials cannot simply order a new aircraft carrier or fighter jet from a manufacturer. Rather, they must design the weapon, negotiate a contract, and agree on a delivery schedule. This process often takes five to eight years. The government thus usually cannot realize immediate savings by ending a project immediately. At the same time, today's budget decisions will take years to show up in federal spending, creating incentives for budget-makers to think short-term rather than long-term.[32]

However measured, defense is a relatively minor player in the US economy today. Scholars have estimated that a large cutback in defense spending would lead to a short-term increase in unemployment as the economy's growth rate slowed. Over the long term, however, a peacetime economy would follow a growth path. Economists generally believe that the US economy can prosper with a greatly reduced military establishment.[33] To some degree this happened with the end of the Cold War; after an initial era of transition, the shift from military to civilian priorities contributed to the strength and duration of the economic upturn of the 1990s.[34]

It has been found that, overall, the effects of defense cuts in industrialized democracies are not as politically unpopular as cuts in social programs. The lobbying on behalf of maintaining or increasing military expenditures is generally not nearly as strong as the mass mobilization that tends to occur with attempts to change health care or pensions. Also, part of the reason that citizens in other countries consider military expenditures less desirable is that the United States spends so much on defense that it provides a perceived public good to the entire world. Polls indicate that citizens in most countries consider military defense as one of the few policy areas on which government spends too much money.[35] The United States, where defense spending tends to be relatively popular, is an exception.

Though defense spending is generally popular in the United States, foreign aid—though only a very small portion of overall expenditures—tends to have relatively sparse support among the public. As a result, US foreign aid has fallen dramatically since the 1960s (see Figure 7.3), from 0.6 percent of gross national income in 1964 to less than 0.1 percent in 1998, with a slight rebound in the early part of the twenty-first century. Whereas the United States once spent more than other industrialized democracies in foreign aid, since the 1970s it has spent considerably less on a per capita basis than other countries belonging to the Organization for Economic Cooperation and Development (OECD). Thus, even though foreign aid might be a

Figure 7.3 US Foreign Aid, 1960–2007

Source: Organization for Economic Cooperation and Development.

politically popular area for advocating reduced spending, current levels are so low that any future cuts would have only a minimal impact on overall spending levels.

The Partisanship of Spending

Since the Great Depression, Democrats and Republicans have generally favored different spending policies. Generally, with the exception of defense, Republicans have tended to support greater cuts in federal spending than Democrats, and have been critical of Democrats' lack of attention to problems associated with the expansion of entitlement programs.[36] Conservative economic theorists tend to oppose government spending on moral grounds, believing that government spending aimed at particular groups discourages personal responsibility. Centralized planning and government-sponsored redistribution of wealth, it is held, strip citizens of the freedom and autonomy to make financial decisions and interfere with competition in a free market economy. Following from Adam Smith, economic conservatives historically have stressed the importance of balanced budgets, believing that budget deficits increase interest rates, thus crowding out private investment and damaging economic health.[37]

The polarization between the parties on spending is greater today than it has ever been.[38] Their different stances on spending legislation are partially class-based. While the Democrats have argued against spending cuts for programs such as Social Security, Medicare, and education, among others, the Republicans have preferred to reduce taxes. Tax cuts may give some monetary benefits to the less affluent, but at the same time they deprive government of resources for programs beneficial to those with lower incomes.[39] Whether to reduce the budget deficit by cutting spending, therefore, may now be viewed as a defining ideological difference between the parties. As a result of this polarization on spending matters, partisan control of Congress can potentially have important effects on the economy.[40]

When it comes to particular programs, Americans generally want to increase spending and tend to reward the party that is most likely to support that position. The experience of the early 1980s, for example, taught the Republicans that opposing taxes was good politics, but that assailing popular domestic programs was not.[41] Politicians will therefore tend to argue against budget cuts based on their inability to justify them to the public.[42]

One measure of partisan support for cutting spending is the Concord Coalition's "fiscal responsibility scorecard," which suggests that Republicans tended to be more supportive of deficit reduction from the expenditure side of the budget than Democrats. As Figure 7.4 displays, from the 104th Congress (1995–1996) to the 107th Congress (2001–2002), Republicans supported the Concord Coalition's position on 43.7 percent of votes in the House and on 48.3 percent of votes in the Senate, while Democrats supported the Concord Coalition's position on 29.8 percent of votes in the House and on 33.0 percent of votes in the Senate. The level of support on spending votes, however, did vary considerably by type of spending.

The largest partisan difference existed on entitlement spending. Republicans were consistently much more likely than Democrats to support reducing entitlement spending, the fastest-growing part of the budget. Republicans supported the Concord Coalition's position on entitlement spending on 63.2 percent of votes in the House and on 58.2 percent of votes in the Senate. Democrats, on the other hand, supported the Concord Coalition's position on entitlement spending on only 30 percent of votes in the House and 29.4 percent of votes in the Senate.

Republicans also tend to be more supportive of cutting discretionary spending than Democrats, though not to the degree as for entitlement spending. From the 104th to 107th Congresses, Republicans supported the Concord Coalition's position on entitlement spending on 38.8 and 50.5 percent of votes in the House and the Senate respectively, compared to 29.6 and 37.1 for Democrats. The fact that Republicans are more likely to support reductions in entitlement and discretionary spending is consistent with the finding that Democrats give higher priority to domestic spending programs than Republicans.[43] But despite the fact that Republicans are more supportive of both entitlement and discretionary cuts than Democrats, they tend to be much more supportive of cutting entitlement spending than discretionary spending.

For defense spending, however, there is a much different relationship. In the House and Senate alike, Democratic legislators are more likely to support reducing defense spending than their Republican counterparts. From the 104th to 107th Congresses, Democratic representatives and Democratic senators supported the Concord Coalition's position on defense spending on 43.5 and 31.8 percent of votes respectively, compared to about 20 percent for both Republican representatives and Republican senators.

Figure 7.4 The Partisanship of Congressional Spending Votes

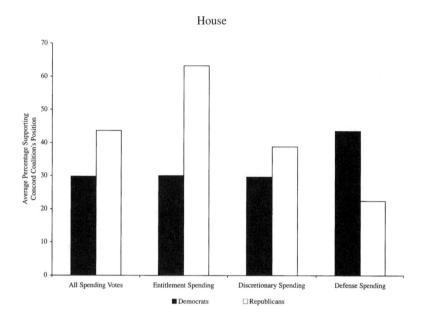

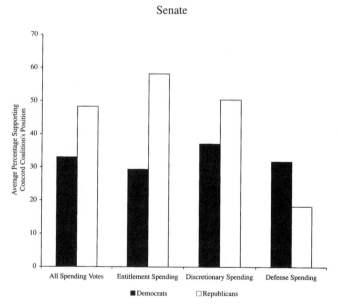

Source: Compiled by author.
Note: Data are for the 104th–107th Congresses (1995–2002).

This suggests that there is no consistent coalition that supports budget cuts across the board. Republicans tend to be more supportive of cuts in the domestic budget, but not in the defense budget. Democrats, on the other hand, tend to be more supportive of cuts in defense, but more opposed to cuts in domestic social programs, especially entitlement spending.

Partisanship is thus an extremely strong predictor of how members of Congress vote on expenditure legislation. This implies that the inability of Congress to produce balanced budgets through spending reductions is not necessarily an inevitable result of the nature of congressional representation. Pork barrel legislation, for example, is an example of spending that would be considered a result of constituency influence, not partisan influence. The fact that partisanship is so dominant, however, denotes that constituency-oriented spending legislation such as earmarks may be less of a factor in congressional voting decisions than is commonly believed. Rather than constituency influence, it appears today that partisan pressure is most prominent in congressional spending decisions. It thus may be the partisan nature of the contemporary congressional budget process that makes cutting spending, and correspondingly balancing the budget, so difficult.

Yet there may also be advantages to a partisan budget process, which must accommodate many conflicting pressures, including pressures from constituencies as well as from within the parties themselves. Budgeting, by its very nature, requires policymakers to think of the well-being of society as a whole. Thus political parties, while they may potentially hinder the budget process, may also be able to encourage a more comprehensive budget process that overcomes the disconnection between taxing and spending.

Notes

1. R. Douglas Arnold, *The Logic of Congressional Action* (New Haven: Yale University Press, 1990).

2. Naomi Caiden, "The Politics of Subtraction," in Allen Schick, ed., *Making Economic Policy in Congress* (Washington, DC: AEI, 1983), p. 103.

3. David A. Stockman, *The Triumph of Politics: Why the Reagan Revolution Failed* (New York: Harper and Row, 1986), p. 401.

4. Patrick Fisher, *Congressional Budgeting: A Representational Perspective* (Lanham: University Press of America, 2005), chap. 7.

5. Gary C. Jacobson, "Deficit-Cutting Politics and Congressional Elections," *Political Science Quarterly* 108 (1993): 375–402.

6. Allen Schick, *The Capacity to Budget* (Washington, DC: Urban Institute, 1990), pp. 111–113.

7. Ibid., p. 128.

8. Aaron Wildavsky and Namoi Caiden, *The New Politics of the Budgetary Process,* 5th ed. (New York: Longman, 2004), chap. 5.

9. Allen Schick, *The Capacity to Budget* (Washington, DC: Urban Institute, 1990), pp. 8–12, 85.

10. Richard Fenno, *The Emergence of a Senate Leader: Pete Domenici and the Reagan Budget* (Washington, DC: Congressional Quarterly, 1991), pp. 44, 134.

11. Anthony Downs, "Why the Government Budget Is Too Small in a Democracy," *World Politics* 12 (1960): 541–563.

12. University of Chicago News Office, "Americans Want to Spend More on Education, Health," January 10, 2007, http://www-news.uchicago .edu/releases/07/070110.gss.shtml.

13. Donald F. Kettl, *Deficit Politics,* 2nd ed. (New York: Longman, 2003), p. 157.

14. David W. Brady and Craig Volden, *Revolving Deadlock,* 2nd ed. (Boulder: Westview, 2006).

15. B. Guy Peters, *The Politics of Taxation* (Cambridge: Blackwell, 1991), p. 74.

16. David A. Super, "The Political Economy of Entitlement," *Columbia Law Review* 104 (2004): 633–729.

17. Kettl, *Deficit Politics,* pp. 65–66.

18. Concord Coalition, "The President's New Fiscal Strategy: Still Out of Balance," *Facing Facts Quarterly* 1 (2005): 1–4.

19. Wildavsky and Caiden, *The New Politics of the Budgetary Process,* pp. 139–140.

20. Schick, *The Capacity to Budget,* pp. 92–93.

21. Irene Rubin, *Balancing the Federal Budget* (New York: Chatham, 2003), p. 49.

22. Congressional Budget Office, *The Fiscal and Economic Outlook: Fiscal Years 2007 to 2016* (Washington, DC, 2006), p. 71.

23. Ibid., p. 10.

24. Ibid., p. 44.

25. Larry M. Bartels, "The American Public's Defense Spending Preferences in the Post–Cold War Era," *Public Opinion Quarterly* 58 (1994): 479–508.

26. Charles V. Pena, "A Reality Check on Military Spending," *Issues in Science and Technology* 21 (2005): 41–48.

27. William Hudson, *American Democracy in Peril,* 5th ed. (Washington, DC: Congressional Quarterly, 2006), chap. 8.

28. Charles V. Pena, "A Reality Check on Military Spending," *Issues in Science and Technology* 21 (2005): 41–48.

29. Christopher Wlezien, "On the Salience of Political Issues: The Problem with 'Most Important Problem,'" *Electoral Studies* 24 (2005): 555–579.

30. Larry M. Bartels, "Constituency Opinion and Congressional Policy Making: The Reagan Defense Buildup," *American Political Science Review* 85 (1991): 457–474.

31. Murray Weidenbaum, "How Much Defense Spending Can We Afford?" *Public Interest* 151 (2003): 52–62.

32. Kettl, *Deficit Politics,* p. 52.

33. Murray Weidenbaum, "How Much Defense Spending Can We Afford?" *Public Interest* 151 (2003): 52–61.

34. Ibid.

35. Peters, *The Politics of Taxation,* pp. 88–89.

36. Peter G. Peterson, *Running on Empty* (New York: Farrar, Straus and Giroux, 2004).

37. David C. Barker and Stephanie T. Muraca, "We're All Keynesians Now? Understanding Public Attitudes Toward the Federal Budget," *American Politics Research* 31 (2003): 485–519.

38. Fisher, *Congressional Budgeting,* chap. 5.

39. Jeffrey M. Stonecash, *Class and Party in American Politics* (Boulder: Westview, 2000).

40. Alberto Alesina and Howard Rosenthal, *Partisan Politics, Divided Government, and the Economy* (New York: Cambridge University Press, 1995).

41. Jacobson, "Deficit-Cutting Politics and Congressional Elections."

42. David G. Levasseur, "The Role of Public Opinion in Policy Argument: An Examination of Public Opinion Rhetoric in the Federal Budget Process," *Argumentation and Advocacy* 41 (2005): 152–167.

43. Tsai-Tsu Su, Mark Kamlet, and David Mowery, "Modeling U.S. Budgetary and Fiscal Policy Outcomes: A Disaggregated Systemwide Perspective," *American Journal of Political Science* 37 (1993): 213–245.

8

DEFICITS AND DEMOCRACY
IN THE UNITED STATES

BUDGETARY OUTCOMES IN DEMOCRACIES ARE INEVITABLY UN-satisfying to most because there are so many players in the process and so many losers in the end. Democracy inevitably makes for messy budgeting. The budget process in the United States, however, is especially untidy. The fragmented nature of US political institutions means that more entities are involved in the process, each with its separate demands. The constitutional design of the US government was simply not designed with the twenty-first century budget in mind. As a result, the federal budget process has been forced to adapt to a changing political environment. Despite the intentions of the constitutional framers, the executive branch has become the dominant player in the budget process. Presidents, however, have generally done an extremely poor job of aligning taxing and spending levels. Unless budgetary dynamics change, deficits in the long run risk overrunning the federal budget, severely limiting the taxing and spending decisions that future generations of US policymakers will be able to make. This in turn will make it more difficult to reduce the increase in economic inequality in the United States.

The Federal Budget Deficit

Ultimately, the disconnection between taxing and spending is problematic for the federal government because spending levels tend to be consistently higher than tax revenues. Chronically large deficits are the obvious indicator that the budget process has gone awry. A structural deficit is one that is endemic to the system, while a cyclical deficit is one that is caused by a temporary downturn in the economy. The deficit in the United States has clearly become a structural deficit. Occasional deficits are not necessarily bad, but persistent deficits are a cause for concern and most economists and policymakers believe that balancing the budget needs to be combined with flexibility in order to respond to changing needs or to downturns in the economy.[1]

To a significant degree, large deficits are the result of the disconnection between taxing and spending decisions. Americans have very different views about whether they prefer the federal government to both tax and spend at 15 percent of GDP or at 30 percent of GDP. Both options are legitimate politically and neither will wreck the economy. Yet if the federal government taxes at 15 percent of GDP and spends at 30 percent, the results would certainly be economically devastating, because the national debt would overwhelm the budget.[2] Nothing, however, legally prevents the federal government from adopting such taxing and spending policies. The federal government, unlike most state governments, can borrow to fund budget deficits. Federal budget deficits, however, are potentially limited by the statutory debt limit. The statutory debt limit, which originated in legislation passed in 1917, requires Congress and the president to set an upper limit on the size of the public debt. Once the debt limit is reached, it is illegal for the US Treasury to borrow new funds. The debt limit, therefore, can be a means to control the growth of the debt. In reality, however, when the ceiling is reached, the limit is raised—this has been done more than sixty times since 1941, rendering the limit practically meaningless.[3]

Historically, the belief that the federal government should balance its budget has been a dominating and stable conviction in US politics.[4] From a historical perspective, the deficits that the nation has been facing over the past three decades are unprecedented. From the nation's founding until the 1930s, the balanced budget rule was adhered to almost religiously, except in times of war and recession. Every year from 1866 to 1893, in fact, the federal government produced budget surpluses. In part, these surpluses were due to the fact that tax policy after the Civil War was dictated not by revenue requirements as much as by the federal government's imposition of high tariffs on imported goods to protect domestic industries. Nonetheless, the post–Civil War surpluses demonstrate the degree to which the balanced budget norm dominated the US political landscape.[5]

By the 1970s, however, after 180 years of generally balanced budgets, large federal deficits became the standard, and a historical abnormality. The transition to large and chronic deficits beginning in the 1970s was largely a result of nondefense spending growth due to the expansion of entitlement benefits (particularly Medicare and Medicaid). While spending levels increased substantially beginning in the 1970s, revenue levels did not, leading to large deficits.

The US government is not unique in running deficits. Most industrialized democracies have tended to run budget deficits in the post–World War II period, because they have found it easier to spend than to tax. Even though governments have the power to tax, summoning the will to tax is often a stumbling block that prevents more balanced budgets. Governments historically have encountered difficulty in mustering the will to levy new or increased taxes, and this tendency appears to have proliferated in the 1970s.[6] At the same time, it is easy and politically desirable for governments to spend money. As a society becomes more economically prosperous, its institutions tend to become more complex and inevitably become too rigid.[7] Thus there are biases in the political and economic systems of modern industrial democracies that tend to drive budgetary outcomes toward deficits.

Though most industrial democracies tend to run deficits, however, deficit levels in the United States in recent years have tended to be considerably larger than those found in most other countries. As Figure 8.1 demonstrates, among industrialized democracies in 2007, only Japan and Italy had larger projected deficits as a percentage of GDP than the United States. The Nordic countries of Denmark, Sweden, and Finland provide an interesting contrast to the United States. All had budget surpluses of more than 2 percent of GDP in 2007, and all have significantly higher tax rates than the United States. This suggests that deficits in the United States may be a product of the political inability to tax enough to meet citizens' spending demands. Regardless, the fact that a number of other nations are currently producing large budget surpluses indicates that deficits are not necessarily inherent to democracies. Specific characteristics unique to democracy in the United States, therefore, may make the country relatively more deficit-prone. Economists across the political spectrum overwhelmingly argue that large budget deficits and the accumulation of a large national debt undermine the fiscal integrity of the federal government. Large deficits, it is believed, will either drive down domestic investment or be financed increasingly by capital inflow from abroad, decreasing living standards of American citizens.[8]

Figure 8.1 General Government Budget Balance, 2007

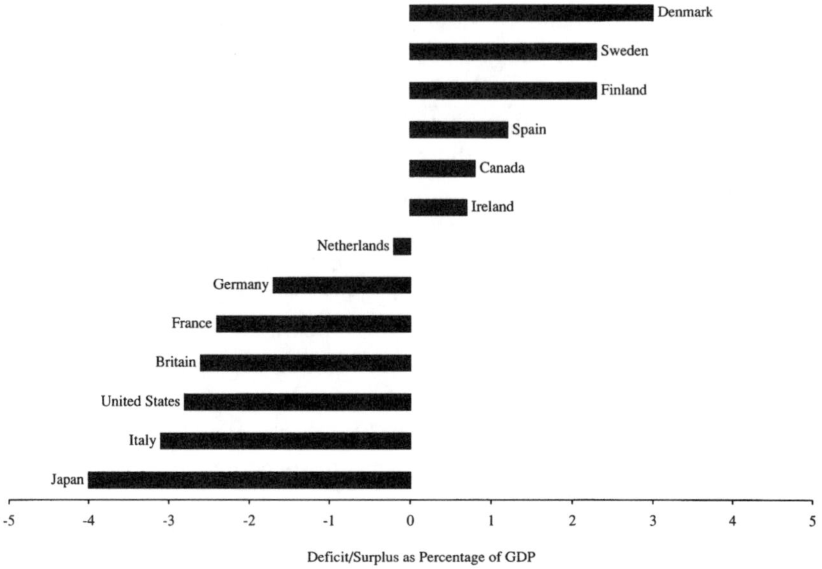

Deficit/Surplus as Percentage of GDP

Source: Organization for Economic Cooperation and Development.

The accumulation of large deficits on a regular basis further burdens taxpayers and undermines future living standards. Since an increase in government debt is effectively equivalent to a future increase in tax liabilities, an increase in the federal debt is not judged to be an addition to private wealth.[9] As a consequence of large and continuous borrowing, net interest comprised more than 8 percent of all federal expenditures in the United States by 2007. Since the 1990s, the federal government has been paying on average about $200 billion in interest per year, up from $53 billion in 1980. Interest payments depend not just on the amount of the debt but on interest rates as well. Since the US Treasury borrows about three-fourths of the debt in medium- and long-term securities (mainly with maturities of two to ten years, but up to thirty years for some bonds), the rate it pays on the debt is a hybrid of current and past market interest rates. It has been estimated that the deficit will reduce average annual household income by $1,800 by 2014.[10] Publicly held debt is expected to increase from 35 percent of GDP today to 72 percent by 2020, and to a staggering 295 percent by 2040.[11] With no policy changes, federal deficits will expand dramatically as a share of GDP, and it is possible that the debt could become so large that the economy will implode.[12]

The fact that the US government is paying such enormous sums just to meet the interest on the national debt does not bode well for future generations of Americans. Large deficits, unless their interest payments are effectively reduced or denied to creditors by the future effects of inflation, will finance current government consumption at the expense of future government spending. That is, instead of buying services, a larger and larger proportion of future citizens' taxes will go toward interest payments. Many Republicans fear that this will eventually result in higher taxes for future generations, while many Democrats fear that interest payments will displace social spending.

Thus, efforts to reduce the deficit will not only impinge on other spending, but also diminish a major portion of available resources in the future. Larger deficits make it politically more difficult to expand government programs, even when there is a broad consensus to do so.[13] Chronic large budget deficits, therefore, have the potential to tie the hands of future policymakers for years to come.

The adverse economic impact of budget deficits is probably most frequently associated with the phenomenon known as "crowding out," which in general refers to the effects of expansionary fiscal actions on private sector spending—the offsetting changes in private investment and consumption of outlays that result when an expansionary fiscal action acts to raise the interest rate.[14] Crowding out is based on the most widely agreed premise of modern economic analysis: when the demand for any commodity rises, and its supply does not, the price will increase. According to the crowding out argument, when the Treasury borrows it floods the market with various forms of government bonds and, in so doing, according to the argument, pushes market interest rate yields above what they otherwise would be. It has been estimated that a family with a $250,000 thirty-year mortgage pays an additional $2,000 annually in interest due to the national debt.[15] Given these higher interest rates, consumers buy fewer homes and automobiles, meaning jobs and income are lost in both of those industries. Higher interest rates also discourage firms from investing in new facilities and equipment, as well as diminish savings that could be used to start new businesses.[16]

Another problem with large deficits is their effect on monetary policy, especially their inflationary impact on the economy. If the deficit is financed not by borrowing from the financial markets but simply by printing more money, there is a greater likelihood of inflation.[17] The sharp decline in inflation during the 1980s despite the tripling of the deficit, however, implies that inflation is not simply a result of deficits.[18] In order to stem inflation, the Federal Reserve is more likely to adopt a tight monetary policy when the deficit is large, which in turn results in less money being available for loans and lower tax revenues coming to government. Deficits and tight monetary policy thus can drive up interest rates and discourage private investment, hurting credit-sensitive industries.[19] The unpredictable reaction of the markets to increased deficits is also a significant concern.[20]

An additional common criticism of deficits is that the cost of borrowing to pay for the activities of the government has led the United States to rely heavily on foreign countries to finance its national debt. Traditionally, the federal debt has been owed to Americans—the public sector owing the private sector. Today, however, much of the interest on the national debt is now paid to foreigners, whose resources play an important role in keeping the US government solvent. Investors from other countries annually purchase more than $230 billion in US Treasury securities, with investors in Japan, China, and the United Kingdom having the largest holdings.[21] As Figure 8.2 demonstrates, today's deficits are funded in large part by overseas borrowing. The percentage of the US national debt that is owned by foreigners is now more than triple what it was during the early 1980s.

Figure 8.2 Percentage of the National Debt Held by the Public but Owned by Foreigners, 1980–2007

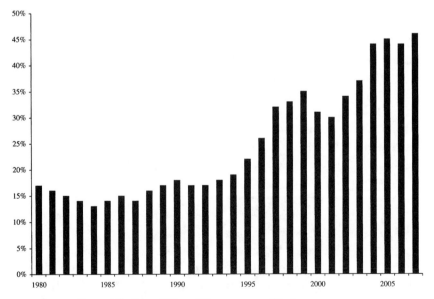

Sources: Concord Coalition; Office of Management and Budget.

The economic impact of public debt may become greater if a large percentage is held by other countries, or by the citizens of other countries.[22] If the borrowed money is not producing substantial economic growth, then the long-term consequences could be hazardous. The debtor nation becomes dependent upon its creditors and to some degree must tailor its policies to ensure a stable environment for borrowing. The economy also becomes vulnerable to rapid movements of capital out of the country. Borrowing from abroad means that debt interest must be paid abroad; rather than being just an internal transfer of funds, it becomes a net loss to the economy. Increased reliance on foreign capital to finance deficits means that decisions of foreign interests have a greater impact on the US economy and give foreign investors a larger claim of future economic resources.

In order to reduce a budget deficit, policymakers must raise taxes, cut spending, or hope that economic growth outpaces the growth of spending. The political battles over deficit reduction have tended to center on the degree to which spending should be reduced or taxes increased. Republicans (rhetorically at least) tend to favor spending cuts, while Democrats, in an effort to prevent cuts to federal programs they favor, often support tax increases. Democrats tend to favor maintaining as much social spending as possible even if that means higher taxes. Republicans, on the other hand, desire lower taxes more than social spending (though they tend to support spending on defense). Thus, Democrats favor relatively high expenditures and high revenues, while Republicans favor relatively low expenditures and low revenues. Balancing the budget at lower levels of expenditures and revenues is quite different than at higher levels.

Potentially, an effectively executed expansionary monetary policy could be combined with a policy of deficit reduction. If monetary expansion were sufficiently strong, interest rates could be pushed downward. In turn, consumer spending and investment would probably rise, pushing up GDP, which in turn would elevate tax revenues. With downward pressure on interest rates, government debt service requirements for new and refinanced debt would also decline.[23] It is much more likely, however, that future efforts to reduce the deficit will have to lean on tax increases and spending cuts. There are simply too many powerful interests (such as the banking industry) aligned against monetary expansion.

The fact that deficit reduction measures appear to be so painful leads some to suggest that the cure may be worse than the disease. Given the serious potential consequences of large deficits, however, it becomes critical for the nation's leaders to work toward reducing the national debt. Since the regular legislative process seems incapable of dealing with the future implications of the budget, it has been suggested that a commission be established to suggest the compromises that are necessary for the long-term economic health of the country.[24] Regardless of how they do it, policymakers must act if they are to prevent the national debt from overwhelming future generations.

Deficits and Separation of Powers

Since Congress is a decentralized body of 535 members, it often appears weak compared to the executive branch, which speaks with one voice. The president has gradually taken on increasing budgetary power while Congress has often seemed unable to gain control over its own diverse institutional self-interests. The institutional advantages of the executive branch, combined with the tremendous rise in scope of the federal government, have resulted in the president becoming the dominant force in the budget process.

Conflict between the branches is still an inevitable aspect of federal budgeting, just as the constitutional framers intended. Many hold that the budget inefficiencies inherent in the US political system are the costs of democracy, whatever the merits of separation of powers. The budgetary rivalries inherent in separation of powers can be seen in the fact that the United States has two budget offices (a feature unique to US democracy)—the Congressional Budget Office (CBO) and the Office of Management and Budget (OMB). The CBO was created by the Congressional Budget Act of 1974 as part of a post-Watergate attempt to limit the power of the executive branch. The CBO was intended to keep a watchful eye over the OMB, which is lodged in the White House. The CBO has guarded its apolitical nature fiercely, hiring an ideologically diverse staff and refraining from public punditry that might cast doubt on its independence.[25]

Congress was designed with the assumption that members would fight for their institution and that budget powers would be especially dear to the hearts of legislators.[26] Prior to 1921, the president's role in determining national budget policy was relatively minimal. With the Budget and Accounting Act of 1921, however, Congress delegated to the president its traditional powers over compiling the preliminary draft of the budget. The shift of taxing and spending powers from Congress to the president goes against the core belief of the constitutional framers that each branch of government would protect its own prerogatives. The framers believed that institutional self-defense would safeguard separation of powers and give life and energy to the system of checks and balances, a model that worked for more than a century. Congress used to be much more central to taxing and decisions than it is today. The committee system, especially the prerogatives attached to Ways and Means and Appropriations before 1974, provided the political insulation necessary to forge the artful compromises that the budget requires. These committees exercised broad control over the budget—they were responsible not only for taxes and tariffs, but also for appropriations and banking and currency.[27]

Budgetary delegation of power is at the heart of the complexities of representation. In an attempt to please their constituents, members of Congress try to direct federal dollars to their respective states while at the same time trying to avoid blame for large deficits. This dilemma encourages Congress to delegate power to the president. This delegation of power to the president, however, has not necessarily improved the budget process, because the executive branch's national budgets are just as deficit-prone as those of Congress.[28] Due to the increase in deficits in the 1980s, members of Congress debated measures to increase the president's power to rescind appropriated funds, including a line-item veto. Ironically, it can be argued that it was an irresponsible budget proposed by the president in 1981 that led to intolerable annual deficits, yet Congress decided to reward the president with additional budgetary powers anyway.

The president is unique in that he is elected from a national constituency. As such, the president is expected to follow the pulse of national public opinion in ways that members of Congress do not. That, coupled with the fact that the president is now expected to be the primary force behind the nation's taxing and spending policies, suggests that presidential budget priorities will be determined in the context of national public opinion. Yet there are inevitably political biases in the distribution of spending. The federal budget is affected by presidential politics. States that heavily supported the incumbent president tend to receive more funds, while marginal and swing states are not rewarded. Presidents, therefore, are engaged in tactical distribution of federal funds.[29]

With the increased budget responsibilities of the executive branch, expectations have been raised considerably. Clearly, the public holds the president responsible for economic performance and the size of the deficit. One study, for example, found that under divided government, the electorate places economic responsibility on the president and largely absolves Congress, regardless of economic conditions.[30] At the same time, the size of the deficit that the federal government produces can be expected to have an important effect on what the president can propose to do, especially in regard to taxes. Thus, not only does presidential tax policy affect the size of the deficit, but the size of the deficit also affects presidential tax policy.

Given the importance of the presidential role in the budget process, it is fair to conclude that the White House plays a significant role in determining whether or not the federal government produces a budgetary deficit or surplus, though certainly many factors (the state of the economy, congressional priorities) are beyond the control of the presidency. Who the president is thus has a major impact on budgetary outcomes. Electoral cycles in fiscal balance are thus a feature of the US economy.

Presidential policy, therefore, may be held to blame for large deficits.[31] An analysis of deficit and surplus totals by presidential administration shows that Democrats tend to do a better job of producing smaller budget deficits than Republicans. Since the Lyndon Johnson administration, deficits as a percentage of GDP have tended to be significantly higher under Republican administrations (see Figure 8.3).

Figure 8.3 Deficits by Presidential Administration

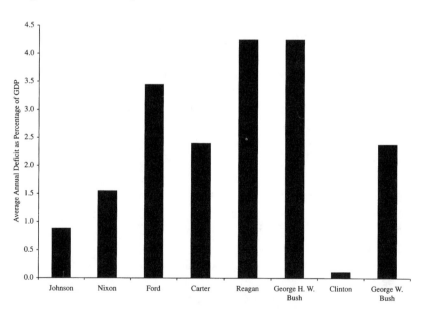

Sources: Compiled by author from Congressional Budget Office data.
Note: Data for George W. Bush adminstration through fiscal year 2007.

Deficits under Democratic presidents since 1965 have averaged 0.88 percent of GDP, compared to 3.13 percent under Republican administrations (see Figure 8.4). These figures strongly support the contention that Democratic administrations are consistently more fiscally responsible than Republican administrations.[32] Making it easier for Democratic presidential administrations to produce smaller deficits is the fact that economic growth tends to be greater with a Democrat in the White House.

Presidents, of course, do not produce budgets in a vacuum. Congress, after all, has the final say in whether or not a budget is eventually enacted, and as a result the White House must consider potential congressional support when constructing budgets. Especially important in this regard is whether or not the president's party has majorities in the House and the Senate, which has been an increasingly rare occurrence since the 1950s.

Divided government may make it more difficult to balance the budget because the president and Congress cannot agree on priorities. Partisanship in Congress may be reinforced by the prevalence of divided government. Divided government creates incentives for Congress to employ so-called wedge issues in order to damage the opposing

Figure 8.4 Deficits by Presidential Party

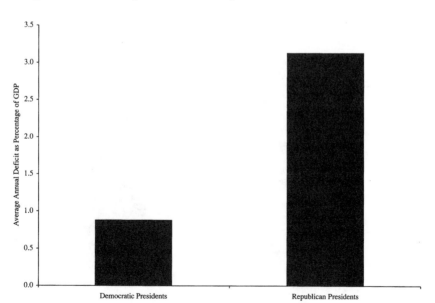

Source: Compiled by author from Congressional Budget Office data for fiscal years 1965–2007.

party in future elections.[33] As a result, divided government may re-inforce the differences in budgetary priorities between the parties. It has been argued, for example, that the large budget deficits from 1981 to 1992 were the outcome of conflicting party preferences under divided control of the federal government.[34] If the president and Congress cannot reach agreement, then an imbalance between taxing and spending will result. Depending on factors such as the state of the economy, either deficits or surpluses are likely under a divided government that cannot reach a budgetary consensus.[35]

Evidence suggests, however, that divided government does not necessarily lead to larger deficits. The George H. W. Bush and Bill Clinton tax increases (in 1990 and 1993, respectively), for example, are both widely regarded as policies that successfully led to deficit reduction; one was produced by divided government, the other by unified government.[36] And since 1965, overall deficit levels during periods of divided government have been only slightly higher than deficit levels during periods of unified government. The average budget deficit under divided governments from 1965 to 2007 was 2.45 percent of GDP, while the average budget deficit under unified governments was 1.87 percent of GDP (see Figure 8.5).

Figure 8.5 Deficits by Type of Government

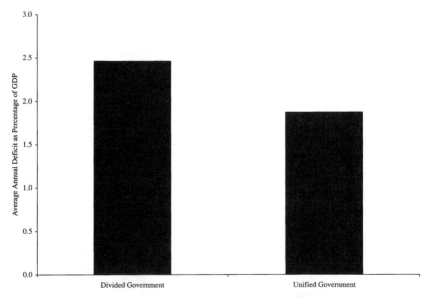

Source: Compiled by author from Congressional Budget Office data for fiscal years 1965–2007.

The federal government has largely adapted to the new budgeting realities by shifting budgeting power to the president. When measured on the basis of balancing the budget, however, the performance of many recent presidents has been dismal. Congress has become so overwhelmed by the budget process that it continues to give up considerable power, though it still has an important role to play. Congress too often influences the budget in negative ways by pressuring for more spending and lower taxes, which leads to larger deficits. Congress needs to actively thwart the excesses of presidential taxing and spending priorities. This is exactly what the nation's architects had in mind in 1787 when designing the Constitution.

Deficits and Inequality

The degree of economic inequality in the United States demonstrates the significant consequences of taxing and spending decisions. Inequality has increasingly become a focal point in the comparative study of advanced capitalist political economies over the past decade.[37] In most affluent countries since the 1980s, there has been a sizable increase in market household inequality.[38] This increase in economic inequality has been especially noticeable in the United States, where it has been shaped by federal budget policy over the past four decades. Taxing and spending decisions directly affect the distribution of wealth in the United States. Economic inequality can be reduced—or increased—by the taxing and spending choices that government makes. Large deficits limit these taxing and spending choices, making it more difficult for the United States to become economically egalitarian.

Figure 8.6 displays the Gini Index for the United States from 1915 to 2007. The index ranges from 0 for no economic inequality to 1 for complete economic inequality. From 1915 through 1940, there was discernible inequality in the distribution of income in the United States, which increased with the Great Depression. World War II and the sustained postwar economic growth, however, significantly reduced inequality. This post–World War II decline in inequality was the result of an increase in real incomes that was experienced disproportionately by lower-income groups. At the same time that inequality was declining, government was simultaneously enacting policies (such as increasing funds for the food stamp program, creating Medicare and Medicaid, and creating the Pell Grant program) designed to create a safety net and reduce economic risk.[39]

Figure 8.6 Inequality in the Distribution of Income, 1915–2007

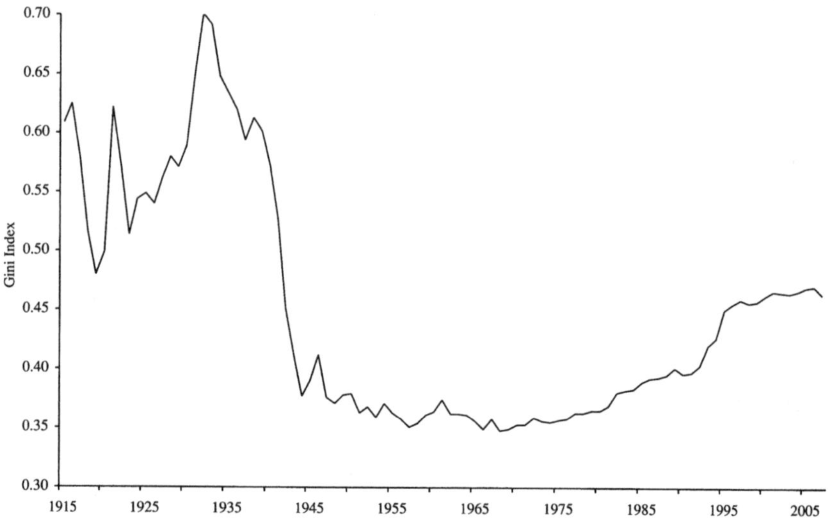

Source: US Census Bureau.

Note: The Gini Index is a measure of statistical dispersion used as a measure of inequality of income. It is defined as a ratio with values between 0 and 1 where the numerator is the area between the Lorenz curve of the distribution and the uniform distribution line, and the denominator is the area under the uniform distribution line. Thus a higher Gini coefficient indicates more unequal distribution.

In the 1970s, however, the affluent began to experience significant growth in incomes while the less affluent realized no income growth, resulting in an unmistakable rise in inequality. At the same time, the advent of large budget deficits—which resulted as a direct consequence of the disconnection between taxing and spending decisions—limited government's ability to address the increase of inequality. This rising inequality since the 1970s has been due to a number of economic divides in American society, including differences in the quality of (and access to) education, health care, and pensions.[40] Inequality has also left an undeniable impact on American politics, with class divisions increasingly influencing Americans' vote choice.[41]

What level of inequality is acceptable is inevitably a political question. Historically, Democrats have placed a greater priority on reducing inequality than have their more individualistic Republican counterparts. Not only have the policies of Democratic administrations been significantly more effective than the policies of Republican administrations in generating economic growth, but Democratic presidents have also been more successful in distributing the benefits of economic growth broadly to people across the economic spectrum (see Figure 8.7). Under Democratic presidents, income growth from 1948 to 2005 was fairly egalitarian, with average real growth rates ranging from 2.6 percent for families at the twentieth percentile to 2.2 percent for families at the eightieth percentile. Under Republican presidents, affluent families fared about as well as they did during Democratic administrations, but middle-class and poor families fared markedly worse.[42] Economic growth during Republican administrations, therefore, has not tended to "trickle down" toward the less affluent, and the result has been a noticeable increase of inequality during Republican presidencies. The higher deficits of Republican administrations have corresponded with an increase of inequality, while the relatively lower deficits of Democratic administrations have been accompanied by a more egalitarian distribution of economic growth.

It has been argued that economic inequality is part of the established order and that political elites do not want to pursue a more egalitarian distribution of wealth.[43] Inequality, of course, is inevitable

Figure 8.7 Income Growth by Income Level: Democratic vs. Republican Presidents

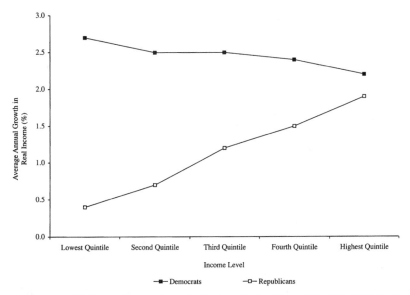

Sources: US Census Bureau; Larry M. Bartels, "Is the Water Rising? Reflections on Inequality and American Democracy," *Political Science and Politics* 39 (2006): 39–42.
Note: Data are for fiscal years 1948–2005.

to some degree in a capitalist system. The US political system, how-ever, may make inequality more problematic. A nation's electoral system plays a key role in redistribution, because it shapes the nature of political parties and the composition of governing coalitions. Pro-portional representation systems redistribute more wealth than ma-joritarian systems, because center-left governments are dominant in proportional representation systems while center-right governments are dominant under majoritarian systems.[44] The institutional biases fermenting inequality may also be more pronounced than they used to be. The political resources that voters need to ensure responsive-ness to budget priorities have eroded over the past couple of decades. The decline of unions and locally rooted Democratic Party organiza-tions, along with widespread disillusionment with the political process, has left lower- and middle-income citizens dependent on media cover-age that rarely focuses on inequality and the long-term consequences of large deficits.[45]

The question of inequality in a democracy, then, becomes one of acceptable levels of inequality.[46] This of course has major political implications. An increase of economic inequality, for example, has been found to be both a cause and a consequence of increased parti-san polarization.[47] There is widespread recognition of the growing economic inequality in the contemporary United States. In 2002, for example, almost 75 percent of respondents said the difference in in-comes between the rich and poor was larger than twenty years ear-lier, and more than 40 percent said it was much larger.[48]

Despite the increase of inequality, however, greater redistribution of wealth through taxation has not occurred. The median-income voter's incentive to redistribute wealth has simply not increased even as overall economic inequality has risen.[49] The tax code has clearly become much less progressive. The nation's 400 wealthiest taxpayers pay 17.5 percent of their total incomes in federal tax. Sixty years ago, this figure was 78 percent.[50]

Though clearly related to tax policy, the fact that the United States has the highest overall level of inequality of any wealthy nation is also a product of spending policy. Public income transfers have been found to be a powerful tool in equalizing income distribution.[51] The relatively high level of inequality in the United States is not due to demography (single parents, immigrants, elders), but rather is a re-sult of the structure of US political institutions and the lack of spend-ing effort on behalf of low-income working families. Government policies and social spending in the United States do not have as much effect as they do in other rich nations, and both low spending and low wages have a significant impact on final income distribution, especially among the nonelderly.[52]

The Outmoded Practice of Taxing and Spending

The federal government's current spending and taxing policies are not serving the United States well. Its policies are simply not intended to create a comprehensive budget for a nation of more than 300 million people. Since taxing and spending decisions are largely made separately from each other, chronic budget deficits have become prevalent. There is shockingly little long-term planning associated with the federal budget, and as a result the country is ill-prepared for the future.

Voters are inclined to see a disjunction between taxing and spending, but the US system encourages the perception to an unusual degree. The structure of government gives few if any elected officials an institutional stake in linking revenues and spending. On the contrary, the structure of the federal government, and the evolution of separate revenue and appropriations functions, reward leaders who act as if these functions are disconnected. The economic philosophies of supply-side conservatives, the growth of sound-bite journalism, and the bitter partisanship of the past three decades have converted federal budgeting into an endemically dysfunctional process.

Tax policy in the United States is largely one of inertia. It is extremely difficult to alter tax policy to accommodate changing needs and circumstances. Since it is politically much easier to cut taxes than to raise taxes, if tax policy is altered at all it tends to be downward. There may be good economic and political arguments for reducing taxes, but without simultaneous spending reductions, tax cuts will result in larger budget deficits. Since Ronald Reagan's election as president in 1980, tax cuts have been disproportionately targeted toward the wealthy. As a result, federal taxes have become significantly less progressive, resulting in the highest level of economic inequality since the 1930s. Tax cut–driven deficits, therefore, have made it more difficult to reduce inequality in the United States.

Spending policy in the United States is made piecemeal, with little regard to how spending affects the budget. The separation of taxing and spending policy encourages higher expenditure levels relative to revenues, leading to deficit-plagued budgets. The future of spending policy looks even more problematic, with the high projected costs of the popular Social Security and Medicare entitlement programs potentially overwhelming the budget, making it difficult to spend on other programs or to reduce taxes in an economically sound manner. Without policy changes, there will be extremely little flexibility in adjusting spending priorities in the future. While projected entitlement spending is too high, domestic discretionary spending may very well be too low. As a result, programs designed to help the economically disadvantaged may be limited in the future, further increasing economic inequality in the country. Future generations of Americans are potentially having their budgetary priorities dictated to them in advance by the lack of foresight of today's policymakers.

Public policy in the United States can be greatly affected by even the smallest taxing and spending alterations. Yet the US political system is not designed in a way that makes producing a comprehensive budget easy. The process of taxing and spending in the twenty-first century requires significant alterations in the way budgets are produced. Under democracy in the United States, taxing and spending decisions are too often made separately from each another. Ultimately, however, tax policy impacts spending policy and vice versa. The trick for policymakers is to examine the big picture, looking at taxing decisions in the context of spending decisions.

Notes

1. Irene Rubin, *Balancing the Federal Budget* (New York: Chatham, 2003), pp. 23–24.

2. Peter G. Peterson, *Running on Empty* (New York: Farrar, Straus and Giroux, 2004).

3. Gary R. Evans, *Red Ink: The Budget, Deficit, and Debt of the U.S. Government* (San Diego: Academic Press, 1997), p. 17.

4. Gary Anderson, "The U.S. Federal Deficit and National Debt: A Political and Economic History," in James Buchanan, Charles Rowley, and Robert Tollison, eds., *Deficits* (New York: Blackwell, 1987), pp. 9–35.

5. Dennis S. Ippolito, *Why Budgets Matter: Budget Policy and American Politics* (University Park: Pennsylvania State University Press, 2003).

6. B. Guy Peters, *The Politics of Taxation* (Cambridge: Blackwell, 1991), p. 112.

7. Mancur Olson, *The Rise and Decline of Nations* (New Haven: Yale University Press, 1982).

8. Joseph White and Aaron Wildavsky, *The Deficit and the Public Interest* (Berkeley: University of California Press, 1989).

9. R. J. Barro, "Are Government Bonds Net Wealth?" *Journal of Political Economy* 82 (1974): 1095–1117.

10. Alice Rivlin and Isabel Sawhill, "How to Balance the Budget," March 1, 2004, http://www.urban.org/url.cfm?id=1000641.

11. "GAO's Long-Term Budget Scenario," *Facing Facts Quarterly: A Report About Entitlements and the Budget from the Concord Coalition* 2 (October 2006): 4.

12. Peterson, *Running on Empty,* p. 34.

13. John Cranford, *Budgeting for America,* 2nd ed. (Washington, DC: Congressional Quarterly, 1989), p. 14.

14. Richard Cebula, *The Deficit Problem in Perspective* (Lexington, MA: Heath, 1987), p. 7.

15. Rivlin and Sawhill, "How to Balance the Budget."

16. Cebula, *The Deficit Problem in Perspective,* pp. 4–5.

17. Peters, *The Politics of Taxation,* p. 129.

18. Robert Sahr, "Using Inflation-Adjusted Dollars in Analyzing Political Developments," *Political Science and Politics* 37 (2004): 273–284.

19. John Kenneth Galbraith, "The Bust and the Bust," in Richard Fink and Jack High, eds., *A Nation in Debt* (Frederick, MD: University Publications, 1987), pp. 136–142.

20. White and Wildavsky, *The Deficit and the Public Interest,* p. 529.

21. Congressional Budget Office, *The Fiscal and Economic Outlook: Fiscal Years 2007 to 2016* (Washington, DC, 2006), p. 18.

22. Peters, *The Politics of Taxation,* p. 107.

23. Cebula, *The Deficit Problem in Perspective,* p. 98.

24. Bob Kerrey and Warren Rudman, "Securing Future Fiscal Health," *Washington Post,* Monday 28, 2006, p. A15.

25. Franklin Foer, "The Closing of the Presidential Mind," *New Republic,* July 5, 2004, pp. 17–20.

26. Jasmine Farrier, *Passing the Buck: Congress, the Budget, and Deficits* (Lexington: University Press of Kentucky, 2004), pp. 223–224.

27. Louis Fisher, *Congressional Abdication on War and Spending* (College Station: Texas A&M Press, 2000).

28. Farrier, *Passing the Buck,* pp. 223–224; Fisher, *Congressional Abdication on War and Spending.*

29. Valentino Larcinese, Leonzio Rizzo, and Cecilia Testa, "Allocating the U.S. Federal Budget to the States: The Impact of the President," *Journal of Politics* 68 (2006): 447–456.

30. Helmut Norpoth, "Divided Government and Economic Voting," *Journal of Politics* 63 (2001): 414–435.

31. Iwan W. Morgan, *Deficit Government* (Chicago: Ivan R. Dee, 1995).

32. John W. Burns and Andrew J. Taylor, "A New Democrat? The Economic Performance of the Clinton Presidency," *Independent Review* 5 (2001): 387–408.

33. Melody Rose, "Divided Government and the Rise of Social Regulation," *Policy Studies Journal* 29 (2001): 611–626.

34. Gary Jacobson, *Electoral Origins of Divided Government* (Boulder: Westview, 1990), p. 379.

35. Morris Fiorina, *Divided Government,* 2nd ed. (Boston: Allyn and Bacon, 1996).

36. Ibid., pp. 169–170.

37. Lane Kenworthy and Jonas Pontusson, "Rising Inequality and the Politics of Redistribution in Affluent Countries," *Perspectives on Politics* 3 (2005): 449–471.

38. Ibid.

39. Mark D. Brewer and Jeffrey M. Stonecash, *Split: Class and Cultural Divides in American Politics* (Washington, DC: Congressional Quarterly, 2007), pp. 24–26.

40. Ibid., chap. 2.

41. Jeffrey M. Stonecash, "The Income Gap," *Political Science and Politics* 39 (2006): 461–465.

42. Larry M. Bartels, "Is the Water Rising? Reflections on Inequality and American Democracy," *Political Science and Politics* 39 (2006): 39–42.

43. Murray Edelman, *Politics as Symbolic Action* (Chicago: Markham, 1971).

44. Torben Iversen and David Soskice, "Electoral Institutions and the Politics of Coalitions: Why Some Democracies Redistribute More Than Others," *American Political Science Review* 100 (2006): 165–181.

45. Jacob S. Hacker and Paul Pierson, "Abandoning the Middle: The Bush Tax Cuts and the Limits of Democratic Control," *Perspectives on Politics* 3 (2005): 33–53.

46. Sam Pizzigati, "Must Wealth Always Concentrate?" *Good Society* 14 (2005): 63–67.

47. Nolan McCarty, Keith Pools, and Howard Rosenthal, *Polarized America: The Dance of Ideology and Unequal Riches* (Cambridge: Massachusetts Institute of Technology Press, 2006), chap. 3.

48. American National Election Studies, "The 2002 American Election Study Dataset."

49. McCarty, Poole, and Rosenthal, *Polarized America,* chap. 4.

50. Pizzigati, "Must Wealth Always Concentrate?"

51. Martha Ozawa and Wang Yeong-Tsyr, "Distributive Effects of Benefits and Taxes," *Social Work Research* 18 (1994): 149–162.

52. Timothy M. Smeeding, "Public Policy, Economic Inequality, and Poverty: The United States in Comparative Perspective," *Social Science Quarterly* 86 (2005): 955–983.

BIBLIOGRAPHY

Alesina, Alberto, and Howard Rosenthal. 1995. *Partisan Politics, Divided Government, and the Economy* (New York: Cambridge University Press).

Alt, James E., and David Dreyer Lassen. 2006. "Transparency, Political Polarization, and Political Budget Cycles in OECD Countries." *American Journal of Political Science* 50: 530–550.

Anderson, Gary. 1987. "The U.S. Federal Deficit and National Debt: A Political and Economic History." In James Buchanan, Charles Rowley, and Robert Tollison, eds., *Deficits* (New York: Blackwell), pp. 9–35.

Anderson, Gerald F., Peter S. Hussey, Bianca K. Frogner, and Hugh R. Waters. 2005. "Health Spending in the United States and the Rest of the Industrialized World." *Health Affairs* 24: 903–914.

Arnold, R. Douglas. 1990. *The Logic of Congressional Action* (New Haven: Yale University Press).

Barker, David C., and Stephanie T. Muraca. 2003. "'We're All Keynesians Now'? Understanding Public Attitudes Toward the Federal Budget." *American Politics Research* 31: 485–519.

Barro, R. J. 1974. "Are Government Bonds Net Wealth?" *Journal of Political Economy* 82: 1095–1117.

Bartels, Larry M. 1991. "Constituency Opinion and Congressional Policy Making: The Reagan Defense Buildup." *American Political Science Review* 85: 457–474.

———. 1994. "The American Public's Defense Spending Preferences in the Post–Cold War Era." *Public Opinion Quarterly* 58: 479–508.

———. 2005. "Homer Gets a Tax Cut: Inequality and Public Policy in the American Mind." *Perspectives on Politics* 3: 15–31.

———. 2006. "Is the Water Rising? Reflections on Inequality and American Democracy." *Political Science and Politics* 39: 39–42.

Bassinger, Scott J., and Mark Hallerberg. 2004. "Remodeling the Competition for Capital: How Domestic Politics Erases the Race to the Bottom." *American Political Science Review* 98: 261–276.

Berkman, Michael S. 1993. *The State Roots of National Politics: Congress and the Tax Agenda, 1978–1986* (Pittsburgh: University of Pittsburgh Press).

Bickers, Kenneth, and Robert Stein. 2000. "The Congressional Pork Barrel in a Republican Era." *Journal of Politics* 62: 1070–1086.

Birnbaum, Jefferey H., and Alan S. Murray. 1987. *Showdown at Gucci Gulch* (New York: Random House).

Brady, David W., and Craig Volden. 2006. *Revolving Deadlock,* 2nd ed. (Boulder: Westview).

Brewer, Mark D., and Jeffrey M. Stonecash. 2007. *Split: Class and Cultural Divides in American Politics* (Washington, DC: Congressional Quarterly).

Brownlee, W. Elliot. 2004. *Federal Taxation in America: A Short History,* 2nd ed. (New York: Cambridge University Press).

Buchanan, James. 1977. "Why Does Government Grow?" In Thomas Borcherding, ed., *Budgets and Bureaucrats: The Sources of Government Growth* (Durham: Duke University Press), pp. 3–18.

Burns, John W., and Andrew J. Taylor. 2000. "The Mythical Causes of the Republican Supply-Side Economics Revolution." *Party Politics* 6: 419–440.

———. "A New Democrat? The Economic Performance of the Clinton Presidency." *Independent Review* 5: 387–408.

Caiden, Naomi. 1983. "The Politics of Subtraction." In Allen Schick, ed., *Making Economic Policy in Congress* (Washington, DC: AEI), pp. 100–130.

Canes-Wrone, Brandice, David W. Brady, and John F. Cogan. 2002. "Out of Step, Out of Office: Electoral Accountability and House Members' Voting." *American Political Science Review* 96: 127–140.

Carroll, Christopher. 2002. "Portfolios of the Rich." In Lugi Guiso, M. Haliassos, and Tullio Japelli, eds., *Household Portfolios* (Cambridge: Massachusetts Institute of Technology Press), pp. 389–430.

Cebula, Richard. 1987. *The Deficit Problem in Perspective* (Lexington, MA: Heath).

Clemmitt, Marcia. 2006. "Bringing Home the Bacon." *Congressional Quarterly Researcher* 16: 538–540.

Coleman, John. 1996. *Party Decline in America: Policy, Politics, and the Fiscal State* (Princeton: Princeton University Press).

Cowart, Andrew T. 1978. "The Economic Policies of European Governments, Part I: Monetary Policy." *British Journal of Political Science* 8: 285–311.

Cranford, John. 1989. *Budgeting for America,* 2nd ed. (Washington, DC: Congressional Quarterly).

Dionne, E. J. 1991. *Why Americans Hate Politics* (New York: Simon and Schuster).

———. 2000. "Why Americans Hate Politics: A Reprise." *Brookings Review* 18: 8–11.

Downs, Anthony. 1957. *An Economic Theory of Democracy* (New York: Harper and Row).

———. 1960. "Why the Government Budget Is Too Small in a Democracy." *World Politics* 12: 541–563.

Edelman, Murray. 1971. *Politics as Symbolic Action* (Chicago: Markham).

Edlund, Jonas. 2003. "Attitudes Toward Taxation: Ignorant and Incoherent?" *Scandinavian Political Studies* 26: 145–167.

Evans, Gary R. Evans. 1997. *Red Ink* (San Diego: Academic Press).

Farrier, Jasmine. 2004. *Passing the Buck: Congress, the Budget, and Deficits* (Lexington: University Press of Kentucky).

Fenno, Richard. 1978. *Home Style* (Boston: Little, Brown).

———. 1991. The *Emergence of a Senate Leader: Pete Domenici and the Reagan Budget* (Washington, DC: Congressional Quarterly).

Fiorina, Morris. 1974. *Representatives, Roll Calls, and Constituents* (Lexington, MA: Lexington).

———. 1996. *Divided Government,* 2nd ed. (Boston: Allyn and Bacon).

Fisher, Louis. 1997. *Constitutional Conflicts Between Congress and the President,* 4th ed. (Lawrence: University of Kansas Press).

———. 2000. *Congressional Abdication on War and Spending* (College Station: Texas A&M Press).

Fisher, Patrick. 1999. "Political Explanations for the Difficulties in Congressional Budgeting." *Social Science Journal* 36: 149–161.

———. 1999. "The Prominence of Partisanship in the Congressional Budget Process." *Party Politics* 5: 225–236.

————. 2002. "The Success of the 1993 Budget Reconciliation Bill at Reducing the Federal Budget Deficit." *Review of Policy Research* 19: 30–43.

————. 2003. "Who Are the 'Deficit Hawks'? An Analysis of the Concord Coalition Congressional Vote Scores." *American Review of Politics* 24: 343–360.

————. 2005. *Congressional Budgeting: A Representational Perspective* (Lanham: University Press of America).

Fisher, Patrick, and David Nice. 2002. "Variations in the Use of Grant Discretion: The Case of ISTEA." *Publius* 32: 131–142.

Fortier, John C., and Norman J. Ornstein. 2003. "President Bush: Legislative Stategist." In Fred I. Greenstein, ed., *The George W. Bush Presidency: An Early Assessment* (Baltimore: Johns Hopkins University Press), pp. 147–151.

Franklin, Daniel. 1993. *Making Ends Meet* (Washington, DC: Congressional Quarterly).

Fritz, Ben, Bryan Keefer, and Brendan Nyhan. 2004. *All the President's Spin: George W. Bush, the Media, and the Truth* (New York: Simon and Schuster).

Galbraith, John Kenneth. 1987. "The Bust and the Bust." In Richard Fink and Jack High eds., *A Nation in Debt* (Frederick, MD: University Publications), pp. 136–142.

Gersbach, Hans. 2004. "Why One Person One Vote?" *Social Choice and Welfare* 23: 449–464.

Gilens, Martin. 2001. "Political Ignorance and Collective Policy Preferences." *American Political Science Review* 95: 379–396.

Glazer, Nathan. 2003. "On Americans and Inequality." *Daedalus* 132: 111–115.

Greenfield, Margaret. 1968. *Medicare and Medicaid: The 1965 and 1967 Social Security Amendments* (Westport: Greenwood).

Gross, Martin L. 1992. *The Government Racket* (New York: Bantam).

Hacker, Jacob S., and Paul Pierson. 2005. "Abandoning the Middle: The Bush Tax Cuts and the Limits of Democratic Control." *Perspectives on Politics* 3: 33–53.

Hanson, Craig. 2006. "A Green Approach to Tax Reform." *Issues in Science and Technology* 22: 25–27.

Herb, Michael. 2005. "No Representation Without Taxation?" *Comparative Politics* 37: 297–316.

Hudson, William. 2006. *American Democracy in Peril,* 5th ed. (Washington, DC: Congressional Quarterly).

Ippolito, Dennis S. 2003. *Why Budgets Matter: Budget Policy and American Politics* (University Park: Pennsylvania State University Press).

Iversen, Torben, and David Soskice. 2006. "Electoral Institutions and the Politics of Coalitions: Why Some Democracies Redistribute More Than Others." *American Political Science Review* 100: 165–181.

Jacobson, Gary C. 1990. *Electoral Origins of Divided Government* (Boulder: Westview).

———. 1993. "Deficit-Cutting Politics and Congressional Elections." *Political Science Quarterly* 108: 375–402.

———. 2007. *A Divider, Not a Uniter: George Bush and the American People* (New York: Longman).

Johnson, Paul, Frances Lynch, and John Geoffrey Walker. 2005. "Income Tax and Elections in Britain." *Electoral Studies* 24: 393–408.

Kamlet, Mark, and David Mowery. 1992. "The First Decade of the Congressional Budget Act: Legislative Imitation and Adaptation in Budgeting." In Albert Hyde, ed., *Government Budgeting* (Pacific Grove, CA: Brooks Cole), pp. 118–138.

Kato, Junko. 2003. *Regressive Taxation and the Welfare State* (New York: Cambridge University Press).

Kenworthy, Lane, and Jonas Pontusson. 2005. "Rising Inequality and the Politics of Redistribution in Affluent Countries." *Perspectives on Politics* 3: 449–471.

Kettl, Donald F. 2003. *Deficit Politics,* 2nd ed. (New York: Longman).

Keynes, John Maynard. 1937. *The General Theory of Employment, Interest, and Money* (New York: Harcourt Brace Jovanovich).

Kingdon, John W. 1989. *Congressmen's Voting Decisions,* 3rd ed. (Ann Arbor: University of Michigan Press).

Kousser, Thad. 2002. "The Politics of Discretionary Medicaid Spending, 1980–1993." *Journal of Health Politics, Policy, and Law* 27: 639–671.

Larcinese, Valentino, Leonzio Rizzo, and Cecilia Testa. 2006. "Allocating the U.S. Federal Budget to the States: The Impact of the President." *Journal of Politics* 68: 447–456.

Lee, Robert, and Ronald Johnson. 1994. *Public Budgeting Systems,* 5th ed. (Gaithersburg, MD: Aspen).

LeLoup, Lance. 2005. *Parties, Rules, and the Evolution of Congressional Budgeting* (Columbus: Ohio State University Press).

Levasseur, David G. 2005. "The Role of Public Opinion in Policy Argument: An Examination of Public Opinion Rhetoric in the Federal Budget Process." *Argumentation and Advocacy* 41: 152–167.

Levitt, Steven D., and James M. Snyder. 1997. "The Impact of Federal Spending on House Election Outcomes." *Journal of Political Economy* 105: 30–53.

Lindaman, Kara, and Donald P. Haider-Markel. 2002. "Issue Evolution, Political Parties, and the Culture Wars." *Political Research Quarterly* 55: 91–110.

Lockhart, Charles. 2003. "American and Swedish Tax Regimes." *Comparative Politics* 35: 379–397.

MacManus, Susan A. 1995. "Taxing and Spending Politics: A Generational Perspective." *Journal of Politics* 57: 607–629.

Martin, Paul S. 2003. "Voting's Rewards: Voter Turnout, Attentive Publics, and Congressional Allocation of Federal Money." *American Journal of Political Science* 47: 110–127.

Mayhew, David. 2000. *America's Congress* (New Haven: Yale University Press).

McCarty, Nolan, Keith T. Poole, and Howard Rosenthal. 2006. *Polarized America: The Dance of Ideology and Unequal Riches* (Cambridge: Massachusetts Institute of Technology Press).

Metcalf, Gilbert E., and Ian Parry. 2006. "Tax Solutions." *Issues in Science and Technology* 22: 20–22.

Morgan, Iwan W. 1995. *Deficit Government* (Chicago: Ivan R. Dee).

Nice, David. 2002. *Public Budgeting* (Belmont, CA: Wadsworth).

Norpoth, Helmut. 2001. "Divided Government and Economic Voting." *Journal of Politics* 63: 414–435.

Ogilvie, Donald. 1981. "Constitutional Limits and the Federal Budget." In Rudolph Penner, ed., *The Congressional Budget Process After Five Years* (Washington, DC: AEI), pp. 101–134.

Olson, Mancur. 1982. *The Rise and Decline of Nations* (New Haven: Yale University Press).

Ozawa, Martha, and Wang Yeong-Tsyr. 1994. "Distributive Effects of Benefits and Taxes." *Social Work Research* 18: 149–162.

Patashnik, Eric. 2000. "Budgeting More, Deciding Less." *Public Interest* 138: 65–79.

Pati, Susmita, Ron Keren, Evaline Alessandrini, and Donald Schwarz. 2004. "Generational Differences in U.S. Public Spending, 1980–2000." *Health Affairs* 23: 131–141.

Peltzman, Sam. 1985. "An Economic Interpretation of the History of Congressional Voting in the Twentieth Century." *American Economic Review* 75: 656–675.

Pena, Charles V. 2005. "A Reality Check on Military Spending." *Issues in Science and Technology* 21: 41–48.

Peters, B. Guy. 1991. *The Politics of Taxation* (Cambridge: Blackwell).

Peterson, Peter G. 2004. "Riding for a Fall." *Foreign Affairs* 83: 111–125.

———. 2004. *Running on Empty* (New York: Farrar, Straus and Giroux).

Pious, Richard M. 1999. "The Limits of Rational Choice: Bush and Clinton Budget Summitry." *Presidential Studies Quarterly* 29: 617–637.

Pizzigati, Sam. 2005. "Must Wealth Always Concentrate?" *Good Society* 14: 63–67.

Poole, Keith T., and Howard Rosenthal. 1997. *Congress: A Political-Economic History of Roll Call Voting* (New York: Oxford University Press).

Quirk, William. 2003. "Social Security Tax and Social Security." *Society* 40: 49–56.

Rivlin, Alice. 1989. "The Continuing Search for a Popular Tax." *AEA Papers and Proceedings* 79: 113–117.

Rose, Melody. 2001. "Divided Government and the Rise of Social Regulation." *Policy Studies Journal* 29: 611–626.

Rose, Richard. 1986. "Maximizing Tax Revenue While Minimizing Political Costs." *Journal of Public Policy* 5: 289–320.

Ross, Michael. 2004. "Does Taxation Lead to Representation?" *British Journal of Political Science* 34: 229–249.

Rubin, Irene S. 2003. *Balancing the Federal Budget* (New York: Chatham).

———. 2006. *The Politics of Public Budgeting*, 5th ed. (Washington, DC: Congressional Quarterly).

Sahr, Robert. 2004. "Using Inflation-Adjusted Dollars in Analyzing Political Developments." *Political Science and Politics* 37: 273–284.

Schick, Allen. 1980. *Congress and Money* (Washington, DC: AEI).

———. 1990. *The Capacity to Budget* (Washington, DC: Urban Institute).

———. 1995. *The Federal Budget Process: Politics, Policy, Process* (Washington, DC: Brookings Institution).

———. 2000. "A Surplus, If We Can Keep It." *Brookings Review* 18: 36–39.

Schier, Steven E. 1992. *A Decade of Deficits* (Albany: State University of New York Press).

———. 2003. "George W. Bush's Presidential Project and Its Prospects." *The Forum* 1: Article 2, Issue 4 (online edition).

Shuman, Howard E. 1988. *Politics and the Budget,* 2nd ed. (Englewood Cliffs, NJ: Prentice Hall).

Smeeding, Timothy M. 2005. "Public Policy, Economic Inequality, and Poverty: The United States in Comparative Perspective." *Social Science Quarterly* 86: 955–983.

Soroka, Stuart N., and Christopher Wlezien. 2005. "Opinion-Policy Dynamics: Public Preferences and Public Expenditure in the United Kingdom." *British Journal of Political Science* 35: 665–689.

Steinmo, Sven. 1993. *Taxation and Democracy* (New Haven: Yale University Press).

———. 1998. *Tax Policy* (Cheltenham: Edward Elgar).

Stockman, David A. 1986. *The Triumph of Politics: Why the Reagan Revolution Failed* (New York: Harper and Row).

Stonecash, Jeffrey M. 2000. *Class and Party in American Politics* (Boulder: Westview).

———. 2006. "The Income Gap." *Political Science and Politics* 39: 461–465.

Street, Debra, and Jeralynn Sittig Cossman. 2006. "Greatest Generation or Greedy Geezers? Social Spending Preferences and the Elderly." *Social Problems* 53: 75–96.

Su, Tsai-Tsu, Mark Kamlet, and David Mowery. 1993. "Modeling U.S. Budgetary and Fiscal Policy Outcomes: A Disaggregated Systemwide Perspective." *American Journal of Political Science* 37: 213–245.

Super, David A. 2004. "The Political Economy of Entitlement." *Columbia Law Review* 104: 633–729.

Synder, James M., Jr. 1992. "Artificial Extremism in Interest Group Ratings." *Legislative Studies Quarterly* 17: 319–345.

Taylor, Andrew. 2002. "The Ideological Roots of Deficit Reduction Policy." *Review of Policy Research* 19: 11–29.

Tohamy, Soumaya M., Hashem Dezbakhsh, and Peter H. Aranson. 2006. "A New Theory of the Budgetary Process." *Economics and Politics* 18: 47–70.

Vandoren, Peter M. 1990. "Can We Learn the Causes of Congressional Decisions from Roll-Call Data?" *Legislative Studies Quarterly* 15: 311–340.

Volcker, Paul. 1987. "Facing Up to the Twin Deficits." In Richard Fink and Jack White eds., *A Nation in Debt* (Frederick, MD: University Publications), pp. 154–161.

Volden, Craig. 2005. "Intergovernmental Political Competition in American Federalism." *American Journal of Political Science* 49: 327–342.

Wahl, Jenny B. 2003. "From Riches to Riches: Intergenerational Transfers and the Evidence from Estate Tax Returns." *Social Science Quarterly* 84: 278–296.

Walker, Jesse. 2006. "Welfare as We Know It." *Reason* 38: 16.

Weatherford, M. Stephen, and Lorraine M. McDonnell. 2005. "Ronald Reagan as Legislative Advocate: Passing the Reagan Revolution's Budgets in 1981 and 1982." *Congress and the Presidency* 32: 1–29.

Webber, Carolyn, and Aaron Wildavsky. 1986. *A History of Taxation and Expenditure in the Western World* (New York: Simon and Schuster).

Weidenbaum, Murray. 2003. "How Much Defense Spending Can We Afford?" *Public Interest* 151: 52–62.

West, Darrell. 1988. "Activists and Economic Policymaking in Congress." *American Journal of Political Science* 32: 662–680.

White, Joseph, and Aaron Wildavsky. 1989. *The Deficit and the Public Interest* (Berkeley: University of California Press).

Wildavsky, Aaron, and Naomi Caiden. 2004. *The New Politics of the Budgetary Process,* 5th ed. (New York: Longman).

Wlezien, Christopher. 1995. "The Public as Thermostat: Dynamics of Preferences for Spending." *American Journal of Political Science* 39: 981–1000.

———. 2004. "Patterns of Representation: Dynamics of Public Preferences and Policy." *Journal of Politics* 66: 1–24.

———. 2005. "On the Salience of Political Issues: The Problem with 'Most Important Problem.'" *Electoral Studies* 24: 555–579.

Wlezien, Christopher, and Stuart N. Soroka. 2003. "Measures and Models of Budgetary Policy." *Policy Studies Journal* 31: 273–286.

Zelizer, Julian E. 1998. *Taxing America: Wilbur D. Mills, Congress, and the State, 1945–1975* (New York: Cambridge University Press).

INDEX

About the Book

How are budget decisions made by the US government? Is it fair to blame skyrocketing deficits on an inability to curtail spending? How—and why—are taxing and spending decidedly separate political processes? Emphasizing budgetary *politics* rather than economic theories, Patrick Fisher offers a clear, thorough overview of how money flows through our government coffers.

A welcome realism pervades Fisher's analysis of budget-making, and numerous case studies of events in recent budget politics bring his arguments to life. The result is a balanced wealth of material for classroom discussion.

Patrick Fisher is associate professor of political science at Seton Hall University. His publications include *Congressional Budgeting: A Representational Perspective.*